Born Again Radical

Born Again Radical

Don Benedict

The Pilgrim Press
New York

Library of Congress Cataloging in Publication Data

Benedict, Don, 1917-
    Born again radical.

    1. Benedict, Don, 1917-   . 2. United Church of Christ—
Clergy—Biography.   3. Clergy—United States—Biography.
4. City churches—United States.   5. Church and the poor.
6. Peace (Theology) I. title.
BX9886.Z8B382   1982   285.8'34'0924   [B]   82-9100
ISBN 0-8298-0371-8 (pbk.)   AACR2

The Pilgrim Press, 132 West 31 Street, New York, New York 10001

To Ann, without whom this
pilgrimage would have been impossible,
and to Kennette, Sandra, Susan, and
Ruth in the hope that the impossible
may become more possible

Contents

Foreword

F OR UNFLAGGING ZEAL, you have to hand it to Don Benedict. For thirty-five years, in a variety of forms, and in diverse places, he has been "Mr. Urban Ministry." But his is not, in the apostle Paul's phrase, "zeal without knowledge." He knows institutional racism as he knows personal racism. He knows that while the gospel is always the answer—to know God is to love the poor—the churches are too often the problem, Christians being all too prone to favor charity over justice. As regards tactics, he knows that "compassion without confrontation is mere commiseration, fruitless and sentimental" (Henri Nouwen). Yet he is patient as well as aggressive; he knows the meaning of the phrase, "the long march through institutions." And on the personal side, he knows that bitterness is a diminishing emotion, that the art of life is to personalize your sympathies and to depersonalize your antipathies.

I first met Benedict in the summer of 1948. It was in East Harlem. He was one of the four founders of the East Harlem Protestant Parish; I was one of a small army of summer interns—theological students for the most part. I can't remember the subject of the conversation that first night, but we weren't far into it—Benedict and the interns—when he leaned across the table, wagging his finger at me. "Coffin," he said, "I don't know how long it's been since I've listened to a mind as bourgeois as yours."

Hiding my hurt as best I could, I answered, "Benedict, on the basis of our very short acquaintance I can see that a few solid middle-class virtues wouldn't harm the workings of your mind one little bit."

Benedict loved it, and I loved him—and learned a lot also. He became a good friend, the rare kind that risks his friendship for the sake of his friend. I'm glad he has written his story; it's a good one. And I hope to underline again his zeal. We live in wretched times that permit little optimism. But if you can't be optimistic, you can be persistent. That, above all else, is what I've learned from Don.

William Sloane Coffin Jr.
April 1982

Preface

THIS BOOK is not, strictly speaking, an autobiography. It is an account of a spiritual pilgrimage interpreting the gospel as a public concern for peace and economic and racial justice. While I am aware that the just society lies beyond history, I have, with but a few exceptions, continued to strive for justice insofar as God has given me eyes to see and ears to hear. Thanks to Reinhold Niebuhr, I finally came to understand the meaning of the "impossible possibility."

Therefore the impossible has not deterred me. I have always felt it fortuitous that I do very little planning in the sense of weighing possible difficulties. In many instances, if I had assessed the consequence and cost, I never would have moved forward. Fortunately my ministry has been blessed by colleagues who have had unusual capability in picking up the pieces. Their faithfulness has enabled me to achieve breakthroughs in matters of justice.

In the writing of this book I am indebted to a host of people. At great risk of omission, I wish to acknowledge those who immediately come to mind: Bill Voelkel, who over twenty years ago urged me to reflect on our experiences in Cleveland; Steve Rose, who assisted me in getting some order and a beginning draft; especially Ruth Gates, who not only rewrote sections of the original but, through use of a tape recorder and cross-questioning like a prosecuting attorney, made me reflect on the meaning of events in a personal way. Without the persistence and encouragement of Ms. Gates this book would not have been completed. There were others also, many of them unpaid, who typed and retyped, nudged and heckled until I produced, including Shirley VanClay, Claire Aldrich, and Deborah Cato.

I am indebted to the board and staff of the Community Renewal Society for continual encouragement and willingness to assist in the preparation of the manuscript.

It is my hope that those who read *Born Again Radical* will gain an insight into the dangerous notion of the Christian gospel. Innocent Bible stories read in churches have a way of transforming life day after day and enlisting ordinary people in crusades against institutional racism and institutional poverty. This book is a story like the stories of multitudes of people who, from time to time, have been captured by the life and spirit of Jesus of Nazareth and within the limits of human frailty have followed him.

Don and Ann Benedict

Born Again Radical

I

SOLITARY

1

THE GUARD reached through the bars to hand me the razor. I was twenty-six years old, and I had been in prison long enough to know what was going through his mind: "This guy is a religious nut. He won't try anything." Nevertheless, rules were rules; he had to stay. But when he saw how my hand shook he probably added, "You never know what solitary will do to a man" and decided to keep his eye on me. The shaking was residue—the aftermath of the night.

It is not true that one can think in solitary. Or, rather, one cannot trust one's thinking here, which is far worse. There is nothing to hear or look at, and the emptiness seems to swallow up deliberate thought. I had intended to stick it out. I had come in to prison of my own free will during World War II refusing to register for the draft. But I could not make the monumental decision I had to make until I was physically free. Yet the decision was partly made when I made up my mind I had to get out. This was the obsessive thought that made my night so wretched, tossing on the mattress, or on my knees in prayer, or trying to walk in the confined space—a few steps; turning, bumping, and scraping the walls; grazing the bars like a caged animal. I told myself the resolve to get out was not a premeditated decision I must justify, and walking out would not be an action but a reaction. I told myself I could come back again to jail. But I had to get out in order to think. I knew that people sometimes went mad in solitary. I had seen some taken out in straitjackets. Could this happen to me? I thought I still knew right from wrong. How long could I hold on to this certainty?

The cell was six by eight feet, with concrete walls and floor, literally bare except for the toilet and sink. There was no window—only a dim recessed light high in the corner—and nothing to sit on but the john. The mattress was brought in at night and laid on the floor. No reading material was allowed and no outside exercise except going down the hall for a shower twice a week. The heavy door outside the barred door was opened only to push meals through the slot. The cells were built in tiers, with walkways along the rows of doors. It wasn't so terrible at first, and I started out feeling pretty good, even self-possessed and self-reliant, because I had a reason for being there. Solitary was the ultimate, and I was defending my principles, demonstrating support for a cause in which I believed. But the cell got to me. As a boy I could never follow the others into a cave or crawl through a tunnel without having an awful fear that I might not get out. This feeling came back in the cell.

This was my second term in prison, and I was facing two and a half years. Would most of this time be in solitary? Being an inmate for ten months hadn't bothered me. But now, after only seven days in isolation, I was wrestling with the idea of reconsidering my whole philosophy of life and accusing myself of giving up my convictions. I still believed war was wrong. Violence and killing were wrong. As a pacifist, I would not kill or cooperate in any systematic support of war. Was I capitulating now just to get out of jail? I still wasn't sure, but this morning I was going to see the warden. I was going to shave. It was a gesture of propriety—possibly of conformity—but also of stubborn pride. I wanted to look neat but also to muster at least the appearance of being unaffected and unbeaten, even though I was going to say the word and sign the papers that would get me out. Getting out didn't mean going into the fighting army. I would be paroled for the purpose of going back to seminary. As a seminarian, I would be exempt and later if drafted could choose alternative service. But this would be capitulation. How was I going to decide? Did I know what I was doing?

I finished shaving, wiped off the razor with the towel, and handed it through the bars. The clang of the massive door cut off distant sounds. I began to pray that when I went through the door I might find a new direction for my life.

2

Everything I had done in my life, it seemed to me, had led to prison and the blank walls of solitary confinement. Solitary was the logical end of the road I had taken, but I couldn't make out where the path began. Childhood associations are misty. Yet there were discernible signposts along the way, and some of them are clear. The Russian primer was one and the good Samaritan another.

I had idly picked up the primer—a little book written for Soviet schoolchildren and translated into English—in the high school library. It explained the plan of what seemed to me a perfect state, with a classless society where no one was rich or poor and everyone would work and share equally. Profiteering would not exist, and all people would cooperate toward the same end. I liked the idea of everyone being a comrade, and I was interested enough to begin a course of independent reading to satisfy my curiosity. My father could not find a job, and we had given up our home in Canton, Ohio, and moved back to Tecumseh, Michigan, to live with my grandmother. There were discussions about borrowing money at the bank, using our automobile as collateral, and I remember the long summers when my father and I walked three miles to the family farm where we helped the tenant farmer in return for vegetables. Everyone in the country was worried.

One Thanksgiving the family gathered at Uncle Raynor's house, where the conversation grew serious when politics came up. My uncle was the county supervisor and a Democrat, whereas my folks were Republican and had voted for Hoover. I listened closely, and as they began to talk about the continuing depression, government spending, and the slim hopes for business recovery I joined in. Before I realized it I was on my feet giving a regular speech. In full-blown oratorical style I attacked the evils of capitalism and proclaimed the merits of socialism. I talked about the proletariat and uttered aloud for my first time the word bourgeoisie, probably mispronouncing it horribly. I spoke of production and overproduction. I saw no reason why a socialist system would not work in a democratic country and said so. When I stopped speaking I expected the crossfire of rebuttal. But there was dead silence. Everyone looked at one another. Then one brief chuckle came. It was like a signal for the general smiles and outright laughter that followed. "Listen to the expert!" said my aunt.

All I could manage was a weak smile. I felt vulnerable, embarrassed. With exaggerated dignity I stalked out of the room and out of the house. Standing on the front porch I heard a burst of laughter. I crossed the lawn and stood leaning against the trunk of a tree, my back to the house. A sodden pile of leaves lay there, swept by the wind into a heap in the fence corner. After a while I noticed that a light frost had begun to cover them, and I realized I was cold. But I wouldn't go back for a coat. I went around to the barn and stayed there.

I was thinking that the depression hadn't happened to me. It had happened to them. I didn't believe I was affected at all. There was little that I wanted, although I knew other kids who wanted things they couldn't get. It wasn't easy to get jobs, but I played on the softball team sponsored by the butcher shop, so from the time I started high school I had a job with the butcher after school and on Saturdays. I could buy my own clothes to help the family finances, and I had just bought my first car, a Model T, for seven dollars.

I stood in the barn doorway wondering why my father had never tried to get work as a laborer. He had left the farm for the city when he was very young, started out painting china in a dish factory, worked as a traveling salesman, and ended as sales manager of a dress company in Canton, continuing to make trips to Chicago and New York. Then suddenly the work of all those years had been swept away. Nobody wanted salesmen, but he kept on writing letters and going to Detroit, still hoping.

I didn't go back into the house.

My acquaintance with the good Samaritan took hold earlier, in the Methodist Sunday school. I was in the fifth or sixth grade, and we were living in Canton. Our class had a good teacher, and that day she had spoken about loving one's neighbor, telling us this was an essential part of the Great Commandment. I had heard about the good Samaritan many times, but suddenly the story opened out for me and I couldn't stop asking questions.

I was struck by its manifest truth. The low caste, the despised person was the one who helped others. I could see that it was the way things were. I imagined myself dying by the roadside, moaning with pain, and people passing by, turning their heads away, then a dark face bending over me, eyes filled with sorrow and pity. I wanted to know all about the Samaritans and why they were despised. I could picture a proud or even a rich man going by, pulling his garments about him so as not to touch the poor wretch lying in the ditch, bleeding to death—probably afraid he would get some blood on him. Or he was in a hurry. But I couldn't picture him as a priest. Why did Jesus make him a priest? And if he really were a priest, I wanted to know why he didn't have any feelings. Did some people lose their feelings when they became important—even in the church? Weren't ministers and priests supposed to practice charity? Weren't they constantly preaching it?

I told the teacher we ought to quit coming to church with the same people every Sunday and start looking for the poor and unfortunate and helping them. She didn't always know what to say but was willing to talk, and we sat there, missing the Sunday service. I asked her if churches weren't full of people who loved God and didn't really love their neighbors. Before, I had always thought the question, "Who is my neighbor?" to be rather plain and ordinary, but now I could see that it was beautiful and magnificent. I began to see that the neighbor was anybody who needed help, and that compassion was the distinguishing mark of those who recognized their neighbors. The feeling wasn't new to me, but now I could put a name to it. Compassion. Compassion moved one to act. Compassion had to be shown.

I began looking at our minister and wondering if he showed

compassion and, if he did, to whom. I told myself if I ever became a minister I would also be a Samaritan. My mother listened to my talk about the good Samaritan and finally said that everyone is a child of God and should be treated as such. Regardless of race, wealth, or station in life everyone should be treated equally. She had explained this to me many times. But the important word for her was conscience. "It is God," she would say, "who speaks to you." That God speaks to everyone in making decisions, and that I was to be guided by my own conscience rather than by what other people said or did was plain to me.

My mother brought me up for the most part. I was an only child. My father was away traveling, worked long hours, and at home seemed much quieter than in company. He was inclined to sympathize with anyone who had troubles. When we went to the ball park I sometimes noticed that his attitude separated him from the crowd. Usually he cheered for the team that was losing or was expected to lose. I didn't think anything about that; it seemed the natural thing for him to do. He was not at all assertive, and I never knew him to be angry.

My mother, born Nina Hagadorn, came from Carlton, Michigan, where she had been valedictorian in her high school class of thirteen members. There was an alcoholic father in and out of the house, and an indomitably puritanical grandmother who formed her principles. She got her first job as a bookkeeper, then moved to Detroit, where she met my father.

She was uncompromising: The traditional standards of honor, justice, and virtue were to be obeyed, not interpreted. My father took the side of the unfortunate person or the losing cause more from inclination than motivation, and I do not recall his doing anything actively. He was not a political person, although he talked a lot about politics.

I always trusted my feelings. My feelings and my conscience were so closely bound together as to be almost the same thing. At first I didn't see any difference, and so there was an ease in doing the right thing. When I acted according to the way I felt, I had the comfortable sense of being right. There were no struggles with conscience because I wanted to do everything well. I aimed at perfection in most things, especially in sports. I would train myself, submit to rigid rules, and practice regularly and willingly. But if schoolwork did not interest me—and little of it did—I felt no guilt in neglecting it. Either they were not teaching what I needed to learn or not teaching it in the right way. Or perhaps the long-range goals of study were beyond the realm of feeling.

3

One place in town where the poorest of the poor lived was called the Old Vendoma. It stood by the railroad tracks, a big, ancient, ill-kept apartment building with sagging walls. What gave the place its raffish air were the windows and the noise. The windows—some with rusty, bulging screens, often with holes in them—were usually wide open, shades askew, the drab, dingy curtains pushed to one side or hooked over a chair in hot weather, or floating their frayed edges outside the ledge. The noise was, all of it, loud—voices in argument, wails of infants, racket and hullabaloo of many children, blare of radios, and sometimes bellows, screams, and the crash of breaking glass. In the forlorn yard the many young children were dressed in clothes that were too big for them. Everybody knew the Old Vendoma and almost everybody made fun of it. The name became a catchall into which people placed anything that was socially unacceptable. The kind of person whose behavior raised eyebrows would be dismissed as probably coming from a background like the Old Vendoma. If a boy obviously needed a haircut, someone would say, "You look like the Old Vendoma." A young man escorting an ill-favored or tacky girl would be asked, "Where did you get her? At the Old Vendoma?" It was only a taunt, for of course we knew everyone and usually where each person lived in our town of 2,000. So it was odd that Louie Atkins, who lived at the Old Vendoma, was able to keep it a secret for so long, but not surprising that he tried. In grade school we didn't think much about where a person lived unless the place was odd or ostentatious.

A couple of times I invited Louie to the church youth meetings on Sunday afternoons, and he seemed interested. But he didn't talk much, and he was too nearsighted to be good at sports. His clothes were a little shabby, but none of us had many clothes. Finding out that he lived at the Old Vendoma made Louie more interesting to me, and I used to ask him what he thought about almost everything. Somehow I expected him to have a different opinion from that of other people, but this was seldom the case.

The summer after my freshman year in high school Louie went with a bunch of us to the annual week-long youth conference for Methodist kids from Michigan. It was held on the Albion College campus, a fifty-mile drive for the two or three cars going from Tecumseh. Each day began with worship, then a prominent speaker, after which we would break up into discussion groups.

Pacifism was usually the principal topic. In the 1930s a strong peace movement was sweeping the country. This was the theme, too, at our weekly church meetings. Those who, like me—thanks to my mother's prodding—were active members gained a thorough grounding in pacifist views, and confidence in defending them. I was absolutely sure I was on the right side, and I liked to bring antiwar arguments into school debates. Before the entire high school I once made a strong attack on militarism in an oratorical contest. Although I didn't know about it until long afterward, the local American Legion post sent a delegate to the school board to demand that I be expelled as an undesirable and unpatriotic influence.

When we stopped for Louie, he came out with his suitcase, and as he walked up to the car I began to feel uncomfortable. I never had this feeling before, but now we were sitting in the car staring up at the Old Vendoma and watching him come out of it. He climbed into the back seat, and someone said, "Hey, you're crowding me!" and a scuffle started. Then the others started talking about where they were going for the summer—vacations, summer cottages, and camps. One boy was going out West to a ranch. I felt that everything they said excluded him, and when I turned around to talk to him he was more formal than usual. They were all from fairly wealthy families and inclined to hang together. When we got to Albion I felt I wanted to spend all my time with Louie. We ate together and sat with each other at the meetings and services. When the time came to choose up sides for softball, the Tecumseh boys always tried to stick together. We usually beat the other teams because we had a strong softball league. But that week I stayed away from them.

High school students were as narrow and prejudiced as their elders. There was always an underlying awareness of social lines not only by the wealthy or educated people, but also by those who resented them. But elitism always made me uncomfortable. I got along well enough with people where there were advantages of superior education or reputed wealth, because I looked at them as individuals, and I liked everybody. But whenever I sensed an attitude of superiority or arrogance, it always made me uneasy. I couldn't talk about it like I could pacifism. It was just a feeling. A noticeable display of affluence made me uneasy in the same way, and I was convinced that all profits were somehow evil. I think I was more strongly drawn to poor people than to the rich; I was never uncomfortable with them. But I continued to have friends in both camps.

My circle of friends included boys who went in for athletics and those who were active in school affairs. My steady girlfriend during my first two years in high school was the daughter of our Methodist minister, but she was two years ahead of me in class. After she was graduated there was no one girl in particular.

Ernie, one of my classmates, was going to run away to fight with other Americans in the Spanish Civil War. He asked me to join the Abraham Lincoln Brigade, as well. Although I didn't want to kill anybody, I wanted to help the Socialists in Spain and so I agreed. But late one afternoon I unwittingly revealed the scheme to the coach. I hadn't intended to tell anybody. Ernie and I knew we had to keep it a secret until we were well on our way, but I made a crucial slip and then had to give away the whole thing.

The coach kept it casual. He scarcely paused in what he was doing, but he began asking practical questions about what I was going to do and how I felt about it. They were good questions, and I realize now, designed to show that I was essentially running away from something rather than irresistibly drawn with a clear purpose.

He said nothing at all critical and conveyed the feeling that he was certain I would always do the right thing. But he began to work me hard, giving me a new position to play, and I could see that he would be terribly disappointed if I left.

Finally I told Ernie I was not going to Spain. I was not cured, however, of wanting to quit school. The aggravation was often intense, but I always ran into the same uncertainty about what I would do after I left. I had no real objective except that of a vague freedom. In the end, Ernie didn't go to Spain either.

After repeal of prohibition, drinking became lawful for adults and much more visible, and fully half the students in our school took it up. By my senior year I was drinking regularly. It was considered sophisticated, and it was soon taken for granted as the thing to do. If we were going to a dance, of course we must get some wine. Anyone who objected was dismissed as a terrible bore. Between dances we would go out and drink wine in the car. Drinking made our fun more hilarious and the people more genuine and less affected. It seemed to form a bond of instant friendship. Alcohol had a diabolic appeal, especially for people like me, and it had the fascination of forbidden fruit, particularly because of my mother's strong stand against it.

At first, drinking was pure pleasure; later, a mixed pleasure, when I had to deal with consequences. All of us often got quite drunk, sometimes sick. Coming home late, I would take off my shoes on the porch and try to sneak into the house and up the stairs without being heard. I bore the headaches with nonchalance and took to chewing gum and Sen-Sen, but I didn't fool my mother. Curiously, my conscience, usually so prickly, did not intrude. The few twinges were soon drowned in a lovely sense of well-being. I was uncomfortable only when I got home, and then it seemed more my mother's conscience pressing me than mine. She said nothing at first, but I could see the storms coming. Finally, I was scolded and lectured on the subject of temperance. My reply was the firmness of my silence.

Despite our regular Friday- and Saturday-night forays my friends and I worked as hard as ever in sports, making the school teams in basketball, baseball, and football. I was class president for three of the four years. I was elected class orator in my senior year and worked hard to prepare my oration. But through this last year the drinking increased. It was irresistible.

Finally, I had a big clash with my mother. It was not over my drinking, but because I had stayed out all night on a date with a girl. It was a double date with Al Breitzke. Al had a steady girl and sometimes would ask me to go along with her best friend. That evening we went to a double feature. It was late when we came out, and Al, who had his father's car, drove to a narrow gravel road, and pulled the car off the road to the side. There was a sharp, rank smell of grass and weeds, and it was so quiet we could hear the leaves rustling and the repeated calls of frogs. I listened. They seemed to be all around the car but more concentrated over toward the right side. Then I noticed in the half-moonlight spears of coarse grass sticking up above the edge of the car door.

"Hey, Al! The car is sinking. We're in a swamp!" I shouted.

There was nothing we could do. The motor would start, but the wheels spun freely in the water. I got out and my feet sank deep into soft mud. All four wheels were in swampy water and the frame was on the ground. We talked it over and decided to stay in the car and wait until daylight. Luckily, a farmer came along about sunrise and Al yelled to him. He seemed to think our plight very funny but agreed to get his tractor and pull us out. The bottom of the car was coated with black mud. We had to clean it off with sticks, and then we took our dates home. It was about six o'clock in the morning when I walked into the house, streaked with dried mud, my clothes damp and wrinkled. My mother was up, and I told her what had happened.

"All night!" she said. "You mean to say you were with her all night?"

"We had to stay. We couldn't move the car."

She asked me all sorts of questions, then she blurted out, "Did you do anything to that girl?"

I was disgusted. "Do anything! We were necking, that's all."

"You realize, don't you, that you will have to marry the girl?"

"Marry her! Marry Donna Jean? Why?"

"You know well enough why! Because you have compromised her. You have ruined her reputation—not to say your own!" Her eyes were blazing and her face had gone white.

I was shocked. "Look," I said, "there is absolutely no reason for my marrying her. Can't you understand that? There's no reason!"

But she went on and on, almost hysterical. Did I realize the story would be all over town? She wouldn't be able to hold up her head in the town if I didn't marry the girl. It was the only thing to do, if I were a gentleman.

"Stop it!" I said. I was terribly angry now. I walked over and looked her in the eye. "I have done nothing wrong!" For a moment we stared at each other. Then I turned to go out of the room.

She called after me. "If you haven't, then why didn't you get out of the car? You could have carried them out. The two of you. You could have all walked home. Why did you stay in the car?"

I didn't answer but left the room and started up the stairs. I hadn't done anything. We hadn't even been drinking. She didn't believe me! My own mother accusing me of something I had not done!

When my father came home the next day I talked to him about it. "Your mother is very unhappy," he said. "It's a foolish mess, but I can't see that you're to blame." He clamped his hand on my shoulder. "Don't worry, Don. We'll live through it."

Trying to be cheerful in that house was impossible, but he did try. He did his best. My mother said nothing more about that night, but she was after me constantly about everything I did. I was nagged and censured, and we bickered over things that didn't matter at all. I couldn't stand it. I knew I had to get away. I could not endure being with her and tried to avoid it by going out more often or staying in my room.

As graduation day approached there were parties and still more drinking. One night three or four of us were on the sidewalk across the street from the candy store. It was fairly early. We were not drunk that night. We were depressed, feeling the effects of a late party the night before, at loose ends, hanging around but not talking much. Reluctant to go home, we drifted along the street. A car came around the corner, and suddenly I stepped back from the others and faced them. "I'm not going home tonight," I said. "I'm going to . . ." The car was almost there, and I jumped off the curb into its path. Somehow, instantly it seemed, with no time in between, I was back on the curb, and their hands were holding me. The car screeched to a stop and the driver turned around, shaking his fist. "You kids!" he yelled. "You ought to be locked up!" Then he shifted gears and went on. I was trying to think, trying to realize what had happened. The others couldn't have been that quick. I must have jumped back. I really didn't intend to do it. Or did I? Or was it pure reflex? This remains an empty space in my life. The others let go of me and waited for me to say something. Finally, I said, "Can't you guys take a joke? I was only fooling." But they were far from laughing. After a while Doug said, "Look, let's go across the street and have a Coke." So we went and sat in the last booth at the back of the candy store.

Gradually, we began to feel better, and we were all talking. I said, "I've got my mother, God help her, as my biggest problem in life, and she's got me as her main shooting target." We all agreed that we couldn't do anything good or right at home anymore, and that the worst of it was not the nagging. The worst thing was the suspicion.

But my life was also filled with good times. Graduation was one of the happiest, a sentimental, romantic time. I had applied for admission at Albion and was being rushed by the Tau Kappa Epsilon fraternity.

There were many soft, summery evenings, and we might just sit on the steps of someone's house or stand around a piano singing. There were times when I forgot my bitterness. But that night at the candy store was a low point. When we left, the others walked home with me to see that I got there.

At breakfast the next morning I told my mother, "Right after graduation, I'm going away. I'm leaving home." She looked at me as if I had gone mad. Then her face changed. She saw that I meant it. "And I'm not going to college." I meant that too.

By the time of graduation the atmosphere had cleared somewhat at home and we talked over my leaving. The feeling of strong opposition, stubborn resistance, of neither one of us giving in was still felt, but we agreed that it would be a sensible thing for me to be on my own. What made it palatable to my mother was the arrangement made for me to stay with my uncle and aunt, Frank and Grace Warrington. Aunt Grace was my mother's sister. I had written to Uncle Frank asking for a laboring job in the lumber company he managed in Rib Lake, Wisconsin. This changed the whole character of the affair. My mother spoke of it as a summer visit. I could hear her saying to the neighbors, "Don is away visiting relatives in Wisconsin for the summer."

A day or two after graduation I took the ferry across Lake Michigan to Manitowoc, where my uncle and aunt met me. Warrie was in the car. Their only child, he was about my age.

It turned out to be a great summer. Warrie became the brother I never had, and Aunt Grace—a calm, unruffled sort— did her best to spoil me. Being a good ballplayer was a social asset in many small towns in those days. I played baseball and softball on the Rib Lake teams and soon got to know almost everybody in town.

Later in the season I asked to be sent to the lumber camp. A mill train ran up to the woods and brought down the logs every day; it was real camp life. We lived in a clearing surrounded by forest, mostly pine and birch, with a narrow dirt road going into it. I worked one end of a crosscut saw and soon began to feel I was in the greatest physical shape I had ever known. Now and then I played softball at the camp in the evenings, and the men began to say, "You can't hit this kid!" So everyone wanted to try it, even those who knew practically nothing about the game. They were all good-natured when I struck them out and would hit me hard, high on the back—congratulating me with the attitude of experienced men toward a younger man of great promise. All of us worked together easily, everyone supporting the team effort, and I found something fundamentally satisfying in the combination of hard, sweating work and the dense, almost spiritual mystery of the forest.

I discovered at Rib Lake that drinking was not a habit with me, only a preoccupation. During the first tough week at the mill and the initial fatigue I forgot about it and then realized I hadn't even missed it. I had no appetite for it, probably because

I was away from my peers. Being with a group of older men threw me back on my own, and I was beginning to discover myself.

Often I went for long walks alone. The woods were still and peaceful, but not silent. They were quiet but alive. Bird calls came clear, every leaf stretched itself for a place in the light, and the sunshine glittered high above in the foliage or fell in long slanting shafts that one could walk through. Sometimes I could hear a rhythmic tapping in the distance. I walked with a feeling of wonder, strangely alert to what I can only describe as a strong consciousness of my own distinct, independent existence and an awareness of a "self" that was, in some ways, unfathomable.

I also began to feel self-righteous. I had become convinced that drinking was morally wrong, and I was at peace with my conscience and with the world. Again, I knew that I was right. I wrote my mother that this was the greatest experience I had ever had. I was on my own and wanted to prolong the feeling of freedom, but also I was thinking hard about the ministry. By the end of the summer I had decided to enter the ministry and to go to Albion.

4

That summer my father found a steady job; this meant I could enter college in the fall. Knowing both his decided optimism and my mother's capacity for saving, I knew the venture would be a tight squeak but that it would work.

My moral rejuvenation at the lumber camp combined with sober expectations of four years of college had enhanced my perfectionism. I resolved not to waste my time, and so I took up an overly moral, overly conscientious attitude that was too strict to be maintained. Everything I enjoyed doing was suspect. I decided to stay out of sports, all extracurricular activities, and to keep a low profile socially.

College years were a time for discovering new ideas and changing my beliefs. I was introduced to biblical criticism and interpretation, which opened new highways of thought for me. Any reference to social justice, peace, equal rights, cooperative ventures, the plight of minorities could bring me to my feet. I was excited by these topics when related to current events or when I thought action was possible; I am less inclined to uphold precepts and principles keyed to some distant, ultimately desirable end.

My resolve to forego activities like debating was broken as the result of a discussion about labor disputes. I suggested one day that compulsory arbitration was the best way to settle controversy and a means of reducing loss through strikes. To me, a labor dispute is like any other conflict in society, except that it usually deals with economics and so the judicial system ought to be used. It seemed better qualified than strikes and public sentiment.

But wouldn't that destroy the labor movement and eventually the unions? Wasn't the judicial approach less human? There were good arguments on both sides.

Most students were hoping for careers in the city, because that was the place where success and a better life could be found. I knew I was going to be drawn to the city, because the unfortunate and miserable lives were there.

I saw social change as a necessity, and I was at the same time nonviolent. But I was coming to believe it was no longer totally a matter of logical persuasion, of trying to convince the American people through reason. What was needed was demonstration, bringing into public view all cases of outright injustice, and keeping this issue before the people. Just getting the message across by preaching wasn't enough; it wanted organization.

Pacifism became a more emotional issue with apprehension growing as the country watched Hitler in Germany, and when people began to predict he would move into Austria, arguments grew hot. I was far more engrossed in reading about Gandhi and about Kagawa, a Christian who lived in the slums of Japan and influenced the entire direct action movement, than in reading my textbooks. On an international student peace day some of us ran up a white flag on the flagpole in the center of the campus, an act that incensed the opposition and the townspeople. Reprimanded by the president, we came away convinced that some of the college officials were more worried about contributions from alumni than they were about world peace.

I felt closer to my fraternity brothers than to any other group. The Tekes were mostly bright, serious men, quite a few with scholarships, and they were more service-minded than business-minded. I do not remember a single black student at Albion. Students came from suburban Detroit and middle-class Michigan towns and were mostly Methodists.

My habit of the lumber camp continued. I would go out for long walks alone at night and was struck by the line between black and white. Blacks lived in poor structures on low land on one side of the railroad tracks, with the more spacious homes of the white people on the heights. I often went along the tracks sensing comfort and plenty on one side, poverty and misery on the other. The first blacks had been shipped north in boxcars during World War I, to work in the factories. I remember one night walking down the tracks and thinking that God must be on their side. The next moment I was startled by the shadow of a huge cross lying on the ground ahead of me. I looked up and saw that the shadow was made by the grade crossing sign and the angle of a streetlight. "A sign," I thought, "and a black shadow that is a cross." I took this as a sign that I was destined to become a minister of God and that I was to be on the side of the unfortunate.

I took many such solitary walks below the tracks, thinking about my vocation. I felt I belonged among the Methodists, but there never seemed to be any really poor or downtrodden people in their congregations. It was true that those who achieve worldly success needed ministering, but so long as whole classes of people were being exploited I felt that other urgencies were not so pressing. This was the practical and pragmatic, the reformer in me, speaking. But another feeling was that God loved the poor not because they were poor, but because God was just. Some of this love was implanted in me, and I was going to try to show it through the Methodist church.

Toward the end of my freshman year I suddenly realized that I was going to have to bury myself in the library to prepare for exams if I was going to catch up to the level I had set for myself. But spring is the season for softball. Each spring at Albion we had Class Scraps. Freshmen and sophomores became two young armies pitted against each other in tugs of war, greased pole climbing, and many games. Any method of winning—fair or foul—was grasped in the prevailing carnival spirit.

I told myself in justification that at least I had stayed out of varsity sports all year. As a pitcher, I remained a perfectionist, and I began training. On the day before we were to play the sophs I was pitching to Jack Trimble, our catcher, to keep warmed up for the next day. An old touring car drove up and stopped. There must have been eight or ten sophomores in the car, and I thought they had probably come over to see what kind of "stuff" I had on the ball. After a while one of them called me over, and I strolled toward them, glove in hand, not at all suspicious. When I got there I was pushed into the back seat, and the car jerked into gear and sped off. I was able to turn my head and saw Trimble standing in the middle of the street, shouting.

There was nothing I could do. My kidnappers had coils of rope and said I was to take a trip by rail. I assumed it would be more than a day's journey, and they said they hoped it would turn out to be an extensive one. They drove along the tracks, looking for a boxcar. Luckily for me, they couldn't find one that was unlocked and decided to tie me up in an abandoned slaughterhouse a few miles out of Albion. It was a pretty good choice. I was bound and left in a room with a very high ceiling and thick walls. The windows were about ten feet above me and were locked. I could shout all day and nobody would hear me. No houses were nearby, and the building was off the road. They padlocked the door and took away all my clothes except shorts and shoes.

As soon as they left I began to strain at the knotted ropes, trying to work my arms and wrists around, and eyeing with great interest a row of large iron meat hooks on the opposite wall. Finally, I wriggled out of the bonds and got one of the hooks off the wall. It couldn't be used on the door, which was massive and tight fitting. But with the rope and the heavy hook I succeeded in smashing a window and got the hook, with rope attached, fast to the windowsill. Then all I had to do was crawl up the wall, chin myself up, and pick out the remaining glass fragments. I went across country as much as I could until I came to the river where I found a fellow with a canoe and persuaded him to take me across. Standing at the edge of town, I wondered how I was to get home without clothes. I was near a cemetery and took the road through it, running. People seemed startled but not outraged, and suddenly it occurred to me that I was wearing the ideal costume for a Sunday afternoon in a college town. They assumed I was practicing for cross-country but wondered why I had chosen to run through the cemetery. I simply continued my jogging all the way home. Among the townspeople I passed, scarcely a head turned.

When I got to the fraternity house I went into seclusion until game time on Monday. Word got around about the kidnapping, and a sizable crowd turned out. That game was one of my best; I struck out twenty batters.

I did not drink at all during my four years at Albion; it was forbidden in the Teke house. I was enthusiastic about Tau Kappa Epsilon. During my junior year I was put in charge of pledging and met every prospect. In the end we pledged more than we had ever pledged before. It was then my job to shepherd these neophytes during the following school year. I continued the personal attention I had begun during rushing and got to know the men well.

But my academic performance was far from triumphant and I came out of college with a C + or B − average.

5

In the spring of my senior year at Albion I drove to New York City, having decided to apply for admission to Union Theological Seminary. Union was interdenominational and one of the best seminaries in the country; it was in New York, where the problems of race and poverty were acute; and its excellent faculty included Reinhold Niebuhr, known for relating the Christian faith to societal problems. Harry Emerson Fosdick, pastor of Riverside Church, also taught classes there.

In New York I rode the subway and walked, observing and

absorbing the city's special flavor and contradictions. I could stand in a single street and see hundreds more unfortunate people and dismal conditions than in any Michigan town.

The high moment of my trip was my meeting with Henry Sloane Coffin, president of Union. Uncle Henry—as he was known among students—welcomed me like the jovial person he was. He wanted to know about my background, but he was far more interested in what I was thinking. Never before had I met a clergyman whom I could admire so unrestrainedly. Dr. Coffin understood that I was struggling with my doubts about the church, but rather than responding with grave concern he took it as a hopeful sign. I came home in raptures over Uncle Henry, and I could scarcely wait for autumn.

My admission was undoubtedly the result of my interview with Uncle Henry, not my grade point average. The seminary is at 122nd Street and Broadway, and I remember the strong contrast between the purposeful atmosphere within those buildings and the aimless wanderings of the unemployed on the streets. The teaching at Union was stimulating, and I discovered most students were concerned about ministering to the people rather than being ministers. This was precisely what I wanted.

My fieldwork was in a community church in Yonkers, teaching Sunday school, working with a youth group on Sunday nights, and supervising boys' recreation. I had never felt happier. I wrote to my mother that this was the greatest experience I had ever had, and that I had learned more in one week than in the four years at Albion. I knew that here I would be able to study without anything else on my mind, and I resolved to keep out of all activities—intramurals included—and begin three years of intense concentration. As a seminarian at Union, I acquired a certain status in the Methodist Church known as "in conference on trial." I had committed myself to go into the Methodist ministry, and I retained this status while at the seminary.

Union students came from all over the world, and it was exciting to find many who felt as I did. David Dellinger was one. I was drawn by his great feeling of compassion for the poor and his strong pacifism. He had been in Spain during the civil war, and he told me that going through a major air raid in Madrid had made him a pacifist.

Dave and I talked a lot about demonstrating. Living what I believed meant individual action and also standing up to be counted with those who held the same beliefs. Both of us saw the value of drama. The following February the two of us went to Washington, D.C. to demonstrate against participation in the war, stressing opposition to sending supplies to England. It turned out to be a huge rally, with thousands massed outside the White House. Franklin Roosevelt finally came out and spoke to us, and later Eleanor Roosevelt.

We had a ride down but didn't know how we were going to get back. We had no money, so we decided to hop a freight train. The idea appealed to me, because I had never done it. It was not so easy. The yards were dark except for the switch lights. We had to avoid watchmen and pick a train that was moving and going north. We couldn't get into any of the boxcars. Finally, we climbed into an old coal car, open, empty, and deathly cold. We wore overcoats, but the cold penetrated, and when the train gathered speed the wind swiped at us like a whip. We tried to get out of its sweep by wedging ourselves into the corners, and during the night we often passed one another stamping over the bumpy floor, flailing our arms. The air was thick with dust, and when the train went through seven tunnels in Baltimore, one after the other, we thought we would choke to death in the clouds of smoke. There was no getting out; the train didn't stop until it reached Philadelphia, where we climbed out, stiff and numb.

My roommate, Meredith Dallas (Dal), Dave, and I were together most of the time, and a few others began to join us. I felt I was really talking for the first time in my life. I had always spoken freely, but now I spoke in freedom, and with the others I began to make decisions with self-assurance.

The poorer neighborhoods of New York drew us, and those of us who were socialists and pacifists began to criticize the cloistered atmosphere in which we found ourselves. Dal had been able to get a job at Union Settlement and Dave was at a church in a deteriorating neighborhood in Newark, so they had outlets for their social philosophy. As we talked it became evident that we ought to find living quarters among the dispossessed—the people we wanted to serve—if our studies were to have meaning. Why not get our own place nearby, in Harlem? I also wanted to demonstrate something. My quarrel was not with the school, but with its tacit elitism. In the gospel there was no place for elitism. The seminary stood removed from its community, with empty rooms in the dorm, while the unemployed walked the streets with no place to sleep.

Merely by living with the poor I would not be doing anything for them. I only was showing I was on their side. I would continue to spend weekends assisting the pastor of a suburban church. We would be placing ourselves in Harlem only geographically, but thereby we would be pointing out to everyone our future paths. Howard Spragg, who had been active in the Young Peoples Socialist League, agreed with our stand, but we didn't expect him to come and live with us. He was somewhat of a loner, burying himself in books. But he was interested in our experiment and often visited us.

Dave, Dal, Jimmy Gleyer, and I went to Uncle Henry with our plan. He was aghast. "You cannot do it. Out of the question," he said. "We will not allow it. Your studies would suffer." Finally, he remarked that under such an arrangement our scholarships would be withdrawn. It was a threat, but we couldn't believe he meant it.

Finding a place was not easy. In Harlem we soon learned what discrimination is like. We were refused apartments because we were white. White people moving into a black neighborhood meant to everybody that we were posing as a front for numbers racketeers or that we were pimps or federal agents of some kind. Reassuring the landlords was impossible. We finally found a place wretched enough to please us—a six-room walk-up on 128th Street and 8th Avenue. The living room windows frosted up in cold weather and elevated trains screeched and roared by. For heat we had only the kitchen stove and a small kerosene burner, so we closed off the front rooms and used them for sleeping.

At school, when referred to as "the martyrs" or "our deserving poor" and repeatedly asked, "What are you fellows trying to prove?" we would retort that it was impossible to study the gospel except in community with the common people. After working late in the library I would walk home along 125th Street, where derelicts leaned against storefronts or slept in doorways and prostitutes often stood in hallways. They would whistle or even grab me by the arm. Occasionally, a man, almost too drunk to stand, would fall forward from the shadows, begging for money for more drink. They were not the hungry men on crowded street corners, ashamed to meet eyes, asking for carfare or a dime for soup. One of them pushed against me one night when Dal happened to be with me. The man grabbed me, thrusting his face close to mine, mumbling incoherently. He was a large, hulking fellow, revoltingly dirty and frowzy, altogether a disgusting sight, steeped in the sour smell of vomit and the stench of alcohol. Instinctively, I sidestepped and jerked my arm away. Then, as suddenly, I stopped, appalled at what I had done. "Chrissake," said the man and lunged off.

Dal and I stood looking at each other. Then a car swung into the street and its headlights swept over a huddled figure on the ground in a narrow area between buildings. Without saying a word, we went in. Grasping the man's shoulder, Dal shook him gently, and we turned him over. "Let's take him home with us, Dal!" I said. The man tried to struggle to his feet as we lifted him but couldn't make it. We took him between us with an arm around each of our necks. When I felt his weight and his weakness I was suddenly overcome. I wanted to weep. But as we straggled on he roused himself repeatedly, each time urging us to stop and have "another little drink." When we got him home Dal made some coffee, and I cleaned an ugly abrasion with soap and water. When I put iodine on it he scarcely felt it. The man was conscious enough so that we could get him into the bathtub and into a pair of clean pajamas.

Howard Spragg happened to be there that night, and he stood in the doorway watching as we bedded the man down. He couldn't resist saying, "What good are you doing? This sort of thing is hardly going to solve the urban problems." He was strong on the systemic approach.

Waking early, my first thought was about the man we had picked up. In the cold morning light I was troubled. There were so many alcoholics. "So I'm to become a minister, am I?" I asked myself, "and walk away? pass them by?" Wouldn't it be better to quit seminary, devote myself to beggars like this man? I could pick them up, offer sympathy and some kind of help even if it were only food and clean clothes and a night's sleep. And pray with them. In a sense I had already half quit the seminary by living in Harlem. But was my living there only tokenism? I hoped not. But did I have the right to be studying while a single unclaimed beggar lay in the street?

I got out of bed and looked out the window at the gray sky. No. Howard was right. I wanted to show compassion *personally*. Howard didn't usually become involved with people, didn't show his feelings. He would never bring home a drunk. But he would work hard in any movement to reform the system that caused injustice and human misery. Howard was right. I would work through the church and try to attack the causes of suffering.

When our man awoke he must have thought he was in jail, for he looked at Dal and me and said, "You ain't cops!" His name was George, he said. He was astonished and delighted to find out who we were and all the time he was with us addressed us as "You preachers." That night he offered to cook our dinner. He turned out such a terrific lamb stew we asked him to cook it every few days. George stayed with us for several weeks, but we couldn't find out much about him. He turned away our offers to help him find a job. "Don't you preachers worry 'bout me," he would say. Then one day he wasn't there and he never came back.

Sometime later Dallas brought home two young black men he had met in a bar who were out of work and had no place to stay. They were trying, they said, to develop a dance team. But after a few days they decamped, taking along our typewriters and most of our clothes. We talked it over. We had taken them in, shared what we had, and offered to hold them over until they could find work. Where had we failed?

That spring we invited the entire Union faculty to an open house in Harlem. The school administrators had not canceled our scholarships, but they did not approve of our living arrangements. Empty rooms meant a loss of revenue for the school. We would not have been surprised if our invitation were ignored by all but a few, but to our amazement at least half the faculty arrived on that day and stood around our dining room table, drinking tea and eating sandwiches and cake. They wanted to see everything. I believe some of them had never walked around in Harlem. Our defection had, to some extent, split the student body. Some students criticized us as self-righteous, but others began to say, "This is the way we ought to live. You can go to Union and not really experience the city at all when you stay within the walls."

In the summer of 1940, Walt Jackson, a fellow student at Union, and I decided to tour what was called the Jim Crow south. Neither of us had ever been there. We bought a Model A Ford for twenty-eight dollars and got letters of introduction to a few pastors of churches along our route.

We wrote ahead to a minister in a small, mostly white coal-mining town in Harlan County, Kentucky. Harlan County was noted for strikes, and the minister was having a bad time, because he had identified himself with the striking mineworkers. We went through a mine to see what the work situation was like and talk with the men. To me, it would have been depressing to work there, and I was amazed at the cheerfulness of those men.

Our next minister was in Crossville, Tennessee. His house had been bombed during some local turbulence. I preached in his church on Sunday and probably pressed the question of racism too hard. The next day the congregation told him if he had any more people like me in the pulpit they would ask him to leave.

We visited the Highland Folk School and the Delta Cooperatives in Mississippi. Here we talked to blacks and whites who were attempting to live together in a cooperative situation, with intense hostility all around them. It was common for their persecutors to drive through shooting from their cars. The people could do nothing but stay in their houses, hoping not to be hit. They were barely surviving and lived in constant fear of lynchings.

Except for the few times we were guests at parish houses, we slept out in our sleeping bags wherever we could find suitable grass.

One morning in Mississippi I was awakened by a loud voice shouting at us to get off the schoolhouse lawn. I opened my eyes and saw an old man with a small boy at his side.

"You jest pick up them things and git off. This-here is school propuhty," he shouted.

I decided to ignore him and closed my eyes.

He shouted even louder. "You're vagrants! And there's a law agin that. Thet yer car down thar with them Noo Yawk Yankee plates?" He couldn't seem to talk without yelling.

"Who are you, the sheriff?" I asked.

"The constable, that's who," he bawled. "Horton," he said to the boy, "run home and git me my pistol."

The boy trotted off, and he turned back to me. "And I'm fixin' to arrest you for trespassin' and vagrancy."

"How do I know you're the constable?" I said somewhat sleepily.

He pulled out his badge. I still wasn't moving, but when the boy came back lugging a gun belt and the constable pulled out a huge revolver, I got up quickly, picked up my bag, and began to walk to the car, calling to Walt to hurry. He was awake but too sleepy to stir. When I got to the car I threw in the sleeping bag and turned. Walt stood there with an amused half-smile on his face, looking as if the constable were something out of comic opera. The constable was holding the gun at Walt's head.

"Walt!" I shouted. "Get your stuff in the car! This guy is serious!" I could see his hand shake as he held the gun.

Walt drove the car, on the constable's orders, to the local jail with that shaking hand holding the gun at his head. Before we were booked we insisted that we were seminary students traveling through the South on a study tour. After four or five hours in jail we were released. The police had verified our attendance at Union, but we were told to get out of town within one hour.

We gradually came into the heavy, humid air of the Deep South and into "Coloured Only" and "White Only" signs on drinking fountains, washrooms, and on the doors of waiting rooms and other public places. On our first night in New Orleans, Walt and I partook generously of the beer in the French Quarter and walked a bit unsteadily toward our car.

Near us was a yard adjoining the bus depot, where buses were being cleaned for the next day's run. We climbed into one of them. A young black man was sweeping the rear of the bus. He paused and looked at us apprehensively as we came down the aisle. Seeing him with that "Coloured" sign directly over his head made me terribly angry and I pointed to the sign and shouted, wanting the whole world to hear, "I'm going to spend the rest of my life taking that sign down!" I went on repeating my avowal while the young man, startled and nervous, kept saying, "Yessa, yessa," in a hushing tone, as if he feared the whole world might indeed hear me.

Our trip lasted a month, and we had little contact with southern people, black or white. But we saw the South. I had heard about the signs, but now I felt their reality. Inside I was far more angry than I had ever been before and more inclined toward radical action. Also I saw how deeply embedded the racism was and realized it would take a great deal more than I had thought to change things. Again the gospel had been privatized, making religion a personal thing and forgetting about it in economics, politics, and business. The national attitude seemed to be, "It's OK if you treat them right personally," and then to go along with the exploitative system.

I lived in Newark for the rest of that summer. Dave had asked several of us from Union to help him develop a summer program at the Jube Memorial Congregational Church, where he had been doing his fieldwork all year. The immediate neighborhood was changing. Apartments in two- and three-flat buildings were being subdivided to increase profitability and blacks were moving into the area but not into the church. We ran a Bible school five days a week as well as other activities for the children, and hoped through our summer program to bring neighborhood children into the Sunday school as the first step toward getting black members into the church. Some of us had part-time jobs in the city. There were about twenty on that summer staff.

H. Richard Niebuhr, Christian ethics professor at Yale Divinity School, came down one night a week from New Haven to teach us, without any charge. We studied the Gospel of John, and this was the beginning of what we called a new kind of seminary and of the eventual development of a structured working and learning ministry. We called it our seminary without walls.

Our work was successful; the only question was how the parish would react. The established congregation was dwindling and the area changing. Would these people accept the change and welcome their new neighbors? No. They resisted. The minister wanted to be a pastor to all the people, but those who formed the nucleus of his congregation had drawn the lines. They did not object to black children in the weekday Bible classes; this was Christian work. But their Christianity did not extend to receiving black people in the church on Sunday. When some of the children came to the Sunday school, there were strong protests from church members. Finally, two of the church trustees stood on the steps and forbade a group of black children to come in, telling them to go to their own church. Tension increased to the point of crisis, and a congregational meeting, after long argument, ended in an open-door policy for morning worship but not for church membership. My disillusionment with the established church increased. The minister decided to leave and later went to a church in Alaska where he found to his dismay that half-breeds were required to sit in the balcony.

6

Congress passed the draft registration law in July 1940. Apart from my nonviolent philosophy, how could I ever serve in a segregated army? We talked in Newark about the draft, and in September five of us decided to go on living there, continuing to work with children and identifying ourselves with workers and lay people. We rented a house and lived in Christian Ashram style, having prayers together; working at painting, washing windows, and various odd jobs; putting the earnings into a common pot. Each of us took a dollar a week to spend. We decided to attend classes half-time at Union.

The draft issue quickly involved practically everyone at the seminary, where we discussed it in relation to the Christian faith. There was a minimal recognition of the legitimacy of pacifism for conscientious objectors (COs). The crux of the matter for us was that while draft registration was mandatory, seminarians were automatically exempt from military service. Certainly we did not want to be drafted into the fighting army, but neither did we want to be excused because we were different from other people or because we were members of a special class. We felt we should face the draft like anyone else, and as pacifists, we resisted involvement in the process of war.

Dal, Dave and I, living together in Newark, knew that the only consistent attitude for us was to decline to register, thereby refusing to be classed as an elite. We would be doing the same thing we did when we moved out of the seminary. Ministers, we had said, are not better than others; they are the servants. We were being protected unjustifiably. If the government's stand was based on an assumption of our pacifist beliefs, that was in error; not all seminarians were pacifists.

Another consideration was my calling to preach the gospel. I believed that it was the incarnation—the good news that God had sent his only Son, incarnate as a human being—that was central to the gospel. This identification of Jesus with all humanity made rebirth and liberation possible. Could I, as a clergyman, preaching this gospel, ever separate myself from other persons? Could I accept any kind of exemption, any favored position solely because I had indicated my intention to become a follower of Jesus? That would be ridiculous.

Finally, twenty-two of us prepared a signed statement as a public announcement of our intention to refuse to register. *The Christian Century* printed our statement; newspapers picked it up, and intense pressure was exerted—especially by our families—to get us to rescind our decision. My mother wrote that she and my father hoped I would reconsider but that they would stand by whatever decision I reached in good conscience. Their reaction was quite different from that of most others. Dave's father actually threatened suicide. It did not change Dave's mind, but other students began, one by one, to succumb to the pressure. We expected opposition from Uncle Henry, but we were surprised to have well-known pacifists like Harry Emerson Fosdick and Ralph Sockman, the nationally known radio preacher, come to talk to us and counsel us to register. Norman Thomas came. His brother, Evan, had been in Leavenworth during World War I for the same offense. Even the American Friends Service Committee tried to dissuade us, holding that alternative service was preferable to jail.

Many people misunderstood our direct purpose of course, but it was clear to me that, aside from the specific point we intended to make, the refusal to register was the most effective and concrete thing we could have done as seminary students to make public our opposition to the war and the war system.

By the time the draft law was signed—October 14, 1940—fourteen students had dropped out of our group. Some had decided to register as COs, which meant they could eventually go into Civilian Public Service (CPS). On the day we refused to register, Roger Shinn left school and enlisted. He agreed with us that he ought not to have this exemption, but he thought if he believed in the war he should enlist like anyone else.

The night before the national registration day the seminary community held a public worship service as an expression of solidarity even though many students held opposing views. On the day of registration eight of us appeared before the draft board set up at the seminary and presented a signed letter stating the reasons why we, in good conscience, could not register. To our amazement, the man who took our communication was a United States district attorney. He immediately served a subpoena calling for our appearance the next day before a New York County grand jury. They handed down indictments charging us with failure to register for the draft. We pleaded guilty.

The eight of us were Dave, Dal, Howard Spragg, George Hauser, Bill Lovell, Joe Bevilacqua, Dick Wichli, and me. Ted Walsh, our lawyer, was a prominent corporation counsel who had volunteered his services. He pointed out something that had not occurred to any of us. Our joint signing of the letter indicating our intentions opened us to a possible conspiracy charge that carried a maximum sentence of forty-three years, rather than the five years maximum for draft violation. For the next month national publicity was intense. Letters came from all over the country, supporting or condemning us.

On the day of sentencing we were allowed to make a final statement to the court. Mine implied that anyone who was a Christian could take no other course. As I look back, I see that my attitude was terribly self-righteous, but at the time I was sure I was acting rightly. The judge sentenced us to a year and a day, with the stipulation that at any time we decided to register for the draft we would be immediately released. All we had to do was register, but we had found this impossible to do.

We were led out of the courtroom, handcuffed together, taken down the back elevator, and put into the paddy wagon single file. Reporters and photographers were waiting, and an Associated Press photo of the eight seminary students being taken to the federal jail at West Street was front-page news in the evening papers. Our one-week stay at West Street was an introduction to the prison system. Six of us were put in one room together and two on another floor. We were told we could write two letters during that week.

If our sole concern had been our exemption, then our logical behavior was to become model prisoners, serve the minimum term, and get out. But as pacifists, even in prison we could demonstrate against violence and racism. I tried falling into the food line for blacks only and was promptly jerked away by a guard and placed with my "own people." That night, lying awake, I heard white guards talking to prisoners, calling them "black nigger bastards."

The second day at West Street I wrote reassuringly to my mother. I had decided that stopping the war system was going to take years of hard work and long suffering, so I suggested she read up on the pacifist movement and its full implications. I told her we were kept busy doing maintenance work, but I didn't tell her what the maintenance work had been that day. Howard and I had been ordered to clean out a cell that housed drug addicts. They were men under the torture of being forced to shake their habit cold turkey. If the officials thought seminarians were squeamish, they were wrong. We would not try to avoid trouble or suffering.

There were other efforts to get us to change our minds. Uncle Henry visited us and reiterated his argument that we were being foolish. The warden called us to the front office and spoke about the terrible ordeal we faced. The only thing he was specific about was that we would not be called Mr. but addressed by our last names. This became a standing joke among us.

Two days later I wrote again to my mother. I kept thinking of how she and my father must feel—good, substantial, conservative, church-going people, bewildered by the sudden transference of their only son from seminary to prison. I assured her that I found prison life enjoyable. This was true. There was time for rest and study, and I made some interesting new friends.

Finally, one evening we were taken to the Danbury Federal Correctional Institution under personal escort of the warden. During the drive to Connecticut he said he had a new, young Protestant chaplain and was concerned about the effect we would have on his ministry. We reassured him but privately felt we would not relish the job of preaching to eight theological students. Warden Edgar Gerlach wore horn-rimmed glasses that made him look like a Ph.D. He was, in fact, a criminologist from the University of Michigan whose reputation had convinced the authorities that he could run the model institution at Danbury. The combination of his solemn self-importance and fussy mannerisms made him, for us, somewhat comic. We arrived at Danbury at 3:00 A.M., and when the guard slammed and locked the cell door behind me and I found myself alone, I felt for the first time that I was really in jail.

For most of the day the doors were open so that we could use a common recreation room. We read or talked to other prisoners between a series of tests and interviews. Following this period I was assigned to the library.

All of us were kept busy writing and reading letters for inmates or counseling them day and night. Most of the time it was just listening to their problems. Men in jail have terrible family troubles. There are usually wives and children on the outside left without support. Each prisoner was allowed to have seven certified correspondents. I could send out two letters a week, but there was no limit on the number I received. My weekly letters went to my parents. The best religious discussions I had ever had were going on here, I told them. If it were not for the forced separation from family and friends, I felt I could stay here and work with these men for the rest of my life, for there was plenty to be done.

Danbury was known as the country club of the prison system. It boasted no walls; none were needed because it was built as a quadrangle. To get out, an inmate would need to climb over a two-story building. Beginning in January I was out in the cold all day on a pick-and-shovel team and felt in fine condition. One day while out with the work crew, digging not far from the main gate, I saw a civilian walking toward us, escorted by one of the men. He stopped and shook hands with Dal, and after talking with him for a short time I heard him say, "Which one is Benedict?" He was the alumni secretary at Albion, paying Dal and me a visit. He had tried to see us through official channels and had been refused, but walking out to his car, he had spotted Dal. The obvious alarm of the armed guard in the tower did not deter him. Over he came for a chat with us. Not every college can boast so persistent and dedicated an alumni secretary.

All through my prison term I planned to return to Union and live in Newark. But in early April the seminary sent us the terms for our reentry. We would be expected to refrain from active opposition to the draft. Returning to Union, therefore, was not to be considered. After that I wasn't sure what I would do.

Many others were in prison for draft law violation, and about twenty of us decided to celebrate International Student Peace Day in April by fasting and refusing to work. We informed the warden, and he reacted typically. Calling us together, he gave a little speech about our "positive" relationship. Then he informed us we had ten minutes to talk things over and change our minds, and left the room. In precisely ten minutes he was back. "You know, fellows," he said, dusting off his knees, "I'm not a very religious man but I've been downstairs praying that you will see this thing my way." Stunned for a moment by this display of piety, we reiterated our intention. Instantly his manner changed, and we were ordered back to our cells.

Our demonstration was set for the following Tuesday. On Monday the warden called all the prisoners into the yard and made a speech—something he loved to do. Pointing to our group, he explained that he had tried to ease our stay in prison. He had been good to us. We had been given better treatment than the others.

"And now," he continued, "these men propose to strike not only against the Federal Bureau of Prisons, but also against our beloved President, Franklin D. Roosevelt. They propose to refuse to work tomorrow. If they carry out this threat I will be forced to take away all yard privileges for inmates—also Ping-Pong, softball, movies, and library privileges."

The men began to stir. It was clearly an invitation for the prisoners to mob us. Then a distinctly nonpacifist inmate called out, "Warden, we've heard your side of the story, now let's hear theirs."

"To the mess hall for chow!" the warden shouted back.

Because of the warden's threat, we had to get our story to the men. We arranged to sit at different tables to tell our side of the case. The warden stayed in the mess hall, pacing the aisles. Whenever he noticed a discussion going on he would call out comments like, "You think I'm a phony, but I'm not!" and this of course helped us in our argument. It was never difficult to enlist support from prisoners in any disagreement with the warden. A prisoner always takes the word of another inmate.

The evening before Peace Day, after the buzzer rang indicating all inmates present and accounted for, the lights did not go out as usual in our block. No one knew what to expect. There was an air of unrest. After about an hour the guards called me out with two other COs housed in the block. We were led to the warden's office, where one by one we were taken in. When my turn came I found the warden wearing a smoking jacket, with a pipe in his mouth and a book in his hand. He politely offered me a chair and then in a friendly tone asked if I intended to work the next day. No, I said, nor did I intend to eat. He repeated the same question and I repeated my answer. Obviously, he was recording our conversation. The record would be evidence if any trouble developed later. After this I was taken to one of the new quarantine cell blocks and locked up. All twenty of us were put into this segregated block after the questioning. On Tuesday we were offered no food, although we would not have eaten it anyway. Our belongings and some books were brought to our cells, and we settled down to spend the day reading.

Wednesday at 5:30 A.M. we were awakened and ordered out for breakfast, apart from the inmate population. As we came through the cafeteria line we noticed that behind each man who was serving stood a guard. The men had been ordered not to speak to us, but they would smile or wink as we passed. The waiter who poured our coffee did so with a decided air of hospitality. "Officer's mess!" he whispered as he handed us our cups. It seemed to me the best I had ever tasted—real coffee rather than the bitter brew of chicory we had been getting. Our segregation went on until Friday, when we were taken to the Disciplinary Committee, a body made up of the captain, the psychiatrist and the prison social worker. The men called it the Kangaroo Court, because an inmate had no chance whatsoever. Each of us appeared and was told individually that we would be continued in the present cell block, allowed out to eat and work, but the rest of the time locked in our separate cells. By the time the committee finished with us the prison population had filed around the quad and into the mess hall. The twenty of us were led to the hall and released for chow. This was our first appearance among the men since Monday night. Standing in the center of the mess hall was the warden, evidently there to observe our reception. As we came through the door unattended, the inmates began to clap and shout. They stamped their feet and roared approval. A few stood up cheering, and the warden quickly left. Afterward we were again locked in our cells.

I had been playing on the prison softball team for some time and had pitched a one-hitter on the previous Saturday against the best team in the town. Another game was scheduled for Thursday of the following week. On this day the prisoners gathered at the softball diamond in the center of the yard. The warden was there, and the game started, but when the inmates saw that I was not with the team a few of them called out my name. The warden paid no attention. The prison team was doing well, and early in the game they were out in front by three runs. Then a group that was getting out in a few days asked the warden to send for me. The men said they wanted to see me pitch again before they left. The warden sent a guard to my cell. I refused to go unless the other men were also released, and the guard pleaded that he was under orders and might lose his job if he failed to bring me along. I consulted a few of the others through closed doors, and they decided I should go out and pitch. I realized that their counsel had a purpose. I pitched three innings, struck out nine batters, and then walked back to my cell.

The next day three of us asked to see the captain of the guard. I acted as spokesman. "We are wondering what is happening," I said. "All of us were ordered confined to our cells for thirty days, yet I was released to pitch a softball game. Just what *is* our status?" He said he would find out from the warden.

We heard nothing more until the following Saturday, when another softball game was scheduled on the grounds. Half an hour before the game all twenty of us were let out and informed we were free to go back into the prison population.

I have never regretted a day that I spent in jail. The men in my dormitory were great teachers. They poured out their troubles. Hardly a man among them had any relationship with a church or minister or priest. They attended services because there wasn't much else to do at that time on Sunday or because it would count in their bids for parole.

In September, after ten months, we were released from prison, with time off for good behavior. It did not mean that we were excused from registering for the draft. If we did not register, we could be picked up again at any time. The eight of us were released together. We assumed we would be met by a paddy wagon and sentenced again. Nothing of the sort happened. We walked out.

I went back to Newark.

7

In the spring of 1942 I went to Detroit to start a movement that would minister to industrial workers. When we came out of prison, five in our group had enrolled at Chicago Theological

Seminary, and Dal, Dave, and I returned to Newark. It was difficult to leave New Jersey while on parole, so I could not go home right away.

If there was a leader of the group that went to jail, it was Dave Dellinger. We lived at a house near the Jube Memorial Church, worked at odd jobs, and tried again to live like the early Christians described in the book of Acts. We continued to take in drunks and homeless men and finally bought a farm, giving us space and facilities for our work with these people. Dave's family and some other friends provided the money.

In Detroit I offered to help Bill Perkins, a minister trying to rehabilitate the Cass Avenue Methodist Church, an inner-city church in a deteriorating neighborhood. I thought by bringing in some of our Newark ideas and experiences I could help. Perkins had worked for years with little support from mission boards or from anyone else, but now the plaster and paint were in terrible condition. My method was to go ahead and start the job and people usually rallied round. So I went out and got the scaffolding. Three or four volunteers from the congregation came to help, and we repainted the entire interior.

My plan was to work on community programs at this church and also begin a storefront project in Detroit. I expected to take a laboring job, because I wanted to communicate the gospel to working people by working along with them. Once, between college terms, I had worked in a foundry that was casting vacuum cleaner motors. I remembered the alienation from the church of the workers and the barrier that came between us when they learned I intended to study for the ministry.

Blue-collar people were paid low wages in those days, but with the war, wages rose in Detroit, attracting many to the city. Both blacks and southern whites had come, and this was a volatile mixture. The Ku Klux Klan came in and increased tensions.

In the fall, when we had finished our work and the congregation came back into the main sanctuary, I and some others settled down in a complex of three storefronts with an eight-room apartment overhead. It was in a mixed black and white community of working people. I had rented the whole thing with the idea of using the main storefront for working with neighborhood children and young people, organizing a milk co-op and later a grocery co-op in the two storefronts behind. Bill Lovell had come to Detroit to work part-time for the Fellowship of Reconciliation, and he moved in. We started with only a few people: a young orthodox Jew, a Chinese chemistry student, and some who were having their first run-in with the draft law. I was convinced that the church needed a movement directed at factory workers and that Detroit was the place to begin so I went to see the bishop about doing this under the auspices of the Methodists.

The bishop's office was in a downtown building. I remember him as a rather fat man, looking exactly like my idea of a bishop, but somewhat severe and tight-lipped. He had a ponderous manner of listening and saying nothing. I couldn't tell how he was reacting, but I began to feel coldness developing. Finally he told me there was no category in the Methodist Church for such a lay ministry. I invited him to create a category. Within a denomination founded by a great missionary wanderer, could not a place be made, I asked, for a concerned lay person who wanted to give his life to the church? To this he replied that since I did not intend to return to the seminary his only course was to drop me from the official rolls of the church.

I got to my feet, upset. I felt that my vision of a movement had been belittled because of the way he spoke when he referred to it as a "project," so I looked him straight in the eye. "What," I asked, "would John Wesley have thought of this?" And I walked out. I was shocked later when, at the next meeting of the Detroit Conference, the bishop announced that I had asked to have my name removed from standing in the conference.

After that, my relations with the Cass Avenue Methodist Church, to which I had been devoting all my spare time, deteriorated. Lovell and I began in earnest to organize our milk co-op as a good way to get blacks and whites into an organization together. It was a service to the people, provided us with a means for getting to know them and build a base for our mission, and it helped our group living in the apartment. Early each morning we drove to the dairy and picked up milk for the day's deliveries. In spring 1943 other drivers showed us the tire irons and heavy chains they carried in their trucks to protect themselves. Rumors of racial trouble had started. Detroit had no black bus drivers or streetcar motormen, and there were constant reports of altercations going on between white drivers and black passengers.

We had begun recreational activities for young people in our main storefront, inviting blacks from various Detroit churches. Our store windows were uncurtained so people could see what we were doing and feel free to come in, but many passersby peered in at us in a way that made us expect protests and complaints.

During a hot spell the riots began. It was no surprise. Bill and I cruised along Woodward Avenue, the boundary between the white and black communities. A white man came out of a store wielding a huge table leg like a club, looking for blacks whom he could bludgeon. One by one other white people ran along behind him, urging him on, or lunging out looking for more victims. Other mobs prowled like hunters, overturning cars, setting them afire, stopping streetcars and searching for black people to be dragged out and beaten.

Police were ineffective, almost helpless. Their squad cars were overturned by crowds almost before they could jump out. Fire engines and police sirens screamed, and the smoke from burning cars made it impossible to get through. Woodward Avenue as far as we could see was chaos, and we turned off to go back to our apartment. We decided to make the regular milk run to the families in our neighborhood and get together what food we could for them. Ours was a poor neighborhood of small houses and as I drove up I saw that no one had gone to work. The men, women, and children were sitting on their porches, silent, while from open windows behind them radios blared out the news. Over the trees black smoke billowed up from Woodward Avenue. I stopped my truck and got out. Usually the children came running up immediately, but today no one moved. Every head was turned, staring at me. I took down a carrier of milk and a few loaves of bread and then walked up to the first house on my route. I stopped in the middle of the walk and waved a loaf of bread. At once they all broke into smiles and the children ran to meet me. People hurried over to buy the bread and other things I had brought.

For three days we hauled groceries into these blocks. Many efforts were made to stop the battles in the city. Firemen tried to disperse crowds with water hoses. Walter Reuther and his union members tried to calm things down by driving blacks and whites together in cars under the United Auto Workers banner. But order was not restored until the National Guard was called in. Ironically, it was with great relief that I watched trucks rolling by with grim-faced soldiers in position behind machine guns, in patrol of city streets.

Shortly after this I went to Chillicothe, Ohio, where I had heard that some friends of mine who had registered as COs were working in a camp under Civilian Public Service. I wanted to start more of a movement, bring in more people, and so I convinced five of them that they weren't doing anything against the war system by merely staying out of it as COs, and that they ought to come to Detroit and join us as part of our staff. To get acquainted in our community, they put on a big children's fair in the local playground. Some young women from another church turned out to help. This is where I met Ann. She was moving among the children, and they seemed to hang on her words and follow her around. It was a pretty sight, and I stood for some time, watching. I was thinking, "There's the girl I would like to marry."

I found out that her name was Ann Cnare, and that she was a teacher living in Detroit. She was someone you could talk to and she smiled easily. I had an idea that she liked me too, but for some reason I did not ask her for a date.

At the time we were in the middle of plans for desegregating Greenfield's, a popular cafeteria on Woodward Avenue. On the designated day we met at the restaurant at lunch time, a group of men and women, five white, five black, each of us neatly dressed. Our plan was to move into the line with a black person first, then a white, and alternate this pattern so that several other customers would mix in between us. When Bob Mitchell, our first black, arrived with his tray at the serving counter the woman attendant, as we had expected, refused to serve him.

Bob then asked politely to see the manager.

"It won't do you no good," she said. "I told you we don't serve no niggers here."

"I still want to see him," said Bob. "Will you be so kind as to get him?"

"Step aside, step aside!" she said. "Can't you see you're holding up the line?" She turned to Bill Lovell. "Can I help you, sir?"

"Thank you, no. I will wait until this gentleman has been served."

She looked down the line. Behind Bill was another black person, then me, and behind me two plump elderly ladies, craning their necks and whispering. The line extended through the doorway, and people could be seen getting into line on the sidewalk. The waitress, exasperated, went down the counter and joined two or three others. They stood talking and looking around at us. The line was getting longer down the street and people were peering in the windows. One of the waitresses went through the kitchen door, and after some time came back with a worried, fussy man in shirtsleeves, who, ignoring Bob, tried to get Bill to give his order. Bill repeated his lines with a nice emphasis. The manager then moved along until he got to me. I stood with my arms folded, looking impassively ahead at Bob as if I had all day to wait. He then went back and told the waitress to serve Bob, which she did in an outraged, impatient manner, plopping the food on the dish and banging the plate down on the edge of the counter rather than handing it to him. The line moved, and we were all served while the manager stood behind the counter watching.

Our black contingent ate together at one table while the rest of us chose separate tables in order to listen to comments of the other patrons. People generally were grumbling about the wait and unconcerned about the black customers. As soon as our five black young people had gotten up and filed out the door, a busboy came over to their table, the manager behind him, pushing him forward. The manager then stood at attention while the busboy, with a fling of his arm, crashed all the dishes to the floor. After a moment of startled silence, the room began to buzz with talk, and everyone watched the busboy sweep the mess into a container and carry it out. Don Smucker, one of our group, who was connected with the Fellowship of Reconciliation, immediately jumped up. He spoke passionately about the shame of treating our fellow Americans unequally while we were supposed to be fighting a war overseas for democracy. Then we walked quietly out in an atmosphere that had become tense.

Later, I went home to visit my mother and father. On returning I found that our five COs had been arrested and taken to jail. The next morning, while in the Federal Building to arrange bail for them, I was stopped by two FBI agents who asked my name. When I replied they said they were taking me into custody. "On what charge?" I asked. "Failure to register for the draft" was the reply.

I explained that I had business to transact, and they agreed to pick me up later at home. After arranging bail and getting my five friends released, I went home and packed a few belongings. The FBI agents appeared on schedule, taking me to the Wayne County jail. I was ordered to appear at the federal court in Newark. Just before Christmas, after pleading guilty as I had two years before, I was sentenced by a Newark judge to three years in prison. Again the judge left the term open. I would be released at any time I was willing to register and return to the seminary or accept alternative service.

I was returned to Danbury, and I walked in feeling again that I was doing the right thing, but there was no exhilaration this time. Nor did I have eight boon companions. The experience of the riot had affected me. The attack on Pearl Harbor. The reality of war.

Many of the old guards remembered me and their welcome was cordial. "Now we'll have a winning softball team," they said. I heard that the former warden had left the prison system. The new warden was a younger man, thought to be competent and likable. I learned, too, that there were more than two hundred COs in the prison and that a large group of pacifists had been on a work strike in protest against the segregation policy. They had been locked in their cell blocks for almost three months but were due to come out soon. Three days later the entire mess hall was opened up so that prisoners could sit at any tables they chose. I had the honor of being the first person to sit with blacks, because quarantine units were always the first to go to the mess hall. The housing units remained segregated.

8

I began to think about my pacifism as I read Reinhold Niebuhr's *The Nature and Destiny of Man.* I had been glad to see the National Guard enter Detroit. Why did I feel so guilty at my joy in seeing that army? My joy in seeing those machine guns? Was I following the pacifist line merely out of intellectual or emotional habit? Some pacifists are willing to suffer violent treatment when standing up for a cause. They feel that by absorbing all the hostility and aggression they set up the possibility for reconciliation, whereas force tends to continue the aggression. Some pacifists would use force if nothing else could be done. But there are many different degrees and different expressions of pacifism.

My pacifism was not a rigid philosophy in the sense of rules, nor was it a hierarchy of options. I simply had a strong feeling against violence all my life. I had always tried to break down the case for force. But when it came to acting I thought I would be ruled by my feeling at the time.

It seemed to me now that to kill in a crisis of self-defense was to strike directly at evil. This was permitted. But no matter how evil their cause, to invoke the name of justice and strike at other people when they might be brought to reason was surely wrong. To use force against misguided persons would be only an indirect blow. And how can one avoid striking through others to get at the center of evil?

Suddenly, a thought struck me, preventing me from going on. Here I was, a deep-rooted pacifist, actually trying to figure out a way to use force justly. Nazism was at the back of my mind. Was there such a thing as a just war? Were the Jews only absorbing aggression? This might be a just war but whom would I have to kill? And if it was a just war, what was my attitude saying? OK, it's a just war, but I won't fight—let someone else do it? I had to abandon that line of thinking

• 45 •

temporarily, but I realized I would have to give more thought to my own pacifism. What was my stand? What was I going to do?

Coming out of quarantine as a known pacifist serving my second term, I was approached by a man called Chick who had been a United Mine Workers organizer. After being put in jail for failure to register, he had tried to get out by registering as a CO but was refused because he was not religious. He wanted me to help in another demonstration against prison as part of the war system. I agreed, and we recruited sixteen pacifists who would refuse to work for the rest of our terms. One man was to quit work each Wednesday so that the warden would have no way of knowing how widespread the strike was. Chick and I would be the last. We would go together, signalizing the end of the line.

When the day came, we stopped work and were immediately put into solitary confinement. This was my second time, but it was not to be like the first. I had no suspicion that this time it would break me down, that I would face a terrible crisis. At first I was elated. I was glad I had stopped reading Niebuhr's book and that I had joined the work strike. It was the right thing to do. I might have held back, overindulging in self-examination. I was glad that I hadn't wavered. I had been true to myself. And for my belief I had now gone all the way to the wall. But by the end of the next day I was wondering how long they would keep me in solitary. Probably just a few days, then back to a lock-in in the cell. I could understand why men in solitary spent their days waiting for the only events in their lives—the rattle of the lock, the swish of the door opening, and the sound of the food tray in the slot.

By the seventh night I no longer felt I was in solitary because of this last work strike. I was there because of my entire past life, and the question that faced me was not whether I could continue in solitary for the term of my sentence but for the rest of my life. There was no way to follow Jesus and mitigate the suffering. There was no way without, in the end, facing crucifixion. I knew this and I had always been prepared for it. I would go out from jail into a system I would resist and I would be sent back. In prison, too, I would continue to follow my convictions, and that meant solitary. There is no way to compromise when one follows the perfect One.

But was I strong enough? Always before I had thought I was, but now I was racked by doubt. From boyhood, I had believed violence was wrong. Now I faced a direct contradiction. The mere demonstration of the power of force in the Detroit streets had stopped the riots. I had to face that fact. Here was the one case that disproved my convictions. Not only could force bring order and peace; it had to be a superior force. This was hard for me to accept. Violence ought not to be stopped by violence. Where would it end? Nevertheless, my belief in pacifism as an absolute was shaken. How could I stay in solitary if I was unsure that what I was doing was right? What if I were wrong? No answer came. All day and through the night I was repeating a litany:

I have refused to fight. *Lord, hear me.*

I have tried to love everyone. *Lord, hear me.*

I have tried to be like Jesus, the perfect One, and the more I have tried the more impossible it becomes. *Lord, hear me.*

Midge Miller, shortstop. *Shot down over Germany!*

Lou Krueger, first base. *Killed at Anzio!*

The harder I struggle, the more bitter I become with others who say they are Christians. *Lord, hear me.*

Ed Breezee, Tecumseh High. *Crashed in the Himalayas!*

Maybe it makes a difference who wins the war. *Lord, hear me.*

I have never compromised. *Lord, hear me.*

I have followed my conscience. *Lord, hear me.*

I have striven for perfection and I have become only self-righteous. *Lord, hear me.*

I have given up all sources of income except the bare necessities. *Lord, hear me.*

When I lose count of the trays will I know day from night? *Lord, hear me.*

I am entirely removed from the world. *Lord, hear me.*

I am utterly alone. *Lord, hear me.*

God, God, are you hearing me? What good can I do here? Does it make a difference? How can I get out? How can I get out of here when I talked the others into striking? Is pacifism the only choice? There is nothing here. There is nothing ahead. How can I go on? There is no ground, no place to step. I don't have enough faith. Why am I thinking these things? Am I thinking these things trying to make myself guilty for staying in solitary? Selfish for going to prison? Am I thinking these things because I am losing my mind? I don't know what I believe. Only that I believe in you. You are my faith. And yet how can I go on? Into nothingness? Or have I already made the step?

I fell on the mattress, lying there, tossing from side to side. Gradually, the sense of the terrible silence changed to a feeling of quiet, then of peace. I thought it must be almost morning. I was exhausted and seemed to be falling asleep. I closed my eyes and began to drift, and then the words came, not a voice speaking, only the words, clear, in my mind: *You are my beloved.* This was the word of God to all people who have faith. For the first time I realized that word was also meant for me. I, myself, was loved by God—loved with all my guilt and imperfections; I felt surrounded and supported by love. And I slept.

I slept for an hour. When I awoke I knew I was going to get out. Not just go back on work detail and get out of solitary; I was going to get out of prison. But by the time the guard came and I asked for the razor I was shattered and shaking again. That hour of calm had left me.

I put on my shirt, and as the door opened I was thinking that when I got to the warden's office I would write a note to the other pacifists. I felt I owed them an explanation.

It was the morning of the eighth day, and I stood in the doorway, blinking. A draft of fresh air came through, and a shaft of sunlight fell across the floor. The light almost hurt my eyes. I turned to look back into that cold, dim cell and felt for a moment intense sadness. Something fine was being left behind. Also certitude. Also my youth. I knew I would never come back.

9

Out of jail on parole I found myself in the state of doubt that is paralyzing. To be thrown into such a state after being so certain, so sure of my own motives, was terrible. I still had my faith in God, and I was clinging to this, but in every other way I was at sea. I could not reason away my doubt. I knew what I ought to do, but I could not bring back the old feeling of certitude that had stayed with me so long.

During parole I went to Chicago where Albert W. Palmer, president of Chicago Theological Seminary, had made arrangements for me to attend classes there and work eight hours a day as an orderly in the surgical ward at Billings Hospital. In my studies under Wilhelm Pauck and James Luther Adams I was preoccupied with the doctrine of grace. I knew that grace was given, that I could never earn the right to it, and that it brought with it the tremendous realization that one had been forgiven and accepted by God. But now I was looking at myself far more critically than I ever had before. Here I was, a guy who, trying to be perfect, had become a perfectionist, looking askance at other Christians who did not see things my way. If anything I did was good, it was through the gift of grace, for I was a sinner. My motives were mixed; therefore, I was not to judge the motives of others. The idea of legalistic standards for Christians fell away when I came to understand the doctrine of justification by faith rather than by works. I was finding the codification for what I had learned in jail and in Detroit. I was beginning to grope toward a better understanding but was deeply dissatisfied by the lack of perfect clarity.

At the hospital most of the patients were suffering from cancer. In one or two cases I was impressed by the incredible things a strong will could accomplish, but on the whole the work was depressing. The hours outside of work and study were the worst. Thinking became a process of wrestling with myself. Going to prison was not a possibility. The extermination of the Jews by Hitler convinced me I could not stay out of the war. Hitler was a force that, like the Ku Klux Klan, was evil at its core. There was no way to stop it without superior force. Human beings were both good and evil, but in the extreme they were capable of great good and great evil—even of the demonic. Hitler was demonic and had to be stopped. I was still a pacifist at heart, but I could never go back to absolutism. Yet, I could not go forward; I was unable to take the first step.

I knew I could not go on like this and finally went to see the counselor at the seminary. I felt guilty about forsaking the nonviolent stand I had held for years in order to go out and kill somebody. I felt guilty about going into the war, and guilty about staying out of it. The counselor was an intelligent man.

He said, "Well, I can talk to you for a long time, and I will if you want me to, but here's what you ought to do: Drop out of school and join the army."

This was exactly what I needed. The next day I went out and enlisted.

10

Going on to Detroit, I found Ann Cnare was teaching deaf children, and I asked if I might visit her class one afternoon. A roomful of small, active children is always a cheerful scene, I thought as I walked in, and this was no different. But after a few minutes I felt within all this brightness a sense of unreality. These children were moving about, playing, doing things, communicating with one another. I don't know what I had expected; I had known they were deaf and I had seen deaf children before but not so many together in a group like this. To grown-ups, children's voices seem part of their happiness. I wondered what difference it made to the children.

But Ann was perfect with them. She had their attention and affection. I found myself watching one boy, a sturdy child with red hair and exceptionally bright dark eyes. He seemed to me to be a child who would have a lot of questions to ask, quick to respond, and physically active. I asked Ann about him. She stood between me and the children when she answered, I suppose because they could read her lips. "Yes," she said, "he is bright, and also extremely sensitive and quick, so he often pretends to understand. I need to persist with him. It's important that I do not use sign language and it's important to persist. Otherwise because of his impatience to communicate he will end by being limited to signing. It's a little like teaching music, where the teacher insists on long hours of practicing the scales and the child wants to blunder brazenly through Bach right away."

Later I watched Ann speak to him. At once he nodded comprehendingly and flashed her a brilliant smile. She put a hand on his shoulder and spoke to him again, distinctly. He shrugged his shoulders, smiled, and answered vocally. As she went on speaking, making him answer or repeat sounds again and again, pointing to and touching parts of his mouth and throat, his smile gave way to an earnest expression, and as she continued he watched her lips and her eyes. What he said seemed to me to be all vowels; he had trouble with his consonants, but his tone of voice was good, not flat as I had expected. I couldn't make out his speech, but she evidently noticed infinitesimal improvements and managed to show this in her manner. When he finally succeeded Ann gave him a big, hearty hug.

My heart went out to this boy, and I wanted to talk to him. He stood before me, bright as a bird, and I asked him if he liked to play ball. He nodded immediately, but I wasn't sure so I made a gesture of throwing a ball, and he gave me a real boy's grin. He told me his age and also counted it on his fingers. I thought he was amazingly responsive.

Ann said afterward that he could often catch what people were saying by expression and manner alone, without the gestures, but the point was to make him speak. With some twinkling in her eye she remarked that I didn't need to raise my voice in speaking to the totally deaf. Later, crossing the school yard, I was quiet and she seemed to know I was thinking about the boy. She turned to glance at me, brushing a lock of hair back off her forehead. "He was not born that way," she said. "It happened when he was five. So he will have a better command of speech and do a little better than the ones who have never heard at all." I took her hand and held it as we went on down the sidewalk to where my car was parked.

I had come back to Detroit for induction and was staying with Walt Jackson, now minister of a small church in a housing project. And right away, without having to look, I had found Ann—just as I remembered her, blue-eyed, red-haired, standing in a shaft of sunlight. She was teaching a Sunday school class in Walt's church. During the two months I spent in Detroit before induction we fell in love. Ann drifted into it, but I had already fallen. I knew from the start. I felt Ann was a woman I could confide in. She was warm-hearted, interested, responsive. With children she was never rigid or demanding, but permissive and accepting. I liked her, too, for the way she enjoyed them, entering into their games, running and playing with them. And Ann was strongly pacifist; she had been a member of the Young Peoples Socialist League, and had done volunteer work for United Auto Workers locals in the city. We could talk. We had many of the same ideas.

Ann had been made to feel that the kind of work she wanted as a profession was closed to her because she was a woman. So she taught school and gave all of her spare time to volunteer work for churches, unions, and later to organizations such as the Fellowship of Reconciliation (FOR) and the Congress of Racial Equality (CORE). All her life she was drawn toward the struggle for equality, particularly the equality of women, and she wanted to get into that struggle.

Once I decided to go into the service I made up my mind to make the best of it. No longer did I torture myself with the old perplexing questions. I was assigned to the Army Air Corps. My doubts had quieted, and I was prepared to be ordered to shoot.

In basic training I found the segregation rigid in housing and mess halls. There were no opportunities to initiate friendly relations with black people. To say that blacks have a racial tendency to show talent in singing and rhythmic bodily movements is nonsense. But I remember the thrill of watching a black squadron march and count cadence with such snap and rhythm and pure style as to make the white squadrons look like aged arthritics. As I watched those recruits I decided that the talent was attributable to pride of race. It was not merely a physical performance. It had spirit.

I never had to shoot a man. My first assignment was as assistant to the chaplain on Guam, where I became an active organizer. After attending a few meetings of the American Veterans Committee (AVC) I was elected chairman for the island, and I started to work in earnest at organizing the chapter. AVC had been formed as a liberal, noncommunist group by persons who felt the American Legion, largely in the hands of World War I veterans, could not speak for us or for the kind of society we wanted. AVC stood for a more democratic army in terms of officer–enlisted men relations. Although there were many officers who were members, the organization had emerged originally around the ideas of Bill Mauldin, the cartoonist who championed the GI against the army brass. AVC was then promoting an unsegregated army and certain reforms at home that made sense to me. Many of its chapters were initiated by men still in service.

I plunged into the organizing of this chapter but was not to finish the job. Through my work as chaplain's assistant I had become acquainted with the ranking Catholic chaplain, who was involved with the Catholic War Veterans. On the day he left I was ordered to Iwo Jima. It did not occur to me to question the order; this sort of transfer was routine. I found out much later that the influence of this chaplain and of the American Legion were responsible for the sudden transfer, if not also for the remarkable assignment as an automobile mechanic. There was nothing to do but follow orders.

I have known many men who came out of the army and went into business for themselves because they never again wanted to take orders. Along with this aggravated passion for independence in the army ranks went a tendency to applaud any confrontation with authority whenever it could be done, short of battle conditions. I enjoy such confrontations. The desire to argue one's opponent into a state of confusion or to broach authority for justice's sake is not unchristian in itself, but the enjoyment of it may be. However, I may as well admit to enjoying it. I have never hesitated to speak out against authority. As soldiers, we had little hope of confronting the ruling power, the system itself. We could see the reason for the impermeable chain of command and the futility of opposition from within an institution so vast and so organized as is the United States Army when one is essentially a patriot and bound to follow orders.

I knew practically nothing about repairing cars but this did not matter for when I arrived the lieutenant in command of the squadron asked, "Have you been to college?" "Yes," I said. "You are now the first sergeant of this outfit," he told me. I was even less inclined for this job, but by that time the war was over and life on Iwo Jima had simmered down to the formalities of getting out. For two months the island was without a chaplain so I had the opportunity to serve, even though I was only a sergeant. It was interesting to notice how many more enlisted men attended the services when they discovered that one of their number was leading them.

In November 1946 I was discharged. The nearest I had come to action was living through four typhoons.

I expected Ann to meet me at the Detroit airport. She had seen me off when we were mobilizing to go overseas. But Ann was nowhere in sight, and I went into the building, expecting to see her at any moment. I walked around the waiting room and, not finding her, went out the main door. Only a line of taxicabs was there, and I turned back again, moving slowly and searching the faces more carefully.

What had happened? Where was she? Why hadn't she come? The crowd was thinning. All the people looked so happy, standing in groups talking and laughing. Disappointed and hurt, I decided to telephone, and my eye was caught by a young woman emerging from a phone booth. She saw me at the same moment!

Ann had been a few minutes late and had rushed to the gate, missing me as I followed the disembarking passengers. The two of us must have passed several times in the shifting crowd, glancing, scrutinizing, peering anxiously at everyone except each other. Finally, she had gone to call her father, thinking there might be a message that I had missed the flight.

We were married on January 25, 1947, in Detroit.

While overseas I had received a letter from Henry Pitney VanDusen, the new president of Union, telling me I was eligible to return to the seminary. I was still interested in the ministry but could see no way to become pastor of a church and at the same time minister to the dispossessed. However, Ann and I talked it over and agreed that, whatever I did, I ought to finish my education. Then I could try to find my ministry in the inner city. Both of us were concerned about the continuing trend of mainline churches moving out of city centers to new housing developments in the suburbs. We decided to begin our life together at Union Seminary in New York City.

II

THE GROUP MINISTRY

East Harlem

11

I RETURNED to Union viewing the church as having human frailties, but also the potentiality for change. In the world in which I found myself pure choice was impossible; one always had to choose with reservations. I saw that any choice I made would fall short of the kingdom of God; yet to choose was necessary and the choice made a difference.

Ann and I moved into the married students dorm, where Bill and Helen (Dibby) Webber lived across the hall from us. With the Webbers and several other married couples we often talked about our future work and about my experience at Newark. We all wanted to reach the people who were excluded from the system. Inner-city churches were staffed by seminary students or part-time clergy who lacked time or energy to develop the strong new ministry that was needed. We found many older clergy who had not been successful in life and who didn't really want to be in the inner city. They had no interest in the social problems and struggled, often alone, in the old buildings for years. We talked about developing a successful team approach. Newark had pointed the way, attracting many students who had stayed committed even after running into so much opposition from the congregation. My experience had shown that poor people and black people could be drawn through vacation Bible schools for their children. I was eager to prove to the churches, before they gave up on the city areas, that we could reach these people.

In the late fall of 1947, with Bill and Dibby Webber, Paul and Audrey Abrecht, and Walt and Idella Harrellson, we began to plan practically for our group ministry. Bill and I were to finish seminary in July of 1948, and we called on home mission executives who we thought might be interested in experimental work in the blighted areas of the cities. Truman Douglass, executive vice president of the Board of Home Missions for the Congregational Christian Churches, was our first choice. We had great respect for him. After preparing a paper outlining our ideas we went to see him. It took him only ten minutes to read the paper, ask a few good questions, and wholeheartedly approve of our plan. But he thought it should be undertaken as an interdenominational project and sent us to Mark Dawber, director of the Home Missions Council of the Federal Council of Churches; he had spent his life dealing with these problems and knew them far better than we did. Our idea intrigued him, and he arranged for us to have ten minutes on the agenda at the January assembly of the Council. Kenneth Miller, of the New York City Mission Society, was also more than interested in our plan, and we learned of the work of their inner-city missions.

Several other city executives expressed interest, but usually they told us about a dying church that needed leadership and asked if we wouldn't consider helping them out.

In January four of us presented our plan to the assembly. As spokesman, I made my presentation brief, but there was so much interest that we spent more than an hour talking and answering questions. They thought it a splendid idea but made no commitments. They felt it should be tried in New York City, because most of the national mission boards were there.

Later we learned that the New York City group had talked it over and were not going to become involved in any "wild scheme" when they already had churches of their own in difficulties and without leadership. Immediate action was necessary, and, after a number of meetings four denominations—Congregational Christian, Methodist, Baptist, and Presbyterian—pledged a budget of $9,500 for 18 months beginning in March 1948.

The last year at school neither Bill nor I could find fieldwork that related to our mission, and we needed funds, so we went to Dr. Miller. He offered us $200 each during the fall semester to survey the religious situation, block by block, in East Harlem. The Society had just done a survey but wanted to follow it up with details. This solved our problem, and it pointed to the real possibility that East Harlem would be the location of our project. The earlier study had revealed the weakness of Protestantism in the area.

It was an area of about a square mile, extending from 96th Street to 125th Street and from Fifth Avenue to the East River, with a population of 300,000. We visited about thirty storefront churches and interviewed school principals, ministers, and social workers.

Even though we still were finishing our studies we decided to begin in East Harlem during the summer of 1948. This way we could work with the children when they were out of school. When it became evident that the $9,500 was all the money that would be available, it was decided that Bill would accept a job as assistant dean at Union, and Ann and I would move to East Harlem as full-time workers. The others would work part-time with us. The pastors of three storefront churches on East 100th Street, the most crowded block in the area, agreed to let us use their premises weekday mornings for our vacation Bible school.

Looking at the street we realized that if we decided eventually to start our church there, our entire parish would be contained in this single block. Four thousand people lived across the street from one another. The structures were six-story buildings that had been divided and subdivided into many apartments. East Harlem was one third black, one third Puerto Rican, and one third Italian.

On a warm July day Walt Harrellson and I came down the street carrying a card table and camp stools. The block was thick with people on the sidewalks, on the curbs, and in the street. Families sat out on the steps, and people leaned out of windows and perched on fire escapes, calling back and forth. The buildings were contiguous, but wherever there was airspace clotheslines were stretched. On some fire escapes mattresses had been put out to air or for sleeping on hot nights. Walt and I set up our table, laid out a supply of index cards, and posted a small placard announcing the vacation Bible school.

Children began to hover around us, watching us get settled, sensing something new. The younger ones peered at us solemnly over the edge of the table. After we got the first little girl to register, we were literally swamped. She was a black girl who was extremely reluctant to sign up for any kind of school until Walt explained that at our school we told stories. Immediately she changed her mind, gave us her name, age, and address, and ran off excitedly clutching the slip of paper we had given her telling the time and place for the first session. After that, all the children wanted their names put down. A woman came over to see what we were doing, then hurried off, calling loudly for her son, collaring him, and pushing him into the line that had formed. Other mothers soon converged on us, frantically urging on their older children. I found myself wondering if they knew for what they were registering. Probably not all. But anything that was being offered or done for children to keep them busy was popular and welcome.

After an hour we had registered 150 children. We had only five teachers, so we packed up the table, explaining that was all we could take and asking them to come to the school on Monday morning. It was soon evident we were dealing with youngsters disturbed by home or street environment or both. The restlessness, tension, and explosive emotions were different from anything I had ever experienced. Also, an airless, rather unattractive storefront room in hot weather is not an ideal place for meeting thirty or forty children. Their response, however, was great. They seemed to understand that here were some people who at least cared what happened to them during the hot summer months. We ran the school five mornings a week for a month. Two storefronts accommodated the elementary and the junior high ages, and in the third, Ann and Helen Hendrickson worked with preschoolers.

We decided to have an evening of closing exercises, hoping

that some of the parents would come to see what their children had learned. It was held in one of the storefront churches on the hottest night of the summer. All the children came and many parents. The store was packed and many had to stand in the street. The exercises were mediocre, to say the least, although one bashful little boy got resounding applause for the shortest speech of the evening: "We learned how to do good and share with others." Afterward we thanked the parents for coming, then made the mistake of passing cups of Kool-Aid. It caused a riot. Children climbed over the chairs, jumped, and ran, spilling Kool-Aid on the floor and furniture. Finally, we moved to the door, where we gave each child a cupful and a friendly push into the street.

12

A former Lutheran missionary who was helping us that summer found a store for rent on East 102nd Street, near a vacant lot where children gathered. The store was only 20 × 20 feet, dilapidated, dirty, and had broken windows. The basement was filled with rubbish and the rent was high—$75 a month. But it was a place to begin.

I became full-time pastor at the new storefront. Archie Hargraves, a graduate of Union who was in the Ph.D. program at Columbia, worked half-time as copastor. Other part-time staff included Bill Webber and four other people from the seminary: Peggy Ruth, a first-year student; Hugh Hostetler, a middler; Walt Harrellson, instructor in Old Testament; and Durward Foster, a senior.

I knew Bill well and valued his advice and administrative abilities. He was energetic but controlled, inclined to look ahead, see all the pitfalls, and predict them. "Now, let's consider this from the standpoint of what is possible and what is not possible," he would say, whereas I was inclined to rush into action and take on more than I ought. I realized this fault of mine could have serious consequences for the group; Bill's mind provided needed balance. But frequently, I was already involved by the time the group could meet to talk it over. In a place like East Harlem, where crises and emergencies occur constantly, it often is not feasible to defer decisions. Yet all of us wanted to be in concert. Bill was pragmatic, meticulous, politically inclined, efficient.

Archie was, in the beginning, our only black staff member. He was tremendously creative, possessing unusual insight, warm and friendly with people, and a great preacher. He had a strong ego—we all did—but did not let it get in his way. He understood what it meant to be black yet had surmounted the hostility so that all of us could level with him and he with us. People were drawn to Archie by his intelligence and gradually became aware of a kind of solid elegance about him as a person. This had something to do with his flair for drama, but it was more than that. I would call it style and presence.

Peg was beginning a lifetime of devotion to the poor and to East Harlem. A pretty woman, a shade reserved in her manner, she spoke carefully and thought well what she said. She had a long, low laugh when amused. Peg was deeply religious and warm-hearted, easily able to relate to the neighborhood people.

Hugh was a Mennonite, with sincere human concern and a direct friendliness. No one took him for a city person; his long, gangly steps were like the rolling gait of a farmer. His faith and hope in people were unlimited. He could see good in everyone.

There were drawbacks in trying to work through the established storefront churches. We wanted to continue our program for children at those locations, but the children were being exposed on Sundays to a ranting Fundamentalism that we felt was undoing our work during the week.

The principal difficulty of ministering in the inner city is that of penetrating race and class barriers. The real function of a missionary is to make the gospel come alive within the context of the racial, social, and cultural patterns of the people, and so we had to learn a new culture. My experiences in Newark, in jail, in the army, and in Detroit had been some preparation. But now my whole life was to be here. We saw the group as an approach and support in maintaining morale in an alien environment. To live in the neighborhood was imperative. To minister to an inner-city community while living in the suburbs is to be a stranger to the congregation. Most of the problems of life occur between 5 P.M. and 9 A.M., and we wanted to be available.

We decided to call ourselves the East Harlem Protestant Parish. Choosing this name, reflecting our identity and purposes, turned out to be a more exacting task than we had thought. "East Harlem" we knew would identify the place in terms of New York City. "Protestant" distinguished us from the Catholics and at the same time indicated our interdenominational character. Whereas "parish" might mean little to the people, we hoped to put meaning back into the word. We wanted to return to Protestantism the outgoing concept of serving everyone in a given geographical community rather than staying with the inbound idea of church as the central place of worship attracting like-minded people from anywhere.

We depended on home mission boards for support and clarified some of our basic concepts in talking to executives on these boards. The interdenominational approach was fundamental, for no single denomination had the resources and leadership needed. It was difficult for denominations to acknowledge neglect of one section of society in favor of another, to admit they had failed in the inner city through lack of leaders, ideas, and money. Perhaps it meant admitting a deeper failure: that their churches had no meaning for a large segment of society. It was difficult for them to hear us, just out of seminary, with little or no experience, say these things. Looking back, I appreciate the great imagination and trust required of the church executives who were willing to take a chance with us.

To build an enduring movement, we would need group strength to absorb the hostilities around us. But we were conscious of the dangers of monasticism, of turning inward or becoming so self-absorbed as to fail to communicate with the world. Most of us expected to spend the rest of our lives in this kind of ministry, and all of us realized we needed disciplines that would hold us together. We finally adopted four major disciplines.

The first was *worship*. We planned a common devotional life, everyone reading and meditating on the same scriptural passages each day. Weekly Bible study was to be a regular part of our group life as was weekly discussion of problems arising out of our work and life together. All questions—theological, philosophical, economic, social, and political—relating to issues in East Harlem were to be dealt with in the context of the Bible. Occasional retreats would provide times for the whole group to meditate on the life and work of the parish.

The *vocational* discipline would give continuity. Each person was committed to the entire group. All moves were to be discussed, and no one would leave until a replacement could be found. But the group could only recommend what one should do.

Economic discipline was devised so that each person would have about the same amount of money. Theologically, it made sense to have the ministry paid on the basis of need. We were not going to attract people because of what we could pay them, but on the basis of commitment. Salaries were calculated according to the number and ages of the children. Every family was to choose a place to live, and rent was to be paid by the group. Vital to the plan was to be the feeling of sharing equally, all suffering or prospering together.

Because conditions in East Harlem made it expedient to work together on political and social issues, the *political* discipline provided for using the collective wisdom of the group. If we voted to take action on an issue, such as housing, or to support a certain candidate, any objector was free to refrain from that activity but was not to oppose the group publicly.

We hoped these four disciplines would bind us in the manner of the earliest Christians. Also the group ministry was a practical way to substantiate and support the individual in living and proclaiming the gospel in the inner city, and the concept grew more and more in my own mind as a necessary expression of the church in our time.

Belonging to the group answered to a deep imperative in my nature, and I wanted this group to be stable and steadfast. I was now embarking on my life's work. The force still motivating me was the experience of compassion and the desire for justice. Each arose out of the other. I had failed to follow Jesus when it meant going on alone. Perhaps now with the group I could.

If I could ever again stay wholeheartedly with one cause, one side or the other among opposites, I would know it. But if not I could go along with the principle of throwing my weight on the side of the oppressed, the poor, and the powerless.

The single-mindedness of my youth now seemed too simple, but I could not repudiate it or free myself from it completely. I still believed in nonviolence, but it was no longer a consuming passion. Would there now be a tendency to begin accommodating to lesser and lesser goals? I hoped not. The uncompromising ideal—although I had found it impractical for me—was not the less ideal, and I would still need some of that old, pure, unmixed passion. Life had become complex, and I was ill at ease with complexities. I needed to plunge into activities that were useful and to be with others who had faith. I had not been called to be solitary.

13

Our first tasks were to prepare the store's interior for use as a church and recreation center and to call on the block people to tell them about it. The storefront concept enabled us to put most of our money into personnel and made it easy for people to approach us. They were accustomed to going in and out of stores and felt a store was there for them. But we found it difficult to convey a clear idea of what our church would be like. When young people began to come in and ask questions and we told them we were preparing the place as a church they envisioned a Pentecostal sect, the only kind of church they had ever seen in such a location. When we explained that this would also be a place for children and young people to get together, they pictured the usual settlement house. They could not imagine a place to play Ping-Pong on Saturday and worship on Sunday.

Some parents were suspicious or fearful that we were a front for shady activities, that the reredos we were building at the front of the chapel hid telephones to be used in the numbers racket. Others decided that because we seemed interested in children and young people we were Communists. One old man told us frankly, "You won't last six months. These people don't want religion."

Among the first to show interest in our arrival were Marcantonio's men. Political power in East Harlem was in the hands of Vito Marcantonio, the district's congressman for almost twelve years, who ran under the American Labor Party with Communist support. Marc fought for better housing and schools and for enforcement of the housing code, and his organizers made a great show of taking the side of the masses. Tammany Hall controlled the city but had been unable to defeat him.

The four of us at 102nd Street made hundreds of calls on the people in the neighborhood. Often we tried to talk to weary, hopeless women over the howls of children with whom they were unable to cope. Others looked at us with undisguised suspicion as we stood in the hallways telling our story. The more hostile would say immediately that they could give no money and seemed surprised or suspicious when we continued to be interested in them after that. Some told us they had gone to churches where nobody paid any attention to them. It was almost impossible to convince anyone that other Christians had given money to support a new church to be formed by the people of East Harlem in their own neighborhood. But we found enough interested people to raise our hopes, and felt there would be a respectable crowd for the first Sunday service, the fourteenth of October. We had decided to begin with a worship service rather than some other function so the people would recognize us first as a church. Our other affairs would then be seen as activities of the church.

We agreed to wear clerical collars at all times in the neighborhood to identify our operation as a church and so we would not be taken as bill collectors, FBI agents, police, or drug dealers. The collar would identify us when visiting in jails and hospitals. In the beginning, with our myths about the dangers of the ghetto, we probably thought of the collar as protection. But none of us was ever physically assaulted. Violence in those days was not random, but direct, with some known human relationship involved.

Eventually we adopted a zip-up work jacket to wear with our clericals so that people would see us dressed the same and think of us as a movement. One member could substitute for another, and we wanted to be distinctive from the usual pastor.

We hung some old drapes given by a friend and set up a communion table, with a Bible and a pair of candlesticks. Behind the table was a cross made of laths and stained by one of the boys.

Our chapel would seat only fifty or sixty people, and on the morning of the fourteenth we donned our cassocks and stood happily waiting for the crowd. First to arrive was Dora Thompson. She was intensely interested in a church connection for the sake of her children and had brought the three older ones along. Peggy had called on her and now introduced her. As the minutes ticked by we realized no one else was coming and we would have to begin the service. Then the door opened and in walked Fala Cruz, who lived upstairs in the adjoining building with her seven children. We all knew Mrs. Cruz. She was short, very fat, and not only spoke so rapidly both in Spanish and in English that it was almost impossible to understand her, but her remarks were interrupted by reprimands to her children. I was sure she was a Catholic and was surprised to see her.

"Buenos días," she said, pushing back from her face the folds of a lacy shawl covering her head and shoulders. "Hace calor! Hot!" and rapped the smallest boy on the head. "Bastante! Enough!"

Her sharp black eyes took in everything as she talked. Suddenly, she struck her hands together, then clapped one hand to her forehead. "I breeng you sometheeng. Uno momento!" She turned and ran out the door, leaving the seven children staring at us. In a few moments Mrs. Cruz was back, heaving and puffing, with something wrapped in a towel, which she handed to me. "Thees ees my churchee now," she said. "Thees you take for churchee." As I unrolled the towel two cockroaches fell to the floor and crawled off. Within was a crucifix on a stand.

"Thank you," I said. "Thank you very much. It is beautiful. Gracias."

"Nada! Eet ees notheeng! Nada."

I placed the crucifix on the table. The entire Cruz family then genuflected in the aisle and filed into their seats.

No other people came that morning. All through the service the Thompson children sat stiff and proper, never taking their eyes from us, while in the row behind them Mrs. Cruz could be heard swatting, thumping, and shushing the squirming boys and crawling baby. I was curious to know why Fala had chosen to come to our church, and a day or so later asked Ana, her oldest girl. She said that the day we opened the store her mother put fifty cents on the numbers and she won ten dollars.

With some embarrassment we began to call on people after this first Sunday service, deciding to begin our children's program soon. Our youth program began after the fourteen-year-old Puerto Rican girl who lived upstairs ran away from home. She was gone three days, and during this time I worked actively with her father and the police to find her. The day she was returned to her father, who was a block captain for Vito Marcantonio, he marched her down to the storefront, hoping I would give her a severe lecture. I asked some questions, and when she made it clear he had not been much of a father, he became angry. "That's enough," he said and marched her back upstairs. With this girl we organized our teen group. She brought her friends and was elected president of the club. A boy who lived in an adjoining building with his older married sister joined the teenage club and became an active member of our parish. We put him through college eventually, and Hal Walker is now an NBC-TV news correspondent in Europe.

One day I noticed a crowd around a doorway on 101st Street. I went over and found that a mother and her four children were being evicted from an apartment she had rented from the superintendent, who acted as agent for the landlord. He had moved to another place and rented the woman the apartment that went with the job. Two months later he was fired and now the landlord needed the apartment for his replacement.

I felt our church should show concern. It would be virtually impossible to find an adequate apartment for a family of this size with no notice; she ought to be given more time. We began trying desperately to find another place. As crowded as they were, the people of East Harlem would always find a way to shelter victims of fires or evictions and to store some of their smaller things. But the heavy furniture would remain on the street, through rain or snow, until the family could move it.

To show the people that a new force had come into the community interested in justice and the people's rights, we decided to hold a public demonstration. We got out leaflets announcing that the Sunday service would be dedicated to the issue of housing injustice. A new group of people came, and afterward Archie and I, still in our robes, lined up the people as they came out so that we could march two abreast around the block to the apartment building. There, beside the piled-up bedsteads, tables, and bureaus we held a prayer service, calling attention to the plight of the family and insisting that something be done to help them. It drew a large crowd on the block. Most of the people had never before seen a church take an interest in their worries. It was a brief affair, but it served notice to the community of our interest. It opened up the neighborhood to us, not so much bringing people in numbers to church services, but it brought people with problems. Everyone in the group ministry agreed we were moving in the right direction.

I moved my desk to the storefront window and would sit there every morning where I could be seen by people passing by. It was not long before I had to be careful about the amount of time I spent there. There was not a person in East Harlem without a major problem. We went with them to welfare centers and housing offices. Parents came to us when their kids were picked up by police or had troubles in school.

In our group meetings we discussed the slow growth of the congregation in comparison with the numbers coming to us with problems. The earliest to join the church had been mothers of the youngsters in our children's program. There were not many fathers, and many had no visible fathers. Parents of teenagers were not as likely to appear in church. Some of the people we had helped began to come and also those who were politically active, but we were not getting the broad general populace. Part of the reason we knew was that, unlike other churches in the area, we offered no easy illusion of escape. Also there was prejudice. Irish would not meet with blacks, nor some of them with Italians; blacks would not meet with whites; and Spanish-speaking people maintained cautious insularity. Archie felt a way to get them together was to work on a common problem with common action leading to community worship.

We chose a house on 101st Street with a badly leaking roof. Whenever it rained the whole house was flooded. The tenants— blacks, West Indians, and Irish—said they wouldn't come to a meeting. But Peg persisted and finally convinced them that together they might get the landlord to fix the roof. Archie decided to revive the tradition of the agape meal, or love feast, which includes scriptural readings and discussion. The people discovered that they wanted more, and the meetings did not stop when the roof was fixed. The agape meals continued, with prayers, songs, Bible reading, and discussion. "In spite of what they told us at first, this was what the people really wanted," said Archie, "but they didn't know it."

At the beginning Archie and I felt the people wanted pageantry, and we used a liturgy quite like the Episcopal one. For the service we wore aqua cassocks. We had a great variety in the songs and changed the accepted liturgical practices in order to make our forms of worship fit the lives of the people. At our first Maundy Thursday service, knowing the congregation would be put off by the ceremony of washing feet, Archie had us shine their shoes instead.

Archie's litany went through modifications and became a living, changing part of the service. It changed from a singsong intonation to a joyful shouting, which gave a sense of response and power. The people needed to feel organized and to gain a sense of power and Archie knew this. He had other litanies, one of which developed as the "I am somebody" refrain. Many years later this idea was taken up by the Rev. Jesse Jackson in Chicago and was used to great effect. I believe it was Archie who started it.

Our first Christmas was disheartening. The store was without heat, and one morning a pail of water we had left had three inches of ice in it. The premises were heated through the same system as the apartments above us, and the people who lived there told us the entire winter would be like this. We decided to take the matter on and investigate it. A city ordinance specified minimum indoor temperatures, but the tenants said they had been to court with the landlord and had not been able to prove their case. We bought thermometers, gave one to each family, and asked them to keep records over a period of time. The records were compiled and a complaint made to the court. In the meantime we discovered the building thermostat was three feet from the boiler and set for 55 degrees during the coldest months.

Several of the men drove to court with me in the carryall. Their families had suffered for years in freezing rooms every winter, and they were now in high glee at finally having the landlord where they wanted him. He was a bad man, they said, and they would like the judge to put him away for life. So fierce was their feeling that I felt called on to point out the relative aspect of justice even in this case. He was wrong but probably had his own troubles: high interest payments to make, tenants behind in the rent, and so on. I also reminded them of the ways some of their children misused the premises, and I tried to explain that no side in any argument is entirely in the right. I could see I was not reaching them and could understand their extreme indignation. This was not the time to explain the paradoxical position of the Christian in fighting for justice.

But they certainly experienced a rough approximation of the relativity of justice. The judge decided the landlord was guilty of negligence. He was reprimanded and fined fifty dollars. He had saved far more than that amount in heating bills, and while the people were irate over the small penalty, at least they had some satisfaction in the court's finding him guilty. After that he did a little better job of heating. The case had its effect upon him; he realized the tenants had the power to cause him inconvenience and expense.

14

In January we rented a second storefront on East 100th Street, and Archie Hargraves became the pastor. It was larger, took less repairing, and we could then bring the children on this block to our church. We had decided to go our own way, because we would be reaching out to an entirely different strata of society.

Besides parish work, a great deal of time was given to the workings of the group ministry. We met every Monday night, and the attendance rule was strict. At times one could not get to the early prayer service every morning, but Monday nights were inviolate. The most important of our disciplines was the Bible study. This was our touchstone, our center.

We began with supper and after the Bible hour went into discussions that lasted far into the night, covering our plans, operations, finances, and problems, and we tried to apply the gospel literally to every solution. Judgments and decisions usually had to be through consensus rather than majority vote. On certain questions everyone had to agree, and this process took enormous amounts of time.

As time went on many new people joined us. We had to make difficult decisions about who to take. They had to be totally dedicated to what we were doing. Eventually, with numbers joining us, we developed a probationary period of one year before a person could be voted in. One of the group was assigned to each probationer as a confidant, and while continuing to participate in our regular meetings, probationers also had separate meetings with a different agenda.

Ann and I were approached by the Methodist district superintendent and asked to work at the Church of the Savior, at Lexington and 111th. In the fall of 1949 our third storefront church was opened on 101st Street, between Archie's church on 100th and the original storefront on 102nd. It was named Church of the Redeemer and Hugh Hostetler was its pastor.

Gradually, as more people came into the group, we were to establish other churches, and each time there was increasing sentiment among the group that we were moving too fast. All agreed on the second storefront, and the new church for Hugh seemed sensible. But there had been murmurs against our taking over the Methodist church at 111th Street. I also was talking about moving the congregation from 102nd Street into the abandoned chapel on 104th, next to Union Settlement and owned by Union Seminary. But the group was cautious. Slow down until we are better organized, they said. They were satisfied with what we had. My argument was that when we had pastors ready we ought to open the churches for them. With so many seminarians and college students joining us and needing assignments, there was no dearth of help. When we had a chance to get a good location we ought to go ahead. Our parish had captured the imagination of young people going into the ministry. Faculty and students at Union were interested. Everyone, it seemed, wanted to work in East Harlem. Whenever we could afford the salaries we ought to expand.

My main argument with the group was over the Methodist church. The whole point of our movement, they insisted, was not to get involved with one denomination. I agreed we could not take an operating church with a congregation that would not integrate, but this one had dwindled to almost nothing. The old white community had left. We needed the space a church building would provide for larger meetings and for our numerous activities. I couldn't see any problems, and finally after a long session the group agreed to take this church, probably because I was so optimistic. As usual, I was too optimistic. The storefront was far superior in our kind of ministry. A particular denomination can be induced to help support a revived church. When their executives see new life in the old building it is easy to get them involved again. But we now had a building that took half our money; less was available for a staff.

About this time Carlos Rios arrived. He had emigrated from Puerto Rico early in 1949 and settled in New York because his mother, a member of our parish, was there. She soon brought him to see if I could help in getting him a job. Carlos was baptized a Catholic, but he had once gone to a church function where a priest ordered him to go home and put on a suit coat and he never went back to the church.

While I was looking for job openings Carlos began coming to church and soon volunteered to read the scripture in Spanish during the service. It was immediately evident that he had real translating ability. Every Sunday after I preached he would translate my sermons. Questions of justice, especially those evolving around cases of police brutality and housing code enforcement, interested him tremendously. I became more and more dependent on him in casework with Puerto Rican families. The parish finally offered Carlos a full-time job, and with his family he moved into the rooms over the chapel we had acquired on 104th Street.

His devotion to people was remarkable. Any time of day or night he would respond, and he made hundreds of friends taking people to welfare or housing offices. Later we sent him to a biblical seminary, and eventually he became copastor at the Church of the Son of Man. Carlos Rios came to be known all over East Harlem as the man to turn to with any kind of problem. If he did not have the answer, he knew where help could be found.

Norman Eddy came to East Harlem in the summer of 1951, after finishing Union Seminary. People sensed his interest and sympathy at once. During the war he had been a conscientious objector and worked in the American Friends Ambulance Service. For Norm, the ministry was mystical, primarily spiritual, and he always stressed this aspect in our work. He believed in intercessory prayer and wanted to set up prayer cells, not only for personal strengthening and enrichment, but as a resort in solving problems. Later Norm married Peggy Ruth. A great deal of dating always went on among young seminarians and college students working in the parish, but Norm and Peg had always been distant at our group meetings, so we were astounded when the announcement came.

After the first year the group decided I was to have the title of executive director. This was a role I did not want; it seemed to me contrary to our philosophy. But we had to have someone designated whom people could call, someone to speak for the group, answer urgent questions, and make on-the-spot decisions when necessary. The reasons were good, but I was apprehensive that it might be one step toward what I wanted above all things to avoid—the slipping away of the group. I could see this happening when we became more businesslike, more organized in divisions of responsibility. We had by this time set up both a parish board of directors to account to the supporting denominations and a parish council among the churches we were developing. At first there was some conflict among the three groups in policy-making, but as the parish developed the council gradually assumed the policy-making powers regarding church programs, while the group ministry continued to function as a support group for the staff. The parish board raised funds and continued to report to the supporting denominations.

Over the years probably two thousand people, including hundreds of seminarians, got their feet wet in inner-city work in this parish. All who came attended our meetings and participated in our ministry as part of the group. In a sense we had created an urban theological academy.

There were three points of view around which discussions most often coalesced. Some, like Bill Webber, were analytic, cautious, efficient, given to detailed practical planning. Those who were like Norm Eddy saw the minister as not so much involved in the action as influencing it, giving spiritual counsel, and working with individual people. They favored raising the people to the level of confidence where they could do things for themselves. Although many saw me as the political type, always wanting to march on city hall, more correctly my point of view was action-oriented. My logic was more intuitive and less practical than Bill's. I would look at a situation, see what was obviously wrong with it, and want to go ahead, impatient of delay. I leaned more toward dash and drama than caution. Never could I understand why others who agreed on what was right and necessary could not move quickly.

Each of these points of view was valid but led to intense discussions and arguments. I was inclined to argue longer. I never liked to give up on an idea.

15

At one time we heard a clash was brewing between two gangs that would bring in a number of brother gangs. This meant that as many as two hundred young men would be involved in a street fight. We met with the leader of one of the gangs in the basement of the church, along with several members he had with him, and set up a general meeting. When the gang members arrived we took a decisively crisp, commanding attitude and laid down the rules: All weapons were to be checked with us as the members entered. It worked. Word of what was in the wind went around, and shortly the leaders of brother gangs showed up. We didn't know how to find the chief of the other major gangs, but Archie thought he had some leads and circled the neighborhood, going through bars and restaurants, and finally found him. Surrounded by several of his young henchmen, the chief walked in, saying, "What's the shit? Let's settle it! I'm the great Ernie." We sat in the background and let them talk it out. The conference went on until 4:00 A.M., but they came to terms. Surely we were babes in the woods in those days! Anything might have happened in our church basement that night.

The Red Wings and the Black Robes were gangs of younger boys. Leaders of boys' or teenage groups could, once we got to know them, draw the others closer to the church. Hugh became our specialist in this work. The boys trusted him instinctively. For a time I had the Black Robes, a street gang of ten- to twelve-year-olds. Bill and I took them for a camping trip in Vermont. With Bill as a loving drill sergeant, the boys were lined up and assigned duties, the route was mapped with precision, and the troops were thoroughly briefed on everything, including exactly what to do if anyone became lost or separated. He kept everyone alert; there was no straggling, no nonsense. The boys loved it.

Later on at our churches we tried to develop these boys into groups that paralleled the gang organization by training them to do things of a positive nature. At meetings we would line them up in military fashion and ask where they had noticed God working during the week: "What is God doing? Where is God doing it? How do we join God?"

Archie and I took a youth group to Washington, D.C. and while there had an unplanned sit-in. This was in 1950, long before sit-ins became common, and it happened at a White Castle restaurant in sight of the Capitol. Sixteen of us walked in at around 8:00 A.M. More than half the group was black, and the restaurant would not serve them. So we asked for the manager, who turned out to be a good Presbyterian layman. He pleaded with us; he would be ruined. We said we would sit. Eventually, the police came, but we sat there peaceably until late afternoon.

In the spring of 1950 we became involved in our first case of police brutality. Witnesses alleged that two boys had been running a crap game on Lexington Avenue when a policeman came along and asked for a few dollars. The boys scooped up the money and ran, but the policeman caught one of them. The boy wriggled loose and started through a vacant lot. The officer pulled out his gun, shot once in the air, then shot the boy twice in the back.

We felt keenly that the churches in the community should protest. When it became clear that we planned a public demonstration, East Harlem Association of Churches and Pastors withdrew support, although some ministers joined us. We marched to the precinct station with a large crowd and held a service on the station steps, with scripture readings, and prayers for the boy in the hospital, for the policeman who shot him, and for ourselves, who were also responsible, in some sense, for violence in our community. Some police told us later they had been upset by the shooting and that the commissioner had called the precinct captain when he saw the story of our march in the newspaper. He had asked who was running the precinct, the ministers or the captain.

Maria Cimino was a neighbor I knew through helping to get her son paroled rather than sent to prison. Her husband, Sam, told me one day that she had been hemorrhaging for about two weeks and that he had taken her to a local hospital where she was examined in the emergency room and sent home with some pills to take. She had continued to hemorrhage and could not walk, so he had called an ambulance. When it came the driver had walked up the two flights of stairs, looked at Maria, and motioned for her to get up and come down and get into the ambulance. Sam told him she couldn't walk down, but that he would help with the stretcher. "I'm not getting any stretcher out tonight," the driver said. He had simply walked out and left Maria there.

"Come upstairs," Sam said to me. "See her. See how she looks." I went up and when I saw her decided to take the chance of getting her to the hospital in my car. This time we took her to Presbyterian Hospital, where she was taken in a wheelchair to the emergency room: when I came back later Maria was undergoing surgery; the next day the doctor told me if she had waited longer, she would have died.

Sephora Jones became frightened one day at the sound of her baby's breathing, wrapped the child in a blanket, and rushed to the emergency room of a nearby hospital. An intern told her it was just a cold and that he would give the baby a shot of penicillin. That night the child became worse, so she called an ambulance and was taken to a different hospital, where a doctor made the same diagnosis, administered another shot of penicillin, and sent them home.

The next day the baby began to choke again. Sephora ran to the police station, and they took her again to the second hospital where a doctor looked at the child and decided that hospitalization was needed. They had no room, he said, but he would call City Hospital and arrange for a bed. Sephora got a taxicab and took her baby to City Hospital. There an intern told her the child was sick all right but did not need hospitalization. All he needed was a shot of penicillin and she could take him home.

Here Sephora broke down. She was almost hysterical, screaming that they had to take care of the baby. "He's dying," she cried. "At night he chokes. He'll choke to death! My baby!" The nurse standing by prevailed on the doctor to admit the child. Presumably, if they did not they would have Sephora on their hands. The baby died three days later of bronchial pneumonia.

I realized that many hospitals had an impersonal policy of discharging their obligation by seeing the patient and giving some treatment. There was no personal interest in the patient, no one concerned enough to see that the correct diagnosis was made. The attitude seemed to be one of trying to get rid of the responsibility. Ambulance drivers were overworked and probably underpaid. But in a city that could organize and administer an efficient fire department, why wasn't the ambulance service better?

No system can be wholly good, but I could not dismiss the difficulties so easily. What ought to be done? Should we fight the system or try to improve it? It will never be perfect. No matter how well conceived the system is, without vigilance the more people who are treated, the less personal the treatment becomes.

My reasoned conviction that justice is always relative would diminish whenever people in East Harlem were suffering or in trouble. Without the group ministry I might have ended up in jail and again in the pit of solitary confinement. I was trying to make sense of the world. Christianity appealed both to reason and to feelings, but reason and passion did not work together in the world of experience. Which was more significant? The dilemma continued for me.

To the people on the block the police were enemies, not defenders. If the police force had taken this attitude to heart, the problems would have been fewer, the risks lessened, the rewards greater. But policemen, too, showed lack of concern. On 102nd Street one night I saw a squad car and an ambulance draw up to the curb and a nurse and two policemen run between two buildings. A woman had attempted suicide by jumping from a fifth floor window and hit her head on a brick abutment. She was still alive and the driver went for a stretcher. As the policeman turned the light on her face, a woman watching from an upstairs window screamed. I thought she might be a relative. The officer flashed his light up at the building and shouted, "Shut up, you bitch, or I'll take a shot at you!" I helped to carry the woman out to the ambulance. Strangely enough, she survived.

After our morning service one day several young Puerto Ricans told me one of their friends had been killed, and they wanted me to come along with them. As we walked they told me the boy was Sergio Rodriguez and many people had seen the shooting. At the corner twenty or thirty people were gathered and started telling the story of the night before. Sergio had been shot by plainclothes policemen. Some of these people had seen it happen. They were sure the boy had done nothing.

The first thing to do was to get the facts straight and statements in writing from the witnesses, so I took the people to our parish headquarters on 104th Street. I separated the witnesses and got them, one by one, to sit down with the secretary and tell exactly what they had seen, then sign the statement in affidavit form.

The story was that there had been a large number of young people at a wedding party on 101st Street the night before. At about 1:30 A.M. the people began to return home. The bride and groom were walking with their friends along Lexington when someone across the street called out a remark about the bride, which brought an outcry from her friends. Eventually, a group gathered, and persons began shouting at one another, then pushing and shoving and fighting. Finally, two detectives in plain clothes who had been sitting in a car down the street came with their nightsticks and raced into the crowd. They hit a number of people, who later went to the hospital with minor injuries, and when they reached the center of the group they grabbed Sergio. Nobody had seen him involved in the argument or the fighting, and several had noticed him standing on the steps of a building, watching the crowd. Somehow he became the victim of the officers' wrath. According to the eyewitnesses, the detectives beat the boy, then dragged him across the street, where they pulled out their guns. One shot him in the lower abdomen almost point-blank. Witnesses said three more shots were fired; one of them went through the heart and killed Sergio immediately. Later that night about three hundred angry people marched on the local precinct, where they were dispersed with fire hoses and shots fired in the air.

While I worked with the witnesses and the secretary two men came into the room and circulated among the people. I soon discovered they were Marcantonio's friends, were already involved in the affair, and were asking people to come to a meeting to be held in a day or two. I immediately decided we would have our own meeting the next evening and asked the witnesses and all others who were interested to come. I also called the American Civil Liberties Union and invited them to send representatives.

Three of the Puerto Rican youths told me they were worried about their friend's family. They did not think Sergio's parents knew he had been shot. They were pretty sure the police had classed him as an unknown. "Why would they do that?" I asked. The three merely shrugged and glanced at one another. Sergio lived on West 174th Street, and two of them agreed to go with me to his parents' house. The family had not been notified, and only the sister was at home. We then went directly to the city morgue. The three of us waited until the slab on which the boy was resting was pulled out; he had been classed as an unknown male. There was a great deal of blood on the top of his head and over the cheek. He had been shot through the abdomen, and a bullet had gone through the left side, coming out under the left shoulder blade. The two friends said it was Sergio. At the 23rd Precinct we informed the police that we were reasonably sure the boy was Sergio Rodriguez, gave them his address, and asked that they notify his parents so that they might make the formal identification.

Later in the evening I went again to the boy's home. The stepfather had gone to the morgue, and the mother was unnerved and almost unconscious. Gathered around her were five other children and some of her friends. I told them what had happened, according to the eyewitness accounts. When the mother understood the time the killing had taken place she cried out. "Why they no tell us? We went to the beach! We did not know," she moaned. "We did not know!" She insisted that Sergio had a wallet and a draft card and other identification that he always carried.

I talked to her for some time and then suggested that the case should go to court. Our church, I said, was concerned about conditions in our parish. The brutality must be stopped, and the men who practiced it brought to trial, made to answer to the people. A united effort was the only effective deterrent to a force continually getting out of bounds. The realization that she and her family were not helpless or alone was a comfort. She wanted us to go ahead with prosecution and readily gave her permission for us to retain legal counsel.

At the meeting early on Monday evening there were at least one hundred people and more outside the storefront who could not get in. We had asked several lawyers to come. One of them, John Sandifer, took the case. He was a brilliant young black attorney from central Harlem who had experience with cases of police brutality. Marcantonio's people had packed the meeting, but with Sandifer on the case I knew they would have trouble taking over; as a further precaution I took the chairmanship of the committee appointed that evening.

At the group ministry meeting that night I was criticized for taking on too much and going too far. With practically no forethought I had pledged to the people that we would bring a complaint and take the case to court. I had assumed full authority. There was no feeling among the group of pulling back. They would go ahead with it. What they wanted to make clear was that I again had rushed headlong into an undertaking that committed the group. It was becoming a pattern.

I was impatient with the discussion and wanted to get down to plans and procedures in the Rodriguez matter. Bill Webber saw this too. But was going to court the only thing to do? We had not thought this out, but now we had gone on record. We might not even get an indictment. He himself was dubious.

"The first thing to decide is how to handle the funeral," he said. "It's bound to be an emotional affair."

It was then that we got down to specific plans, and it was late when we finished. Archie and I were to officiate, and we wanted to keep it within the bounds of good taste. A march from the funeral parlor to the church was to be quiet and orderly.

When we arrived at the funeral parlor, wearing our cassocks, two or three squad cars were in the street and many people stood waiting on the sidewalk, unable to crowd into the place. Inside, every seat was occupied and many people were standing. Coming through the crush I noticed several plainclothes officers. The police were obviously nervous and this was a situation that could explode. We were aware of this, and the service had been planned and my homily prepared carefully to avoid inflaming this crowd of resentful, outraged people—not by trying to repress their feelings or urge them toward restraint, but by proceeding with great deliberation and dignity. The solemnity in ritual observances of grief and respect at times like this often holds back anger.

When I came out of the funeral parlor an officer who seemed in charge turned to me and said, "We are not going to permit this march." "You had better let them proceed," I said in solemn tones. "I know these people, and they feel strongly about it."

"We've got orders against it," he said. "They've got to go in cars."

I assumed an air of even graver concern. "Well, officer," I said, "these people are excited. Are you going to turn them loose right here? We don't have the cars to take them, and if you try to disperse them now, you are asking for trouble."

"Well," he said, eyeing me. "Well, all right. But you will have to reroute it." We were not to pass the police precinct.

After some time the march started, with a police escort. It proceeded slowly and the people were much quieter than expected. Watchers gathered in somber groups on the sidewalks as we passed.

In the chapel, when I began the homily, a young woman rose from her seat and came forward slowly until she stood directly before the casket. A slight but dramatic figure in a long, flowing black garment, she looked down at the casket and stretched out her arms. She began moving around the casket, leaning over and stroking it lightly, then more fervently, knelt and caressed it, flung herself over it, embracing it again and again. It seemed to be some kind of passionate farewell that grew more and more impassioned and even sensuous. She held back nothing of her feelings but made no cry, no sound. I had never seen anything like it. I was trying to preach to a congregation watching this strange and mysterious pantomime. I half expected someone to come and lead her away. But no one moved. All the people had not crowded into the chapel; there were numbers outside, no doubt restless, talking to one another about the senseless brutality responsible for this death of a youth, keeping their indignation rising. But inside the chapel this mood had been suspended. The people were caught up in an awesome drama, making them self-forgetful and dreamlike.

When I finished, Carlos came forward as usual and began to translate, but at this the young woman stopped her strange ritual, turned away from the casket, and shook her head at him, making negative signs. She threw out her arms, waving and fluttering her fingers in a voodoo sign. But when Carlos went right ahead, the girl walked over to Mrs. Rodriguez and wrote a note and gave it to her. After reading it Mrs. Rodriguez came over to me, whispering that they wanted Carlos to sit down. They did not wish to have a Spanish translation.

When the casket was taken out the girl followed close behind it. At the cemetery entrance she got out, rushed through the gates, and ran off, flitting among the tombstones and evergreens, her skirt billowing and a black scarf streaming behind her. She knew exactly where to go, for when we arrived at the grave site she was standing there, her head bent and hands clasped before her.

After the short service I got into the back seat of a limousine with Sergio's stepfather and found the girl in black seated at my left. I turned to Rodriguez. "Has this girl been deaf and dumb since birth?" I asked. Immediately the girl herself replied. "Oh, I can speak all right." I learned that she was a cousin of the dead boy, and a spiritualist. She explained that when Sergio was killed she became possessed by a strong feeling, as she called it, that she would be unable to speak until the body had been buried. The moment this happened her voice was released. I wished she had not spoken and had remained a mystery.

After the funeral we worked on getting the affidavits in the proper form to present to the district attorney and on preparing a petition to the mayor and district attorney for a grand jury investigation. Newspapers had featured stories of two detectives who had fought their way out of a mob in East Harlem and had to shoot a person in so doing.

There was trouble all along the line. We finally got to see an assistant district attorney, Heffernan, who was second in charge of the homicide bureau. He told us nothing could be done for at least a month, when the man assigned to the case returned from his vacation. The documents were locked in the files, and we would have to wait for his return.

I thought this was the usual dodge. I was determined not to submit, and I think he could see this in my face, for he looked at me rather warily as I took the petitions out of my briefcase, riffled through them, and placed them with some emphasis in the center of his desk. "I do not think the people of our neighborhood are going to wait that long," I said. "This matter must be brought to the attention of a grand jury immediately. These are the signatures of more than two thousand people."

He went out of the room and came back with the records. We sat down to go over the file and discovered that there was no medical examiner's report attached. I remarked that I thought this highly irregular. A full week had gone by since the shooting.

Heffernan called the medical examiner, who gave him a brief summary of the conclusions. The report, I was assured, would be typed immediately and sent over. Later I was to learn that it made no mention of the head injuries. Heffernan then took us to the office of the chief of homicide, Monahan, who later became the police commissioner. He assured us they would see that something happened.

In the meantime Peter Jones, one of our summer student workers, was able, through his father's connections, to get us an appointment with District Attorney Hogan. Five of us spent an hour with Hogan, who promised he would personally see the case through the grand jury. A week later the people who had been witnesses began to get notices. Many were alarmed by the subpoena and terrified at the thought of appearing before the jury. We had to reassure them, furnish babysitters, and in some cases go to their homes, argue with them, and finally escort them in our cars. In the end eighteen people were brought to testify as eyewitnesses.

We lost. Monahan telephoned two weeks later to report. The police had three witnesses of their own—two taxicab drivers and a bus driver—who had testified that the police had been attacked by a mob and had to shoot their way out. The grand jury believed the testimony of these three rather than the accounts of eighteen Puerto Rican Americans. It was not clear to any of our witnesses that the three drivers had been in the vicinity on this night. Bus drivers needed to maintain good relations with the police and taxi drivers' permits were issued by the police department.

Housing was the constant problem in East Harlem. Apartments and buildings were often in terrible condition—sinks stopped up, toilets leaking or overflowing, open and hanging wires, inadequate heat, peeling paint, cracked and fallen plaster, leaking roofs, ratholes everywhere, unsafe fire escapes, loose tiles in hallways, bent and broken stair rails. Yet because of the population density, apartments were in demand and rents were high. Although the city government was unresponsive and corrupt, at least the city had a rent control ordinance that spelled out standards for various rent levels. Enforcing these standards was difficult. Lawyers for the owners were adept at stalling, knowing we could rouse the tenants when there was an immediate crisis but the people would fall away when the case dragged on and when they had to take days off from work to testify in court.

A mass attack led by the church would provide a religious base to sustain the necessary energy over an extended period. We began a campaign that involved three of our churches and the Church of the Ascension, which later became part of the parish.

Five or six blocks having the worst conditions were designated, and our Better Homes Month campaign was inaugurated with a parishwide worship service. At the service we laid the groundwork and talked about the Christian home and the need for families to have decent places in which to live at rents they could afford. We discussed exploitation by landlords as well as our own responsibilities in maintaining our homes in good condition. Our strategy was to have individual parishioners call on the people in the community and get questionnaires filled out providing statistical information that would indicate the numbers and depth of the problems and that could be used to exert pressure on city officials. Each questionnaire, signed by a tenant, would constitute a request for an inspection by the city housing department.

A series of religious events was scheduled during that month, and on four consecutive Saturdays we rallied our parishioners around a sound truck on a particular block and sent them out two by two. Each Thursday evening we assembled for a worship service and a meeting, when the people reported results in statistical and dramatic form. Over three hundred participated in the drive. We discovered hundreds of housing violations and numerous cases of rent-gouging and illegal bonuses demanded and paid to obtain apartments.

To close the drive we held a mass meeting at Ascension Presbyterian and invited Robert Wagner, the borough president, as well as the housing commissioner and a representative of the health department. After our presentation the health department woman responded by giving a simplistic talk, emphasizing that the people ought to clean up their houses. The commissioner of housing pleaded lack of sufficient numbers of inspectors. Wagner was the only one to take the matter seriously, although he did not promise any sweeping changes. When he became mayor, however, a new department for enforcement was organized and many things happened. Perhaps our reports at the meeting made an impression.

After the city took possession of properties designated for urban redevelopment there were periods of time before the people were moved and the buildings torn down. Often the city was lax in its responsibilities to these citizens. One day in late December, during a cold spell, some of our parishioners told Carlos they had no gas or water in their building. I went over with Carlos and found pipes had become rusty and clogged and the city had turned off the water and gas. There were at least thirty children in the building, many of them infants.

We got seventy people down in the lower hall for a prayer meeting, after which the children and older people were loaded into the carryall and the others walked. At the housing authority office there was a flurry of activity among the clerks and a noticeable tenseness in the air. Frightened secretaries were taking papers off their desks and stuffing them into the drawers. One was closing and locking the safe. As we sat in the waiting area some of the people told me that this was the first warm place they had been in for several weeks.

The project manager talked to five of us in a meeting room that had a large table with several chairs around it. "Out of the question to move the tenants," he said, and then launched into a detailed account of the difficulties of making any repairs. Finally, he said that if we would wait two or three days he would try once more to clear the pipes. All he could do was try again. But he would not guarantee anything. I pointed out that there were empty apartments in the project and these people were freezing. Why couldn't they be moved? "Because these people are not eligible to be moved into those structures," he said irritably. "We've been through this before. The regulations—"

"Eligible!" I said. "Regulations! Do you realize that there are thirty children in that building, eight of them under six years of age? They all have bad colds. One went to the hospital with pneumonia."

"Wait a moment," he said in a milder tone. "I'll call

downtown." He went out of the room, and when he came back he said, "Well, we can get plumbers out there in two days. That's all I can do." I told him that was no good. If he could do nothing today, we would be forced to go on downtown. I assured him we were not going to wait and we were not going to drop the matter. We would take it all the way to the mayor's office if necessary.

He left the room again and returned with thirty keys. "These are the keys to other apartments on the site," he said. "They have heat and utilities. But so far as moving all those people—" He fluttered his hands in a gesture of helplessness. "I have no money to pay for moving expenses."

Quickly and foolishly I said, "Then we'll move them ourselves" and took the keys. I was delighted and relieved and even in high spirits at the thought of helping the people to move. But I soon realized the immensity of the task: thirty families on six floors of a dilapidated old tenement, many of the people confused and upset, and in the dead of winter.

We hired one big truck and used four carryalls. We organized the deacons of our churches who were in a parish meeting that night and got students from Union Seminary and other people in the community to help. Starting at about three in the afternoon, we were still at it by three o'clock in the morning. It took a day and a half longer before we finished the job but just before the coldest weather of the winter descended. The people in those buildings never forgot what we did.

Because of complex overlapping bureaucracies and the many regulations governing housing projects we did not always succeed. There could be little progress without influential political allies in city government.

16

My introduction to active political campaigning came in supporting a local man who defeated Congressman Marcantonio. Television was beginning to be used, but most of our campaigning was done with sound trucks on street corners.

Our group ministry had chosen to work with the Liberal Party in East Harlem. Republicans were few, and the Democrats were allied with Tammany Hall. The Liberals were a small splinter group, having left the American Labor Party when the Communists were gaining control. In supporting the Liberals we in no way involved the church or the parish. We respected the right of all parishioners to make their own political choices.

Not to participate in the political life of one's community is wrong, for many ethical choices are made directly through democratic elections. The Christian cannot stay out of the political process because it is not all good any more than he can forsake the world because it is imperfect.

When I was asked by the Liberals in 1952 to run for the council my first impulse was a burst of enthusiasm. The voices of East Harlem would be heard. I could reach the sources of power, even exert some power, in representing the people on such issues as housing, schools, police brutality, drug traffic, ambulance, and other city services. This was a chance for the neighborhood. My second impulse, which followed immediately, was to laugh. I could not possibly win, and I ought to flatly decline. But I did not. The first impulse was still there. I wanted to try it. But it was a choice that should be submitted to the group, so I told the delegation I would let them know.

The next evening when we met at our apartment I gave the group the surprising news. The reactions were mixed. Then Bill asked, "What do you want to do, Don?"

I told him I didn't know. On the one hand I was inclined to try it. I couldn't think of anyone else in the political lineup who would do anything for East Harlem. On the other hand would I be able to win?

Bill asked everyone for an opinion, then got up and walked around while giving his usual neat summary. If I ran on the ticket and won, I could do a lot of good. Ergo, I should run. I could not be elected, however. Therefore, I should decline. But I did have a third choice. I could run fully expecting to be defeated. Knowing I was going to lose anyway, I could bring out the issues, try to push the majority party in the right direction, rouse the people in East Harlem, make them conscious of the issues, get them to take on political responsibility and begin expressing themselves. We had no money for campaigning. The opposition had plenty. Of course, I would run as an individual citizen and they would support me as citizens, not as the group ministry. I would be missed in the parish. They would divide up the work and make changes. Archie was in Chicago. Carlos would be needed to work with me. On the whole, after considering everything, Bill's advice was not to do it. I could not accomplish much, but if I wanted to take it on it would be a matter of only three or four weeks of intense campaigning. And I must be resigned to defeat. We talked a while longer and I decided to run.

Running in any race knowing I would not win was too cold-blooded an approach for me, and I had to concentrate on the positive objectives. I would run on the ticket ostensibly for councilman, but my goal would be to build a base among the powerless against the machine in future elections. I could point out the relevance of Christian faith in making political decisions. I had to go in confidently or not at all. So all through the campaign, while I asked the people for their votes, I had to picture a faceless Christian-principled councilman elected sometime in the future—perhaps years in the future. The machine was bound to win, but it would roll in with dented fenders in our district, and I would make those dents.

Our campaign was amateurish but enthusiastic. We had no money, and to raise funds for a losing campaign was impossible. I borrowed some money from my mother to buy an old milk truck and equip it with a sound system. Carlos was my manager. The conditions were appalling: Out of 200,000 citizens of voting age in the district only 60,000 were registered to vote. The state literacy test kept most Puerto Ricans away from the polls.

We had little literature—a few posters and mimeographed handouts. Our students helped to make banners with our motto: Sweep Clean with the Reverend. Television was out of the question, so I spoke on street corners, where it was practically impossible to get people to stop and listen. I gave at least eight speeches a day during the height of the campaign.

One night a man out walking his dog stopped on the sidewalk to heckle me. He kept at it for some time, then to my relief left, disappearing into the doorway of an apartment building behind the truck. As I continued talking I noticed people looking up, and suddenly there was a loud plop behind me. The man had gone upstairs, filled a large bag with water, and dropped it out the window. It exploded on the sidewalk, splashing many but hitting no one.

Another time some young men set off a package of firecrackers. The bangs resounded in the public address system, drowning my voice. I tried to go on, raising my voice to a shout. At this, the perpetrators gathered together and began to sing in full voice, to the tune of "The Star Spangled Banner," "In the rocket's red glare, Benedict was still there." Along with my shouts and the amplified bangs of the firecrackers, the noise was deafening. Finally, I came to my senses. People were laughing and there was no point in going on.

Messages in various forms came from the Democrats: a rock crashing through our storefront window, a rash of telephone threats, and an attempt to set fire to our campaign truck. In a way these were encouraging signs.

One sunny Saturday afternoon not too long before election some of the seminarians organized a parade, led by a Scottish seminary student playing the bagpipes. Bringing up the rear were Fala Cruz and her seven children. Mrs. Cruz trundled a rickety baby carriage, salvaged from some dump, that she had plastered with our banners and slogans. She bounced along in high spirits, waving at everyone and calling out, "Vote por la familia!" "A vote for the reverend is a vote for the family."

On election eve we assembled at our party headquarters. Some of the workers were at the polling places, waiting for the count. The work was done and we were exhilarated. We were exhausted, but it was an upbeat feeling, for there was a spirit of camaraderie and a consciousness of accomplishment. I knew some of the neighborhood people were expecting me to win. They always had, right from the start.

I knew better, but now, at this moment, I began for the first time to be eager to hear the results. I even began to feel that somehow I might win. It was just barely possible. What a victory it would be! What a sensation! I saw myself in the city council of the great city of New York. I saw myself on my feet in the chamber, giving my maiden speech. I found myself wondering how being elected would affect my life. My father would say, "I knew you would do it," and my mother would be terribly proud of me.

Then our workers started to arrive, one after the other, and it was soon evident that this was a typical election. The machines were working smoothly. Carlos, across the room, looked at me sadly. There was no doubt now, and I experienced a sick feeling in the pit of my stomach. The feeling of defeat. Every Liberal candidate had been defeated. But we continued to chalk up the figures to see how badly we had been beaten. We found that our district was the exception. We had lost, but the Liberals in our district had three times the votes they had in the previous election. We had done what we had expected to do. The marginal effects of the campaign would be good, for we would be looked on in the neighborhood—and even by the party in power—as a movement that was to be watched for we were going to be concerned about what the officeholders did with their power. But I could understand why a candidate who has lost would not want to run again. My reason told me I had won. But my gut feeling was that I had lost, and I was far from happy.

Years after I left East Harlem, Carlos Rios ran on the Democratic ticket for state senator and won, becoming the first Puerto Rican to hold office in the state. After that he ran for city council and won. He became the first Puerto Rican councilman in the city of New York.

17

Around this time I was uneasy about the group. At least I thought it was about the group. Others in our ministry went through such periods, with symptoms varying from a temporary withdrawal into reticence or passivity to outright objections and complaints.

Recently, Norm had been saying that we were becoming a closed corporation, too dependent on one another. The group was a buffer against the surrounding culture. We were like foreign missionaries living in their compound and not experiencing the same life as the natives.

One night I couldn't sleep. Was I becoming overly sensitive to group criticism? I certainly received my share of it. I was not like Archie who had a way of shrugging it off. Then suddenly, I realized my trouble was not with the group but with Bill Webber. Bill and I were in conflict. I had to face it. I got up and out of bed, got dressed, and went out. I soon passed the dark windows of our first storefront on 102nd Street. Walt Harrellson had been with us the first year. I remembered his complaint, "We see too much of each other. The group is too close." Walking on, I turned corners and crossed streets aimlessly.

Why did I feel this way about Bill? There were plenty of conflicts with the others. Joking references had been made to my "imperialism" and "kingdom building" and sober references to my being not religious enough. But I felt more like a minister when some people thought I wasn't behaving like one. When I laid the pile of petitions on Heffernan's desk and forced him to look at them, it was better than preaching. It was like laying down the ten commandments.

Still, none of these conflicts with the group or with individual members worried me. But the strain between Bill and me was different. I couldn't get at the roots of it.

Not long before this I had concluded that we ought to start a training center for seminarians, ministers, and volunteers in inner-city work. The group flatly turned it down as too large an enterprise for us. We had more immediate and urgent tasks. On the contrary, I had argued, it was very logical. Seminaries were not doing it. Training was part of our operation, but we were limited in the number we could accept as colleagues. The inner-city situation was national, and the solution would require many years, thousands of men and women, and several training centers.

Bill saw my points but was adamant against the idea. He stressed the fact that there would be institutional problems we were not aware of and with which we had little experience. If the seminaries wanted to set up such a center, they could handle it. They had the institutional experience. It was Bill who had squashed it. My disappointment had been extreme. Sometimes the group's decisions seemed influenced only by the desire to preserve the group.

Even though, in this instance, Bill had not persuaded me,

was it because he usually could that I felt at odds with him? I recognized that he was reality-oriented. I was not; I was more of a dreamer. I would get started with a rush, but the momentum was always checked when the group got together. Sooner or later I had to face his questions, inwardly impatient and frustrated because, at heart, I probably wanted to run the group.

Our opposition was not because of Bill's organizational abilities. I was sure of that. I was fairly good at coordination, organizing, getting people involved and working together. But I just wasn't given to predicting and guarding against troubles and setbacks like he was.

The conflict, I thought, had not so much to do with our goals as to what those goals related. Mine related to the perfect; I saw the way things ought to be. Bill's related more strongly to the reasonable. I recognized that he was right but nevertheless was irritated at knowing I would have to alter my course. Perhaps this was part of the explanation. But also I loved the group, and I was committed to the people in it.

All of this was clear. I hadn't discovered anything new. There was something lying much deeper that I had not touched. I kept walking until dawn.

18

In 1951 Dr. Neil Hansen of the Chicago City Missionary Society asked if we could assign one of our group to go to Chicago to launch a parish program. We picked Archie, but after he had been there a few months we decided another member should go also. The new parish ought to have a group ministry from the beginning, rather than start with a single pastor. So Ann and I were selected to go to Chicago for six months. With our two children we moved into Hull House, which was in the general area of the new parish.

Some of the same problems were found as in New York, but because the Missionary Society had taken the initiative, we did not have to raise funds. We also inherited the feelings of the churches toward the Society, and it was more difficult to begin as an interdenominational venture. Even though Chicago City

Missionary Society was in the truest sense undenominational, it had for a long time been labeled a Congregational venture, because it had been founded and supported in the beginning by members of that church.

We noticed at once in Chicago a greater hostility among the races. Ann went to call on a woman whose child might be included in a playschool for preschoolers. She knocked on the door and heard some noise inside the house but no one answered. Then a voice within called out, "What do these white sons-of-bitches want with us now?"

In some ways the housing situation was more appalling than that in New York. The crowding was similar, but in Chicago the neighborhoods were more depressing, perhaps because the houses and buildings were mostly of wood, which warps and sags and needs paint, and one could not help dreading the danger of fire. Chicago had no rent control, so landlords were able to retaliate if tenants tried to take action. If inspectors were brought in, the landlord either raised the rent or ordered the family to move. If a tenant fixed up an apartment, the landlord usually raised the rent, because the premises were in better condition.

Two Mexican couples who wanted a church in their neighborhood spoke of various churches they had attended but found they could not feel at home. We heard this phrase often.

Our first service was different from the one in East Harlem. The church was packed. We had learned the lessons of many personal contacts and good publicity in the community. About half were visitors from outside the parish who came out of curiosity, but we had forty or fifty community people. By the time we left Chicago, in August 1952, this storefront church was thriving. Summer workers had come, and our work with youngsters had begun to bring in the adults. Block groups for Bible study and social action had been organized. People for whom church in the past had meant little or nothing were being attracted. So Ann and I went back to New York feeling that the parish would grow.

In Chicago people would often ask, "Who is in charge now in New York?" Ann and I had trouble convincing them that no one was in charge. We worked as a team, and our trip to Chicago proved this. We returned to find the church at 104th Street flourishing. I was immediately plunged again into the housing struggle when Charles Abrams, a New York newspaperman and an authority on housing, telephoned to ask if he could bring a friend to talk with me and look at some of the conditions. During our tour we went into a hallway on East 100th Street, and while we were there a man turned into the courtyard and went into the basement. Something about the man made us decide to follow him. I shall never forget the awful sight that greeted us when we reached the cellar— numbers of people living in coal bins. I couldn't believe it. The heating system in the building had been converted to use oil, and the bins had been turned into rooms. In the four bins we counted twenty-five people living; seventeen were children. They had one toilet and one washstand for all of them. The rent was forty dollars a month for each family. Charlie Abrams' story was prominently featured in the *New York Post,* and authorities quickly pounced on the landlord and got the people out, but we never could find out where they went. This is one of the hazards of bringing pressure. We hoped the people were not moved into a place equally as bad.

My name had been mentioned by Abrams, and we were served with an order to get out of one of our storefronts on the ground that it was not an authorized place of public assembly. Some of our board members went with us to the Department of Housing and Buildings. The order would probably be extended to force us to vacate all our churches. When Dr. Newell, director of the Methodist City Mission Society (later Bishop Newell), pointed out that the Democratic Party used storefront locations for political clubs and we presumed such clubs would also be closed down, the commissioner decided a mistake had been made.

Outdoor theater was a method we began to use in East Harlem. Theater has the advantage of reaching people emotionally, and we thought it would be a more useful tool against narcotics than preaching. Street drama, we thought, could reach young addicts and those headed in that direction.

Maryat Lee, a Union Seminary student who had worked with us part-time, wrote and produced a play entitled *Dope*. To gain an authentic feeling, Maryat lived close to a family in which one member was an addict, and her characters seemed to be ones we saw every day on the street. Original music was written by Otto Thompson, a resident of the block, and his orchestra played for the performance.

The plot was simple: A pusher who thinks himself very smart because he is able to get people hooked builds up a nice business, and everything goes along successfully until he discovers his sister has become an addict. The audience was left with the feeling that users were nothing but suckers to the pushers. Because no one in East Harlem ever wanted to be known as a sucker, it was hoped that this stigma would condemn the drug habit.

The play was produced five nights at five different vacant lots, and about 7,000 people saw it. Jackie Robinson lent his name, and on the last night he appeared at the performance and gave a talk that had a tremendous effect on the young people. Windows and roofs, heavily populated on these nights, were the equivalents of box seats. A prominent theater magazine hailed the play as an attempt to bring drama back to the streets.

Public-school teachers told us for months afterward that some of the children would act out portions of the play in school. The word junkie became the worst name one child could call another. Years later people who came for help would tell us they had seen the play, and this meant it had helped convey the idea of addiction as a disease that could be treated and that help could be found.

A Good Friday play became a traditional part of the parish Easter program, bringing the people into the action. Once Archie took the part of Christ. The scene with Pilate washing his hands had built to a great climax; the guards had been ordered to take Jesus away, and the march to Golgotha had begun. Golgotha was a vacant lot two blocks away, where a service was to be held. Archie was dragging a huge cross through the street, with the crowd following, and as he moved around the corner onto Second Avenue, a black man emerged from a local barroom. Archie, in his long white robe and staggering under the cross, passed close to the befuddled man. Knowing Archie, I suspect he must have given the man a probing and significant look, for as the crowd streamed by, the man suddenly fell to his knees and swore aloud he would never take another drink.

In describing an area like East Harlem, people usually assume the residents are depraved or immoral or hopelessly ignorant. But there have been heroic struggles. To many, the parish came as a ray of hope in darkness. Gradually, some moved into nicer areas and earned higher wages. Others, who realized their lives would be spent in East Harlem, settled down to establish a worthwhile existence. There are hundreds of people caught up in the fellowship of the church who are now living a new life in Christ.

19

What was life like for Ann during these years? What kind of a life for my family? Every day I was engrossed in the problems of others and never dreamed of having any of my own. In a sense I thought of Ann and the children as part of myself. I forgot myself in my work. So I forgot them too. Later, when the girls grew older, it became a family joke. They would say they never could count on me, because whenever anyone was in trouble, off I would go. But it was no joke.

Not until years later did I find out how Ann felt. She felt excluded and alone. People ask what it was like to bring up a family in East Harlem. Ann bore the brunt of it. In the beginning we moved every three months, trying to find an apartment close to the storefront. One summer we lived in a balcony over the gymnasium of the Church of the Savior. Kennette was a year and a half old, and her crib was in a space partitioned off from our room. She was always afraid there, but we did not realize how bold the rats were until the night she screamed. Ann was there in a flash and heard in the dark the thud and the scurrying noise. The baby was terrified, and Ann was sure the rat had been up on the crib and had jumped down. We moved Kennette into our bedroom after that and stuffed material under the door every night. Also, we followed the East Harlem custom of leaving all the lights on at night, hoping to keep the rats away. But I killed one in the kitchen one night with a mop handle.

Not long before, I had called on a neighbor who had come home that day from taking three of her children to the hospital for treatment. I looked at them as they slept. They had huge patches on their heads where they had been bitten by rats the night before.

Kennette was born in January 1948; Sandra, in November 1949; and Susan, in April 1953—all in New York City—and Ruth, in August 1955, after we moved to Cleveland. When Ann was operating nursery schools in the parish she took the children with her to the nursery. Kennette remembers one time when I couldn't pick her up at school and the bus brought her back. As the driver stopped, one of the children called out, "Who lives here? It looks like a slum!" Feeling shattered, Kennette got up from her seat and climbed down from the bus. For some time afterward she was bothered by the realization that she lived in a slum but didn't mention it to us until years later. To most children, all the places in New York look alike—just buildings. But in our area there was the garbage and the number of people on the streets—many of them visibly troubled and hopeless.

Ann was entitled to a distinct voice in the group ministry, but the men ran things in such a way that she felt left out and that we were not treating the women seriously. Not all the wives felt this way. Bill and Dibby also had children, but Dibby seldom came to the meetings. Wives in the group were not considered to have a serious part to play; they were involved, but it was not considered a vocational involvement. Ann expected to be treated as a person, not as someone's wife. She had her own ideas, not necessarily agreeing with mine, and she felt the women ought to have equal say in decisions. Yet when one of the men made a decision it was assumed that his wife agreed. I was the biggest culprit. I was preemptive, presumably speaking for both of us or, worse yet, assuming the decision was only mine to make. At meetings when Ann began to talk I would often interrupt her, and not even to carry on the topic. I would change the subject completely, as if she had not spoken—a terrible thing to do—and I was totally unaware of it.

Ann did what she could, getting involved in the housing problems and working in projects with teenagers, children and mothers, nursery schools, health programs. She worked in the plays and supervised fieldwork of seminary students. At 104th Street, where she started a preschool program, the group hired a seminarian to take over and gave this person the status of a paid worker. No one had considered giving Ann this status or listing her name as a worker.

When she suggested a program at one of our meetings, it would usually be looked upon as in the women's province, separate from the main concerns. For example, we might be discussing drug addiction, and Ann would say, "We ought to get them before they are teenagers, when they are little, if we want to change their lives." Rather than collaborating, the attitude of the group would be, "Well, then, why don't you do it? Go ahead." Getting the kids out into the country, going camping, was her idea as much as mine, but Bill and I took that over and ran it without her. Ann's attitude alienated her from some women in the group she wanted to identify and be with but who felt she ought to be content as a wife, as they were.

So Ann had great sympathy for the women she saw in East Harlem who were without status even in their homes. There was one who worked in some sweatshop and wanted to place her children in the nursery school. "No," said the father. "They get American ideas. No school. I stay with them." The woman went to work and came home to more work left there for her to do. The husband was on hand. He stayed with the children, but that was all.

And there was Edna who did not show up for cooking class, so Ann inquired about her. Mitzi, who lived across the hall from Edna, said, "No, Edna won't be coming now. Her man is back. She has to stay in bed." "What do you mean?" Ann asked. Mitzi explained that Edna had to stay in bed with her nightgown on all the time the man was in the house.

Hispanic women, both wives and daughters, were terribly

constrained by their macho husbands and fathers. Carlos' wife, Candida, and Ann had agreed to teach one another. Ann was to learn Spanish from Candida and teach her English, but most of the time Candida spoke in English about her problems. She was not allowed to go anywhere. Carlos went everywhere. He would not take her out. She had to be always at home. He would come home at all hours and she had to get up at once and cook meals for him. When Ann once said to her, "Why don't you just tell him to go and make himself a peanut butter sandwich?" there was for a second a flame, a spark in Candida's eyes. But she shook her head. "No, no. I couldn't do that."

My routine days were spent taking people to housing offices or clinics in the mornings, calling on residents in early afternoon, and working with children and young people when school was out. In the evenings there were meetings or Bible study. Emergencies, personal and family tragedies constantly occurred, and conducting our special campaigns in social and political matters occupied long spells of time. From the very first we had many people coming and going. The year's program ran from October to the end of May. During the summer the college students were there in droves. Hundreds of persons were involved every year and assignments had to be worked out for them.

I was totally involved in parish activities; and it was years later when I faced the sad truth that I had forgotten my family. The realization was a tragic discovery for me. There is nothing I can do to make it up to them—or to myself, for I am the greatest loser. Of course, my wife and daughters know me very well. My character is clear to them. They know I throw myself into what I am doing and that when I am working on a project I think of nothing else. They have been indulgent and understanding. But this is no excuse. I guess I have never thought much about living—that is, living my own life—and that is probably wrong. I feel guiltier about being away from them than I do about my ignoring the women's rights issue. But that, too, is part of it. I think if I had been with her more, away from my work, I would have been more understanding, had more insight, and Ann's predicament might not have happened.

20

When a tornado strikes the response is typically American. The President declares the place a disaster area, the Red Cross and other organizations mobilize relief measures, and help comes from all over the United States. Churches and other groups collect funds and supplies.

What, I thought, would American citizens be willing to do if they knew—if they really knew—about East Harlem? The disaster here was greater. Not a sudden storm and recovery, but day after day of deterioration and distress spread over years and lifetimes. Why not focus the attention of the nation on East Harlem as a monstrous ongoing disaster area? Get the President to declare it a disaster area and ask the country to respond? Broadcast the story like news of a cyclone and wake up the country to a tragic and shameful condition? Get Congress to appoint a committee? Stir up government departments? Organize marches on Washington? The idea would be to institute a kind of Marshall Plan for East Harlem.

Rather than suggesting this idea to the group ministry at once, I decided to work it out to have an organized plan to show. Under the title Operation Tornado I began to set down the details and soon realized we would need statistics and facts. The investigation would touch all aspects of life in East Harlem: housing conditions, population, ethnic groups, employment and unemployment, job discrimination, health matters, cultural aspects, economics, political factors, schools, rat control, tenant-landlord courts, welfare, police, churches, social organizations and agencies. Accordingly, I outlined the first stage of Operation T, assigning specific tasks to each person in our group for the first few months, and listed areas of concentration for the first year.

I presented it to the group with the feeling it would be rejected. I was no longer in the early stages of euphoria. But as I began to talk about it the idea seemed to regain brilliance.

There was not much to be said: It was all down on paper. On the subject of education, for example, I had a set of questions to be answered. What do people in East Harlem want from education? What does education offer them? What are they getting from education now? What changes should be made? Are there other things they should want from education?

The population question would be approached by investigating who was coming to New York and who was leaving and why. Resettling would be studied, as well as getting churches to coordinate movement to rural areas. One project would study development of facilities on a community rather than a borough or city basis.

Current housing conditions in East Harlem would be compared with those in other parts of the city. There were many other areas to be examined and studied as well as procedures to be evaluated, and I suggested the plan be flexible and open-ended. Like Abraham, we would begin a journey not knowing precisely where we were going.

Briefly, the idea was to start with a study of local conditions and needs and problems; go on to prove the catastrophic implications of these conditions with facts, figures, and case histories; build public awareness; through an organized campaign increase understanding of the Christian faith and of the meaning of fellowship and the neighbor; and draw in a network of outside institutions, groups, and individuals who could serve and contribute, who could rush to the rescue before the storm and prevent the devastation.

"I am calling my plan Operation Tornado," I explained, "because there is great danger—in fact ultimate catastrophe. The important thing is to make the whole country realize that this tornado is coming. It's not here yet. It hasn't struck, but this is one that can be predicted."

They read it over and at first seemed flabbergasted. Then they began asking me questions, but no specific objections or criticisms came. Then someone said the word grandiose. They all took it up. "Yes. Too grandiose!" This was the decisive criticism. Operation Tornado had been leveled.

Nothing is too grandiose as far as I am concerned. I believe the plan was rejected because they felt we were not the ones to do it or do it properly. I didn't feel this way. My feeling was to go into it. Go ahead and start it. But I would need the whole group and more.

I did not sense any negative reaction to the plan as I did at other times. The group had rejected itself. They could not do it.

How long was I going to try to overleap the possible? Probably forever. The group was correct but not absolutely. Someone has to start impossible things.

Suddenly, my mind went back to the night I had walked the streets over my conflict with Bill. There was nothing wrong between Bill and me. I was being myself and so was he, and so were all the members of our group. Freedom will always demand a basic respect for people who insist on being themselves and it was important for me to listen as well as be heard. But it was important for me to be heard. I had something to say. Sometimes I forgot the group and did things on my own. Even then I was part of it.

To this day whenever I see the people of that old group, they say, "Don, do you remember Operation Tornado? That was really something!"

Cleveland

21

On a warm summer night in Cleveland, Ann stood on the front porch of our house on Franklin Boulevard. In her lovely quiet voice she recited the Lord's Prayer for the benefit of Ralph Novacek, long addicted to drink and well soaked this night, as he leaned over the railing, pouring whiskey slowly from a bottle into the shrubbery. The house was the third from the end of the block and light came from the street lamp on the corner. Although it was almost midnight, a few cars passed, going fast; the street was a thruway for traffic to the suburbs. "The kingdom and the power and the glory, forever and ever." Ralph stopped pouring. Scarcely hesitating, Ann began again. "Our Father, who art in heaven . . ." "Oh, hell," muttered Ralph under his breath, and he upended the bottle. "Amen," he intoned, as the last of the whiskey gurgled away. After a minute he straightened up, tucking the bottle under his arm.

"It's empty," said Ann. "Shall I throw it away for you?"

Slowly his lips protruded. "Nooooooo," he said, dragging out the sound, hugging the bottle tightly to his chest. Then he held it out, peering at it, his face growing angry. "You're not getting any more bottles away from me! See this? Empty. 'S kind of friend you are!" Clasping the bottle to him again, he lurched down the steps.

I begin this account of our life in Cleveland with Ralph and Stella Novacek because their difficulties were typical. Our parishioners there were mostly industrial workers, and one of the most serious problems among them was alcoholism.

I was away at a meeting that night until late, and Ralph, who had lost track of Stella, had come to our house a few times. Earlier he had appeared with a bottle of whiskey and had insisted that Ann take it, along with his car keys. Then he came back later and demanded the bottle. Ann said no, somewhat fearfully, expecting him to be angry, which he was.

Finally, he tried to convince Ann that all he wanted was to see the bottle. If he could just see it, then she could throw it away, he promised on his word of honor. Almost out of patience, she went for the bottle, and when she came back he was sitting on the steps. She held the bottle behind her as he got up. "Where'sh it?" he asked, and when she held it up he looked at her.

"Tell you what," he said. "Jus' between you 'n me. Shhh-shay a prayer. Lesh pray. Dump out the whiskey. Lash bottle. All gone," He grabbed the bottle and uncorked it. Quickly Ann began the prayer before he could change his mind.

Stella was the first one of the two whom we met. We were holding a New Year's Eve service in the hallway of the church, and as it was ending she wandered in from the street, sat down at the piano, and started to play. People glanced back curiously as she launched from one tune to another. Her hat was on one side of her head, her hair untidy, eyes watery and unfocused.

When I went to talk to her she began to struggle to her feet.

"No, no," I said. "Don't get up. Stay where you are. We're glad to have you. Stay awhile. Play a few more tunes."

She kept saying she had better go. She had left her husband in the bar across the street in the next block. "Juss came out for some freshair and a walk," she said, then paused and lowered her head. "Trouble is, Ralph and I. We drink."

"That is trouble," I agreed. "Tell me about it."

"Reverend." She fell silent for some time. "Reverend, I'll tell you what. You're gonna get an earful."

I spent about two hours with Stella that evening, but I didn't learn much about her. Although she talked a good deal, she couldn't focus on any subject but her drinking habit. She was repetitious and mostly contrite, but now and then she would come out of it, boasting that she could easily go without a drink for six months and that her problem was not a lack of willpower. And in the next breath, "But a person's got to have a li'l fun once in a while. Life is so doggone dreary." Then she promised to go home, sober up, and come to see us again, bringing Ralph with her.

Weeks went by until we saw Stella again and met Ralph. But after that they kept us going. They seldom came together; it was usually one, after losing track of the other, who would come looking for me.

One day Stella slashed her wrists and I was called. When I got there an ambulance was waiting. She had gone almost crazy after she had been given a sedative, and the attendants were trying to get her into a straitjacket. I went along with her to the hospital and stayed with her, but even after this experience the drinking habit continued. The two were always in trouble, always looking for help.

At heart, Ralph and Stella were sociable; they liked people around them and yet realized they had driven family and friends away. We saw many types of behavior among alcoholics. One of our regular but less frequent drinkers was a lanky man in his late thirties, a loner, who had a job at a nearby restaurant. Whenever he went to work drunk his boss would send him home, but instead he would come to my office and sit silently in a chair, stretching his long legs straight out, so that everyone who came in had to step over him. I would go on with my work, and after a few hours he would get up and leave. There was an unexpressed feeling of companionship between us. I sensed that he wanted to be *left* alone but not *be* alone. He never came to church, but I would see him in the neighborhood and we always talked cheerfully. I never referred to his problem and neither did he. But he drifted away. The people he worked with at the restaurant only knew he had not left a forwarding address.

By far the most time spent performing any one pastoral duty was that given to working with alcoholics. Alcoholism is a tragic disease, because everything one does seems wasted, thrown away. Promise after promise is given and broken. Again and again they return, always dependent, often importunate and disagreeable, frequently repugnant. Patience gives way, and one's Christian faith is severely tested.

I thought of alcoholics as people who had become dependent and needed someone or something to lean on. Many were attracted to fundamentalist religion. We always encouraged them to join Alcoholics Anonymous, which has many elements of the Christian faith, and numbers of people did find there the support they needed and consequently were able to function. But the failures came back to us. The work was good for me, because it required extreme patience and taught me acceptance.

It was a long time before Ralph and Stella could understand emotionally that the big push had to come from within rather than without, but then they joined Alcoholics Anonymous and were members for nearly twenty years, finally straightening themselves out. The problem is one which never ends. It has no real cure, and many are beaten and ruined by it.

22

We had begun to think about opening a parish in another city in the spring of 1954 when five of the best students who were to graduate from Union wanted to join our ministry. We had tried Boston first, then Detroit, but Cleveland had given us the best opportunity. John Duffy, secretary for social work at the Cleveland Church Federation, had suggested we come there. During a visit to survey the possibilities the Baptists promised several thousand dollars and the Congregationalists showed great interest. When the Rev. Richard Pacini, at the Fairmount Presbyterian Church, said they would give five thousand dollars we felt we could raise ten thousand dollars the first year, and so we decided to go.

Our original group ministry in Cleveland was, in addition to Ann and me, Dorothy Bethel, a bright black woman who had become Archie Hargraves' education specialist in East Harlem; Russ Williams, a black Presbyterian minister from Jersey City who helped in my political campaign in East Harlem; and Bill Voelkel, who was to work with me as copastor. We picked two locations. One was a storefront at the corner of East 22nd Street and Woodland Avenue. The neighborhood was one of the neediest and most neglected by the church; the Baptists who were nearby felt a responsibility and were happy to have us come in.

The second location was the building abandoned by the First Congregational Church, which we obtained for a dollar a year with the use of the parsonage, where Ann and I could live. In its early days this church had been a stop on the Underground Railroad. The women of the congregation had organized a day school long before the public schools were opened. At one time First Congregational Church had been one of the city's wealthiest churches, but now the neighborhood had totally changed. In 1947 a tornado had destroyed most of the trees, and the old mansions stood shabby and decayed in their denuded grounds. No blacks had moved into the area; the most recent influx had been that of Appalachian and southern whites, who were now the predominant groups. When the congregation moved to Lakewood the church had made a strong effort to minister to these new residents and had failed. As a result, the building was closed and empty.

I felt at home when we pulled into the driveway of the big house on Clinton Avenue. It was good to see the fenced-in yard and to picture our children playing safely on our own grass. The first morning we explored the large parsonage in high humor.

We began our Cleveland group ministry at the storefront church on Woodland Avenue, in the heart of a black neighborhood. The community had a large number of children, and we worked furiously on the interior, so we could open a summer vacation Bible school. Wonderful help came from people at the Fairmount Church, especially Jo Morris, who was there almost every day. I remember her up on a stepladder, with her hair tied in a scarf, painting walls and partitions. The owner of a bar across the street gave us some old fluorescent lighting fixtures.

Over the storefront more than a hundred men lived in a dormitory-style lodging house. They worked for the Nickel Plate Railroad and many were alcoholics.

When the store was ready we rented sound equipment for the old milk truck and toured the streets, playing hymns and announcing our new school. Some of our people ran along with the truck, handing out leaflets. About seventy-five children came to the first sessions, and our staff worked with children and teenagers that summer.

In coming to a new city I thought the most important thing for me to do was to encourage and consolidate broad support for our work—both financial support and the goodwill of the denominations. I spent the first two months mostly talking to denominational executives and Cleveland ministers. Although concerned about the church's relation to the inner city, they were bogged down with meetings, financial drives, denominational programs, and keeping up with the growing development of new suburban churches. They felt that unless the churches kept moving into the suburbs they would never be strong enough to help the inner city with mission funds. But as people keep moving into segregated communities the church has the constant problem of finding money and energy for bringing the gospel to those left behind. Suburban ministers saw this clearly; their congregations did not. It was difficult to convince suburbanites that they had a responsibility for an inner-city ministry.

Later we deliberately brought parish people to denominational meetings. They felt terribly conspicuous and out of place among sophisticated middle-class people. Some of our people were on welfare. The church could help break down the cultural, economic, and social barriers, but I didn't expect people to be evangelized into faith across these barriers.

When we took over the old First Congregational Church we immediately renamed it St. Paul's. The building was a huge Gothic anachronism that did not attract the neighbors as a storefront did. They could not see into it so easily. Also, this was a different kind of community—white unskilled factory workers.

The area was depressed sociologically but with fewer of the dispossessed people who characterized East Harlem. Here the children were not so free to roam the streets; we had to begin with the parents long alienated from the church, although not altogether from the Bible. But alienation fell away when the people realized they would be forming the congregation, that they would be the church.

The congregation, starting anew at St. Paul's, was free to develop its own style and there were no critics. Nothing remained to set limits or lines of division, and the people accepted one another. Alcoholics, the mentally retarded, the social outcasts—all were welcomed. We attracted no people of wealth.

The members of this church worked with the black members of our other churches when they came to parish council meetings. This was important in the 1950s, when there were few opportunities for interracial cooperation. There were some racial tensions, but the word of the gospel prevailed.

Many things were wrong with our house on Clinton Avenue. It was eight blocks from St. Paul's, and we finally got the parish to sell it and buy another place that was only three doors from the church. It was such an impressive house that everyone referred to it as the Manse. There was a separate entrance to the second floor, where Bill and Joanne Voelkel lived, and on the third floor young volunteers from the Church of the Brethren were housed.

But the Clinton Avenue house persists in our memories. We began to have real family life there, and we stayed long enough to see our fourth daughter, Ruth, come into the world.

In March of 1955 we began to reach out to two other areas. One was a pocket of black people living on the flats in some of the worst housing in the city. Yet the flats were picturesque. Great ore boats floated along the canal of the Cuyahoga, pulled by tugs. At night they made a slow procession of lights moving across the dark city skyline. It was even lovelier at dusk on a winter day, when snow covered the ugliness and across the river the lights came on early in all the tall buildings. Every window on every floor would be lighted.

Snowflakes were blowing about as I got out of the car to visit a family on the day before Christmas. One of our parishioners had given me the address and told me these people had no food. It was an old stucco house, tall and narrow, converted into apartments. On the second floor each bedroom was now a separate apartment. I knocked on the door, then noticed it was padlocked on the outside. The family had gone out so I rapped on the next door. A man opened it, and I asked if I could leave some food with him for the neighboring family. He agreed and I went to the car, brought up a couple of baskets, and put them inside the door. Three children were sitting across the room, and an evergreen branch trimmed with a bit of tinsel was set up in the far corner—not a tree, but a branch that might have been lopped from a balsam tree and thrown away. I noticed that the two boys, about six years old, were twins. One was much livelier and I spoke to him, but he paid no attention. The two went on playing with a piece of knotted clothesline that they were tugging between them. "He can't hear you. He's deaf," said the father. "The other one can't see."

A little girl, about four or five and very thin, sat by herself near the window. He saw me looking at her and said, "She tries to talk to them, but they don't understand too good."

"Look, can you use some groceries?" I asked.

"Well." He seemed embarrassed. "I don't like to . . ." Then he gulped and looked directly at me. "I sure could."

As we unloaded a box and some baskets he told me he had diabetes and was unemployed. I noticed that he kept looking at a doll my daughter Sandra had left in the back seat of the station wagon. As I walked behind him up the stairs I was thinking that I had no right to give it to him, but after we set the groceries on the kitchen floor I went down, picked up the doll, hurried back up, and knocked again at his door. When he opened it and saw the doll in my hands, he said, "Oh," very softly. But he didn't take it. He asked me to wait and in a moment came out, putting on his jacket. Then he took the doll and stowed it under the jacket so it couldn't be seen. "Thank you, thank you!" he whispered. "She's never had one." His eyes were sparkling.

I went home troubled about explaining my high-handed

generosity to Sandra. But I needn't have been worried, for Sandra, like most children, had a sense of the higher levels of justice. After supper I told her I had met a little girl that day, describing the girl, her twin brothers, where they lived, and the Christmas branch, and I explained that because the people were poor, the little girl had never had a doll. I ended somewhat lamely, "You see, Sandra, your doll was in the back seat of the car."

"Priscilla?" said Sandra.

"Yes, Priscilla," I admitted.

She was silent for a minute. Then she said, "Did you give Priscilla to her?"

"Yes," I said.

"I'm glad you did. If I were there, I would have let her have Priscilla," said Sandra.

That spring Ben Andrews, a retired Presbyterian minister, and his brother, who owned some vacant land on the banks of the flats, proposed to donate the funds for a playground if we would run it. When we agreed they bought the house next door and rented it to us for a dollar a year. Grant Williams moved in and began the program with a vacation Bible school on the playground.

We also wanted a location near the Lake View Terrace housing project, because the young children who lived there could not cross the main artery to get to the church on West Franklin. Finally, we were able to rent two storefronts at a dollar a year for after-school programs and a vacation Bible school.

A year later the Cleveland Baptist Association asked us to survey the community around an old church across the river in the business community, the Euclid Avenue Baptist Church. The congregation was disbanding, but the Association felt some responsibility, having been there for more than a hundred years. We discovered there were ten thousand to twelve thousand unchurched people in the community and decided to begin a program. We also moved our parish headquarters into the church office, which gave us a central location near the offices of the Cleveland Church Federation.

Six months later Elam Weist, of the Evangelical and Reformed Church, suggested we provide leadership for their church at 65th and Lorain, which had been without a minister for two years. Several nearby ministers objected to our coming on the grounds that the area was already overchurched. Yet we found an unchurched secular community of thousands with serious economic, emotional, and social needs.

23

Clevelanders Jo and Howard Morris were among our greatest benefactors and friends. Jo had come with the group of volunteers from the Fairmount Church to help open our first storefront on Woodland Avenue. She devoted herself to our parish and could relate to inner-city people with ease.

Howard was a deeply loyal person, a man of few words and dry humor who took early retirement to work in our parish as business manager and treasurer. Knowing he approved of our parish convinced wealthy Clevelanders that they should support our work, and we acquired a farm where we could take city children. When we built a church Howard found the right people to help, and he was instrumental in getting us a solid board of directors.

There were many other lay people who helped us and gave devoted service. Cleveland people responded from the day we arrived, and Ann and I developed warm social relationships. We were accustomed to being seen as the odd people who lived and worked in the inner city, but in Cleveland we were welcomed and taken into homes in a friendly manner.

Paul and Betty Younger were old friends; I had married them in the East Harlem parish. Betty had joined the group ministry and worked at 104th Street while Paul was in the army. They came to serve the Fidelity Baptist Church on Hough Avenue. Paul was intensely radical but, unlike most radicals I have known, cheerful and humorous. With great optimism he plunged into every cause, believing that somehow the Holy Spirit would work things out.

Among all the wives, Betty and Ann were the most articulate

on women's rights and many years ahead of their time. Our three children were attending the city's public schools, which were operating in double shifts under a board of education that did not believe in borrowing money. Ann and Betty knew how bad the schools were. They inaugurated Save Our Schools, a citizens' committee that used the churches as centers and organized parents into informed and active groups. They investigated schools, went to school board meetings, wrote letters and circulars, and brought school problems into the open. Betty and Ann became friendly with the school superintendent and various board members, and their citywide committee succeeded in arousing parents and causing concern about the schools. This was the parish's first attempt at broad citizen organization, and it was interclass and interracial. Paul and Betty continued their involvement in public school matters long after Ann and I left Cleveland.

After a few years Bill Voelkel began a training project for students at Oberlin Graduate School of Theology. He stayed in the group ministry but was relieved of the copastorship. I got in touch with Walt Ziegenhals and asked him to come as copastor. Walt had started at 100th Street in East Harlem while he was a student at Union. He was a fine organizer: methodical, with good ideas, personable, and affable. His wife, Harriet, the daughter of a Lutheran minister, was a graduate of the School of Sacred Music at Union. She brought a love of people and of choral music to our Cleveland ministry.

24

If we were to do a small part of what needed to be done, we had to have more money. At the start denominations were not putting in enough so we went directly to laypersons. Handling administrative affairs meant I was drawn away from direct engulfment in the fundamental conflicts that can bring about better social conditions. I felt the pull, but who else would run things? Someone had to work at raising funds and I was the one to do it. And would I have been content to take a back seat? Or would I have been willing to make someone of great promise in the ministry over into an executive?

In the Inner City Protestant Parish—as it was called in Cleveland—the group ministry concept was carried on. We had the experience of East Harlem behind us. But in Cleveland, as in New York, the parish ministry and staff mushroomed in a short time. Again long agonizing meetings began to drain the group's strength, and I realized I was fast losing patience with the endless dialogue about what seemed to me simple questions.

We criticized one another quite readily and openly. Paul Younger was censured for not paying enough attention to his church. It was generally agreed—or assumed—that his pastoral services were haphazard because he was always involved in some activist cause or welfare crisis. One time, instead of sitting in at our meeting, he was sitting in at the school board and got carried out and put into a paddy wagon.

Bill Voelkel would often talk about the way we used our time and insist an analysis be made. According to Fred Jenkins, we were not really building up our ministry unless we were more involved in the sacraments. Paul would respond that we were not building up our ministry unless we were working on systemic change. Someone would insist we ought to stay in the community and get involved with the people's problems. The importance of parish duties would be stressed. Several would argue that to build up the church, we had to spend time there. Then another outcry would be heard.

Another frequently argued subject was the authority of the executive director. Are we under authority or are we an association of people? Political unanimity was almost nil, but all agreed we should be involved in some kind of political action. But what? Which direction do we take? And the questions of economics recurred. Some families had summer cottages, others did not. Should this be permitted? The Jenkins received one hundred dollars a month from their folks to build up savings for their children's education. Was this fair? Were we going to share all the way or not?

Our group held regular sessions with Gerald (Jerry) Strate, a psychiatrist in private practice. He gave us a chance to step back and look at ourselves and our work. Jerry was the chief listener, except to encourage someone to keep on with the subject. Or sometimes he would say, "I think this fellow needs hospitalization!" He was curious about the difference between the religious commitment and the professional commitment.

We all had people we were worried about. For example, each of us had been "adopted" by at least one alcoholic. Jerry warned us, "You can't do anything. You can't go after them. You have to wait until they come to you." But most of us wanted to find some way, set up some mechanism, to help.

We could not seem to help the younger ones. If a person had been an alcoholic for at least fifteen years, we found longer periods of remission—perhaps they worried about their health or just ran out of energy.

Ann thought it might be a hormone thing. None of us was willing to give up. Experience proved it was hopeless, but was anything hopeless? Jerry said we were admirable fools.

They were great evenings, helped by the ease we felt with Jerry and the interaction that touched off sparks of recognition. It was the opposite of confrontation and more of a common search. Although we talked constantly about our work and, in the process, really about ourselves, the final effect was that of a refreshing intermission, a letting up and letting out. These sessions left us stimulated and hopeful and made the group seem less restrictive.

Because our churches were so geographically separated total parish organization was difficult and the parish council accomplished little. But the active association of blacks and whites from the east and west sides of the city at council meetings was of value, although the immediate interests of each church tended to pull the council apart. But this group was able to focus on the public school system after Betty and Ann inaugurated their citizens' action committee.

In the late 1950s denominations moved toward accepting more responsibility in the inner city. The Woodland Avenue storefront church eventually formed into St. Philip's, and it has since become affiliated with the Christian Church. Except for the two storefronts started on the flats, our congregations were in old church buildings; this increased the support of denominations and gradually reduced the need for tight functioning of the group ministry as a support group. The denominational orientation was unlike our experience in East Harlem and seemed a hopeful sign.

We had a continual problem with repairs at St. Paul's. One day a providential windstorm knocked a huge belfrystone loose, and it crashed down through the gymnasium stairs. When the official inspection report condemned the building Walt Ziegenhals and I felt great relief. Our decision had been made for us. Although building a new church structure in a low-income, inner-city community was something no denomination would have considered, our congregation and board wanted to take on the challenge.

We enlisted the support of the United Church of Christ and they responded positively, although our parish board had the final responsibility for securing the funds. This meant Walt and I would do the fund-raising, but we felt we had enough backing to go ahead.

A year later I received a call from the Chicago City Missionary Society. Neil Hansen was retiring and the search committee wanted to interview me for the position of executive director. Under Hansen the society had totally funded the West Side Christian Parish that Ann and I had helped Archie and Inez Hargraves to start in 1952. An endowment gave the Society independence and had enabled it to serve an inner-city population. But I wanted to find out the current position of its board with respect to the denominations and also the general character of the board itself.

Walt did not want me to leave, but he could carry the funding project through. I believed my role in Cleveland was coming to an end. My particular talents lay in recruiting young pastors and in organizing a parish. I thought the parish now needed institutional leadership and management. The group ministry decided that at least I would undertake the interview.

My own feeling was that I wanted to go to Chicago. I thought I could do something in a big city headed for racial conflict, and my work in Cleveland had settled down to the dull, demanding mechanics of administration. I discovered I could stay with an organization up to the point where it becomes a functioning institution but I did not then want to manage it. Even if I did not go to Chicago, I would soon want to be a pastor again in a storefront church or go on to organize an inner-city parish somewhere else. The Chicago opportunity was worth the attempt. It would be a huge task, but I would have the energy to give. Perhaps more was to be accomplished there than I could ever finish. Perhaps it would be the job that would hold me.

I knew Neil Hansen opposed the merger of the Congregational Christian Churches and the Evangelical and Reformed Church—and that the search committee was looking for an administrator who would keep the Society somewhat apart from the Congregational Christian Churches, which had begun it. But how far apart? This was the question. When I arrived Dr. Hansen briefed me on every member of the five-man committee, and this gave me the feeling he was inclined toward me as a candidate. He and his associate, Dick Schwenke, had compiled a history of the Society, which I eagerly read. It emphasized the Society's independent orientation, which made it more attractive to me.

My interview with the committee was lengthy. I told them I had not been looking for a change but wanted to hear their plans for the future.

Several weeks later I was called back. The search committee had recommended me. After dinner with the board members I went to my room while they discussed the report of the committee. Three hours later John Ballman knocked on my door. He said the argument had not been about me, but rather about the general direction in which the Society should go. I learned later that the board was split over whether the Society should relate to the new United Church of Christ or maintain its independence. Strangely, my election as the new executive director helped reconcile the opposing factions. Reassured by my consistent ecumenical stance in East Harlem and Cleveland, half the board felt sure I would remain independent. The others had discussed my candidacy with Truman Douglass of the United Church. He convinced them I was basically loyal to the denomination.

To leave Cleveland was not easy. As a family, we felt settled in our west side blue-collar community. The school situation was now tolerable, and Ann, still earnestly involved in working toward reforming the system, had been asked to run for the school board. We had many friends who had a deep concern for the future of Cleveland. Our children were approaching their teens and had their own ties. Leaving the group would not be easy for me, but I kept telling myself the parish was well established with six churches doing significant work, with a staff of competent young clergy and their wives committed to the city. The denominations were increasing their support and interest. So when Ann and I found a house in the Hyde Park section, we moved to Chicago.

I knew that in my new position I would be giving up the pastoral relationship with people. I would function as the chief executive officer of an institution and would manage staff, raise money, set budgets, and deal with boards and committees. But I looked forward to the new job. I felt I could use the financial strength of the organization to good effect. There would not be the familiar immediacy of the inner-city neighborhood. I would be working from another base, but it would be for the sake of these neighborhoods.

I did not expect the group ministry—in East Harlem or in Cleveland—to end. But this has happened. Gradually, over several years, it gave out.

In East Harlem the group lasted for ten or twelve years, but it became increasingly difficult to raise the money to support the ministry and staff. The inner city was not a priority of the churches.

But Peg and Norm Eddy remained in East Harlem and are still there. So are the Calverts and the Webbers, and all three families brought up their children in the neighborhood. Norm and Peg had a church, erected a building, and he eventually organized an ecumenical nonprofit housing venture. Peg now runs the Spiritual Life Center in East Harlem. Bill is president of New York Theological Seminary, and Dibby is General Secretary of the Division of Health and Welfare of the United Church Board for Homeland Ministries. George is pastor of the

Church of Hope, which also has missions in Africa, and his wife, Buffy, is now going to law school.

In Cleveland, too, where it seemed so strong and everything went so well, the group did not last. Walt Ziegenhals, who was there to see it, gives three reasons for the breakup: "First, we lost our charismatic leader. Second was the difficulty of trust. Each one of us was dependent on the others to stay committed to the group and to its disciplines and economics. This was to be for life, yet we sensed it was not. We had begun to look at one another and wonder if the others were committed enough. Also, the children were growing up and would be reaching college age, and everyone in the group was forced to think about financial stability. The third reason was that the group had served its purpose."

But Walt never talks about the group's weaknesses without mentioning its strengths. "There was a certain status and power," he says, "that we could not have had as individual pastors. The Protestant denominations considered us something special. Collectively, we gave a stronger witness to our commitment to the city. And we had a spirit among us we could not otherwise have known, for it brought together people of no particular natural affinity in a commitment to one another. This spirit attracted others."

The lesson to be learned, according to Walt, is this: Whatever brings such a group or order into being, whatever its enthusiasms at the start, however devoted and consecrated, the group will never endure without compulsion. Compulsion can be benign. Faith and love can be as compelling as fear—probably more so in the end. But strong bonds are needed. If the discipline is relaxed, it weakens gradually for all. When one member leaves, the group may find its faith in the whole association weakened.

It seems to me that to live a life predominantly motivated by strong Christian love is not easy in our society, but it should be easier in a group. Certainly a group ministry can be instituted anywhere when it is needed. It has touched many lives, and there are people all over the world today affected by what was begun when Dave Dellinger invited Meredith Dallas and me to come to his fieldwork parish and spend the summer teaching the Bible to black city children. This was the beginning. We failed to get the blacks and whites together, but the spirit of the group kept some of us going back and trying to continue living that kind of life.

III

THE SOCIETY

25

M Y FIRST DAY at the Chicago City Missionary Society was one of the hottest of the summer. As I waited on the platform for the Illinois Central train my lightweight summer suit was oppressive. When the morning greetings and a few introductions were over I walked into my office, closed the door, and stood looking out the window feeling a bit of loneliness, for I was really on my own.

My mind went back to East Harlem. During our last semester at Union Seminary, after Bill Webber and I had surveyed the East Harlem neighborhoods, I remember saying to him, "Why hasn't there been a revolution?" We saw the connection between the ghetto and the major forces in New York City which had created that ghetto—mostly through a chain of pragmatic decisions geared to economic necessity. The neighborhood people were unaware of their collective potentiality and outside the ghetto few who were aware of the conditions saw themselves involved in the causes.

Whenever people accept a system without reflection they allow it to assume the compelling force of an absolute. To act without reflection was, I thought, impious. Certainly one of the advantages of the group ministry had been our recognition of the duty of reflection and of acting accordingly. I disagreed with those who argued that religious faith follows passions more and reason less. As Christians, we have the gospel prompting us to question, to appraise, to judge the world and ourselves. Whatever our sentiments, religion ought to cause us to reflect on our acts as they relate to others and to the state of the world.

People create the systems, motivated by good and evil. And so motivated, they cannot be wholly to blame. The task was to prevent systems from becoming destructive. This understanding kept one from blaming the victims. Odd as it seems, people often blame the poor, the powerless, and the unsuccessful. They believe the poor to be a hopeless problem, a low class of people who will not work, will not cooperate, who are a drag on the economy, rather than realizing they are a class created by it—and a danger sign. The task, then, was clear: To raise them up and set them on their feet. But how?

I was now one of the bureaucrats, a part of the establishment I had always confronted. Should I try to turn the Society's staff into a group ministry with a common discipline? Somehow I could not bring myself to do it.

I moved away from the window and sat behind the desk to get the feel of the place. The room was sunny but bare. Strange that I noticed this. During my years in the group ministry I had never been very aware of my surroundings. I suppose they were generally rather shabby, with crude partitions, calendars and memos pinned up, and desks always cluttered—not clear and clean like this. On the wall opposite me were several rectangular shapes faintly lighter in shade than the general color. Neil Hansen's pictures and degrees had hung there, and suddenly I was struck by the feeling I might be here for a long time. Like others who had private offices, I would hang up my own pictures and certificates, bring my photographs, and scatter around some mementos, perhaps a few softball trophies. I didn't remember ever feeling so settled in one place.

26

In 1882 a group of committed Christian laymen founded the Chicago City Missionary Society because of the terrible condition of the poor in the city. Caleb Foote Gates, a successful

Chicago businessman who was sensitive to the needs of people, became the Society's first president. "Toiling for money merely for the sake of money I despise," he said, "but the possession of money with a heart to use it for the good of others is a rich gift."

Gates served on the auditing committee of the Chicago Theological Seminary and took great interest in the work of seminarians. His enthusiasm led him to work at the Randolph Street Mission, where he was superintendent for nearly two years. After his experience in this "destitute district" he began a plan for greater mission work.

The masses of immigrants arriving with their troubles brought civic-minded groups and churches to form charities. By 1885 more than 100,000 immigrants, often frightened and inexperienced, came to Chicago every year. Many were easy prey for unscrupulous exploiters.

Several missions were operating under the direction and support of individual Congregational churches, but they fell far short of the need, according to Gates. "In my judgment," he said, "there should be on every half-mile square of the neglected portions of this and every other city of our land a center of religious work, not in any strictly denominational sense or way, but Christlike, all-comprehensive. . . . I would have in charge a suitable matron or man to welcome all wanderers that crossed the threshold, and make their call a pleasant and profitable one." Caleb Gates showed great concern for black people. During the 1860 campaign of Abraham Lincoln, whom he supported, he proposed freedom, education, and land ownership.

In 1880 Chicago was a growing city of thirty-five square miles, and churches were for people who could afford them; those who could not were unchurched. At this time the work ethic taught that religiousness led to success and success was a sign of religiousness. Being poor was seen as being heathen. Churches followed their prosperous members as they moved to outer areas.

In 1882 a committee that included Gates and Prof. Samuel Ives Curtiss was formed by the Congregational churches to consider the "religious destitution" of the city and what could be done about it. The report, according to Gates, "almost staggered our belief," detailing crowded sections, high crime rates, and poor living conditions.

The Missionary Society began with a committee of six laymen and one minister: C.F. Gates, S.M. Moore, Robert E. Jenkins, F.S. Hansen, W.E. Hale, O.W. Norton, and the Rev. Burke F. Leavitt. This committee had authority to employ a superintendent of missionary effort and to apportion the expenses among twenty-three Congregational churches. The task, in the words of Caleb Gates, was "to save to industry, sobriety, virtue, and religion the neglected classes of Chicago." The work, he said, "ought to be done simply, 'in Christ's name,' and without any regard to denominational lines; but if we cannot secure that union of all Christians . . . let us as Congregationalists and citizens at least enter some one district." The committee began by visiting the field, talking with people in their homes, and getting to know the districts of the city. Existing missions continued; the new missionary effort was not to affect these, but to go where the churches could not.

Over the ensuing years neighborhood missions were developed among Poles, Germans, Bohemians, Scandinavians, Welsh, Chinese, and blacks. Sunday schools were established, as well as kindergartens, preaching services in native languages, mothers' meetings, and industrial schools. Weaker churches were supported and new churches founded. The work was done by people from the churches who gave their time and money, and the Society acted as manager, broker, and catalyst.

Victor Fremont Lawson, publisher of the *Chicago Daily News,* became interested in the mission work of the Society soon after it was founded. He began to make regular contributions when he became aware of the Society's services to the families of his newsboys. As a youth, Lawson was fond of baseball and he played with the Atlantics, a Chicago amateur baseball club. Born a Lutheran, he joined the New England Congregational Church on Dearborn Avenue and Washington Square. According to Lawson's biographer, Charles H. Dennis *(Victor Lawson: His Time and His Work* [Chicago: University of Chicago Press, 1935]), the *Daily News* "gave proof of its sympathy for wage-workers subjected to injustice." It was "recognized by the local public as virile, outspoken, and fearless."

When Chicago Theological Seminary planned to establish a chair of social economics, in 1892, Lawson guaranteed the salary of Graham Taylor, called to the position. Dr. Taylor, an unconventional professor, took his family to live in a crowded tenement among immigrants, where he established Chicago Commons, a social center. Lawson wrote to the president of the seminary, "I have been moved to make this contribution not merely on the general ground of aiding the seminary, but more particularly on the ground that it has seemed evident from the circumstances you mentioned to me that I should be thus able to make it possible for you to say to others, who do not take the same view of Professor Taylor's sociological work that I do, that their contributions would not need to be applied in any degree whatever to a line of work concerning which they did not feel any personal responsibility."

Victor Lawson died in 1925. His tombstone does not bear his name but is a granite sculpture of a crusader. He left a trust fund of $1,300,000 in his will to the Chicago City Missionary Society, augmented by one fourth of the residue of the estate after all other special bequests. This was the largest bequest in his will, totaling approximately four million dollars.

The board of the Society was astounded. The Lawson trust tripled the Society's income, and it provides today half the annual budget. It made the difference between an effective but chronically needy agency and one able to carry out its visions. Victor Lawson's bequest made the Society, although church-related, free to lead the way in new directions in Christian witness.

27

Even though the Society was the child of Congregationalists, since 1952 there had been no formal relationship. The board of directors was relatively conservative but included businessmen like Tom Ayers (who eventually became president of Commonwealth Edison Company), who realized the importance of dealing with urban problems. No women or blacks were on the board; nor were there any black employees.

The first thing I had to do was discuss the missionary

situation in Chicago with the board of directors and acquaint them with my ideas. I suggested to the board members that we ought to ask ourselves the same question of eighty years before, "What is to be done about the unchurched masses in the city of Chicago?" We had to put this question into a wider context. In the inner city we could see the process that was going on throughout our whole culture.

It was a culture, I said, that had lost its belief as well as its ability for self-discipline. They no longer felt God was judging them or they felt God was dead. There was no transcendence or meaning, no loyalty, no emotional involvement, no real community. I cited several examples of the emotional isolation, self-absorption, fear, and the spectator attitude toward life that I had noticed.

Now, I continued, our society was trying to legislate integration and decent housing. Resorting to law in order to preserve community revealed our spiritual decay was not restricted to the inner city. It was only seen there in its stark reality, the advanced stage of the decay of our whole civilization.

So we had to do more than merely reflect the church as it was, or as we had known it. We had a pioneering task in relating the gospel to the inner city. And by getting involved with the inner city, we might be able to say something to the world that could not be said by any other institution. The task would demand all the thought and energy we could give it, and I hoped it would become clearer as we moved along.

Many board members were startled by my remarks and got the impression I was a doom-sayer, but I wanted to begin drawing the lines of demarcation without delay.

In coming to Chicago, naturally I had storefront churches on my mind. With the Society's financial backing I could start many more. But soon I began to think about community organizations. City churches were being run by people from outside, and suburbanites were coming in to serve at the settlement houses. I wanted to involve local people, but residential congregations were divided by race and class, acquiescent or blind to poverty and racism. Perhaps the solution would lie in organizations outside local congregations.

Christians were talking about organizing congregations around issues of social change. They would gather around particular issues or create a congregation in the midst of an issue. Missionary congregations, willing to function with some anonymity in society, might inaugurate a religionless Christianity.

I, too, was looking for ways of gathering people around societal issues, but in the context of theological reflection. In Chicago, although the Society had a responsibility for nurturing local congregations, it also had a mandate to address broader systemic issues beyond the neighborhood arena. The concept of a world agenda had captured my mind. Oppressed people in the cities were like people all over the world who were struggling for justice. If God was active in the world, was the world agenda not being set by God's activity? All over the world, then, new forms of congregation would be rising in prophetic witness.

First I took stock of the Society's finances and current programs. In 1960 it had an annual budget of $230,000 and a new-work reserve of $250,000 accumulated by underspending current income. Programs receiving support were three neighborhood houses: Pleasant Valley Farm, near Woodstock, Illinois, a rural retreat for city children; Casa Central, a ministry to the growing Latin population, directed by Rafael Martinez, a Society staff member; and the West Side Christian Parish, which Archie and I had started in 1952. The parish was then under the direction of Dave Wright and included three storefront churches.

Dick Schwenke, Neil Hansen's first assistant, had been with the Society from the beginning of his ministry—at that time almost fifteen years. He knew its history thoroughly and I found him quick to understand me and catch my thinking. Dick was a resource in acquainting me with the inner workings of the Society and with Chicago sociology. We soon became a team.

I wanted to find people who were theologically trained, with competence in secular disciplines, who could explore the relevance of the Christian faith to the emerging urban culture. In spring 1961 I went to Union Seminary to recruit interns for several inner-city churches and to interview students for new programs. I told them I did not have specific jobs to be filled and asked what they wanted to do. I wished to find people who were interested in something and to let them do it. After the interviews four young men, each with a different interest and talent, decided to join the staff. John Roberts was concerned with the problems of youth; Steve Rose, journalism; George Ralph, drama; John Noble, labor. The four were hired as exploratory workers on the basis of their interests. I tended to hire highly motivated people, then to allow considerable freedom.

I also hired Jim Mason, who had been doing research and planning in a Lutheran agency. Eventually, he was put in charge of Pleasant Valley Farm.

The youth and labor programs were short-lived. John Roberts tried for a year to devise a program using the First Congregational Church as a base. He made some contacts and brought youth gangs to Pleasant Valley Farm but after a year decided to move on to the Cleveland parish.

John Noble soon found that relating Protestant churches to trade unions would involve more than meeting with union executives. One of his reports, which revealed that he had joined union members in a picket line, was read by our board members. The traditional Protestant antipathy to trade unions welled up, and at a specially called breakfast meeting in the Society offices the executive committee voted to disband the exploratory labor program by June of 1962. It acted so summarily that I had hardly stated the case when the vote was taken. Obviously, the committee had reached a decision before the formal meeting. When I told John of the vote he decided to leave at the end of the year.

Later I was shocked to learn that officers of the board had spoken about the possibility of bringing back Neil Hansen as a consultant, to prevent such "far out" programs from being attempted in the future. I knew that if he came back as an adviser I would leave, but what bothered me was that the executive committee had met in private session and I had not been invited. I felt such clandestine proceedings could destroy the entire organization, because trust would be lost.

But this did not happen. In fact, long before this incident I had decided that new blood was needed on the board. During the first three years, through close attention to the work of the nominating committee, we acquired twenty-seven new board members. Some members had resigned as they noted our new direction, and attrition accounted for others. These arrangements were made amicably. At the time I came, board members saw their function mainly as trustees of the Lawson money, never thinking they might have to raise additional funds. They were operating like a foundation making grants. It was a closely knit body of men, and I think the Society had almost become their church. When Tom Ayers was elected president, in 1962, things changed. We had great confidence in each other.

At the Society's 1961 annual meeting when a $50,000 surplus was reported for the year, the board members were so joyous that I could not bear it any longer and burst out, saying I thought it was a disgrace. They were mostly people with business and financial backgrounds, who tended to conserve funds and to think of a surplus as a sign of good management. "If we are saving the money for a rainy day," I said, "it can't get much rainier! In civil rights this is as dark a time as we have had so far in this city."

My outburst astonished them, but they had to discover how to spend money, not just save it. They were conscientious men and women, and they changed their thinking when they began to realize that their job was to plant money in projects. Their foresight and prudence would be useful in this capacity.

An exploratory venture begun in 1961 was the drama program, to relate the church and areas of culture from which it had become alienated. George Ralph gathered a small community of writers and actors around the St. James United Church of Christ on Chicago's north side. The company he organized was absorbed by the Community Arts Foundation and became a seedbed for creative work in Chicago theater. It is now known as The Body Politic.

Steve Rose, like the other seminarians coming in without a program and no specific duties, decided that, as a journalist, his main task was to interpret issues of racism and urban blight to mainline church people, especially suburban lay people. He came to me with a proposal for turning the newssheet of the

Society into a small magazine. I agreed, and *Renewal* quickly became an influential national publication. Beginning in 1963, each issue was confined to a single topic explored in depth. Editorial attention was given to structural problems of reforming the church, to communicating the problems of inner-city people to others, and to issues on the church, ministry, women in the church, civil rights, urban renewal, and poverty.

Some readers assumed that *Renewal* expressed the Chicago City Missionary Society's point of view. They could not believe we would support a magazine to create free dialogue on issues. Some contributors wrote that because of views expressed in a certain article they would no longer support the Society. Others were drawn to the work of the Society through this openness in trying to find solutions to urban problems.

Earlier I had invited Helen Archibald, who was with us in East Harlem, to join the Society to develop a Christian education curriculum for inner-city children. This curriculum, "Good News," was widely distributed through the major denominations.

Although I had given up the group ministry as a working approach, I was convinced of the value of the concept, particularly of the meetings that had united us. The intern and exploratory staff met at my home once a week for dinner, followed by Bible study and reflection. We began to have weekly sessions with James Saft, a psychotherapist, on problems of individual work situations. I hoped we could hold these sessions without seeing ourselves as a group ministry; unfortunately, without this commitment, there was not the same constancy and perseverance. We did not have the disciplines, and within a year the group meetings ended.

The primary problem for inner-city people was housing. As in New York, those without power existed in dilapidated and unsanitary housing. Economic forces operating in a system based on welfare rather than on full employment at a living wage meant that public housing was the only answer. Mayor Richard Daley used federal money to build massive housing projects, which many called vertical slums.

When we looked at the magnitude of the problem of housing

for the poor, it was obvious that the Society did not have the funds or the personnel to make an impact. Under the housing code (Sec. 221 (D)3) nonprofit corporations could build middle-income housing through mortgages provided by the federal government. This was a way of challenging the worst conditions indirectly. The purpose of the statute was to help stem the white exodus and assist middle-class black families to find decent dwelling space. Many black families were being forced back into the ghetto because of income limitations. In April 1963 the president of the Society appointed a low- and moderate-income housing committee. We hired Jim Twomey, an Episcopal layman who was a housing expert. In May 1964 we formed the Community Renewal Foundation as an independent entity under a fully ecumenical board, with support from Jewish and Catholic agencies as well as the Church Federation of Greater Chicago. The subsidy was a forty-year FHA loan at three percent interest, which was below market rates, but it took the Foundation over a year to convince the city council that 221 (D)3 housing should be built on land designated for urban renewal. This was necessary because of competition in bidding for the land against for-profit corporations. A 131-unit development was created in the Hyde Park-Kenwood renewal area for $2.4 million. It was the first time Chicago authorities had designated land for nonprofit middle-income housing. The site was important, because it would enable the Foundation to attempt to keep white families in a section from which they had been moving.

Although the statute also provided for renovation of existing dwellings, because of frustration over the sheer magnitude of housing problems—particularly enforcement of building codes—we took advantage of Illinois legislation which provided that courts could appoint receivers to manage buildings in situations where landlords had failed to comply with those codes. Used carelessly, this law was merely a means of swapping among landlords, and it tacitly encouraged kickbacks on various contracts, such as electrical wiring. Nevertheless, the Foundation entered the receivership business. The successful rehabilitation of our first building pointed to an open future for a disinterested, nonprofit third party in this field.

City officials took notice. Here was a rehabilitated building with rentals within the limits for low-income families. We were soon given receiverships of ten buildings. In May 1964 Mayor Daley arrived at a building reopening to congratulate the Foundation, present a key to the first tenant, and announce that a dormant city agency, originally set up to perform the same function, would be put into action.

The real impact of the Society's program was the threat it presented to recalcitrant landlords. The possibility of the appointment of a receiver who will make repairs but also take the rent for eight or ten years while the rehabilitation loan is being repaid, acts as a deterrent to neglect by slum landlords. For every building where a receiver is appointed, three may be upgraded as a result of this threat.

Yet it was clear that receiverships dealt with only the end of the judicial process. The prior process of code enforcement remained a problem. In 1964 the Foundation retained Richard Newhouse (later Illinois state senator), a black attorney, on behalf of slum tenants. A housing complaint form was developed and circulated through the churches, and Newhouse processed these through the Foundation to protect the identity of complainants. Newhouse won a key court case that established the right of tenants in class action suits to take landlords to court. Before that only the city could prosecute for these city code violations.

The Society was then contributing about $25,000 or $30,000 annually to the operating budget of Community Renewal Foundation and had also set aside $100,000 in a building fund, as seed money for housing projects. This enabled the Foundation to propose $14 million worth of housing.

In eight active years of operation the Foundation created over 500 units of new or rehabilitated housing, all for low- and middle-income tenants. Total costs—beyond services recoverable from the Department of Housing and Urban Development (HUD)—were approximately $250,000, or a subsidy of about $500 per unit provided by the Society. We found that some of the most respected leaders in real estate were willing to be helpful, among them John Baird, whose grandfather had served on the Society's board.

Two major factors led us to drop this program. One was the failure of the county or state to provide adequate tax relief. Some states have tax abatement plans to encourage such developments. In the case of our Hyde Park West building the taxes had been figured at something like 17 percent or 19 percent in the estimates for the project, but when the building was finished taxes were set at 43 percent of gross rentals. With controlled rents, there was no way we could become solvent, and therefore the building was in default from the moment it was opened. The other factor was our feeling that a downtown organization had no business owning and managing neighborhood projects. Even though we had set up corporations in which some community residents were members, they were not truly representing community endeavor. HUD would not recognize local housing groups; it would grant programs only to organizations with longevity and assets sufficient to carry forty-year mortgages. We felt our new efforts should go toward assisting local neighborhood groups to develop housing corporations. By the 1970s, HUD had learned that recognizing local groups as developers was practically the only way to discourage vandalism.

In 1963 church concern for the cities reached the point where national programs were begun. Truman Douglass asked if I would take a leave of absence from Chicago to direct a national United Church of Christ project to be known as Urban Emphasis. Encouraged by the momentum in Chicago, I accepted and, having secured a year's leave from the Society, established an office in New York. I kept my residence in Chicago, intending to return regularly for short periods. It was a staggering blow on my arrival in New York to be told by the church's president, Ben Herbster, that there was to be no national fund drive for urban work. For years I had watched the church raise money for suburban church development, but now, when the needs of the cities had come to the fore, the church had decided to cease all national fund efforts. I was committed for a year, however, and since nothing was going to happen nationally, I decided to tackle the state conferences with a consciousness-raising campaign.

At meetings with conference staffs and boards of directors as well as staffs and boards of instrumentalities I asked what they saw as the most pressing urban problems in their areas. These were written down on newsprint and paralleled by a résumé of current church programs and interests. Invariably there was a dramatically negative correlation. After this, small groups were asked to discuss ways in which to address the world's agenda, and I usually concluded with a strong plea that the churches establish structures outside the local congregations to gather Christians around the emerging urban issues.

During that year I think I may have increased the consciousness of some regarding the urban issue, but in my zeal to sound the alarm I did some guilt tripping. Many of us who fought for justice in the 1960s used guilt as a technique; rarely did I fail to come down severely on the suburban churches. I was so convinced that action beyond the local church was the next step in dealing with race and poverty that I neglected to give a full measure of appreciation to the positive work going on in local congregations.

During this period I became concerned again about the need for training clergy specifically for city work. The clergy, whether in residential congregations or specialized ministries, needed knowledge and skills for dealing with urban problems, and the best method was to combine study and reflection with action. The most significant learning process could take place only while involved in ministry. Denominational leaders agreed that a supplement was needed to seminary training, to immerse students in the environment, the politics, and the organizations of inner cities.

The originators of the Urban Training Center for Christian Mission in Chicago were Walter Kloetzli, a Lutheran minister; Gibson Winter, professor of ethics in the Divinity School of the University of Chicago; and me. The Society wanted to play a catalytic role and began to approach foundations for support. We negotiated for the Carpenter Chapel Building next to the old First Congregational Church at 40 North Ashland Avenue. The structure housed Casa Central, several other programs, and originally the Chicago Theological Seminary. It was easily converted into classrooms. C. Kilmer Myers, author of *Light the Dark Street,* had done significant work with youth gangs as an Episcopal priest in New York's lower east side and accepted the post as director.

A distinctive feature was "the plunge" for all new students at the center. Each was given several dollars and told to go out and live in the city for three or four days. It had a profound effect on those who did it. The areas designated were Madison Street to Ashland Avenue, Clark Street to North Avenue, South State Street, and 57th Street to 63rd Street, Stony Island. The students were expected to rely almost exclusively on verbal communication in making their way, and one rendezvous was arranged midway through. On several occasions board members of the center underwent the same plunge and were convinced of its validity as an educational experiment.

A year or so later Kim Myers became a bishop in Detroit, and the board hired Jim Morton, an Episcopalian with inner-city experience in Jersey City, as director. Archie Hargraves had come to the center as Director of Mission Development; and Dick Luecke, to direct a study program in theological reflection. Another who joined its faculty was the Rev. C.T. Vivian, of the Southern Christian Leadership Conference, and through his efforts many southern black clergy came to Chicago for training.

During the 1960s the center trained over a thousand black, Latino, and white clergy for work in the city. Many who came were pastors who returned to their cities to put into practice what they had learned. The center helped develop organizations and leadership in many communities and aided Martin Luther King Jr. and the emerging civil rights movement.

I have often regretted that the center had to be closed. It lasted ten years but by 1974 denominations were decentralizing their structures and thinking in regional terms, and the training center was a national facility. Although white clergy could no longer figure in the organization of ghetto communities, there was a continuing need for educating black and Latino clergy in community organization work. But white churches were not willing to support black clergy in predominantly black denominations, and foundations could not continue grants past the experimental stage. However, I still am inclined to urge the establishment of such in-service training centers for students or clergy engaged in city parishes.

In 1965 the Society, in conjunction with the United Church of Christ, made a television film that alerted people to the impending crisis. The film was built around the idea that for some the city represents freedom and mobility; for others, captivity, immobility, and slavery. For some there is choice and for others, as the film's title suggested, there is but one city, *A City of Necessity*. The film was produced by Robert Newman. One sequence showed a black girl against a background of slum properties rocking back and forth in a creaky swing in a garbage-strewn city lot. Over the image we dubbed in Mayor Daley's voice proclaiming, "We have no ghettos in Chicago."

When the film was released the mayor's press secretary called me, demanding that we cut out this portion. I told him I would consult our board, but before I could even call the executive committee together I had begun to receive telephone calls from many of the most influential board members suggesting that we ought not to alienate the mayor. Our committee decided that the issue was not important enough to warrant further political confrontation, so the scene was cut from the film in several local showings, although copies shown outside the city were unchanged.

28

Chicago's ghettos stretch in three directions from the Loop. To the south, the oldest black district has been enlarged by the construction of what is described as America's most oppressive public housing. A smaller Hispanic settlement exists to the northwest, and the west side ghetto extends for miles from the Roosevelt-Ashland Avenue area not far from the Loop all the way to the western suburban line.

The Roosevelt-Ashland area, where we had started the West Side Christian Parish, became in the middle 1960s the location of a Society-supported community organization to be known as the West Side Organization for Full Employment (WSO). Casa

Central and the Urban Training Center operated a few blocks north. Further west, in Lawndale, we had commissioned a new staff member, Louis Mitchell, to begin a program with indigenous black churches. He was able to give help to the storefront churches in the area and instituted a training program for pastors. Mitchell's efforts to get these churches to organize and deal with community issues laid the groundwork for what later became Pyramid West.

John Purdy, a layman in suburban Hinsdale, told me one day that he wanted to do something more worthwhile with his life.

He felt that the churches' loss of the dispossessed had weakened their ability to be a reconciling force in urban life and that increased residential segregation had cut many children off from blacks and the poor. The "bridge of reconciliation" was John's concept of a program to bring suburbanites and inner-city people together.

During the training period, volunteers heard accounts of the work of particular agencies and listened to inner-city residents describe life in the city. This program was marked with successes and failures. In some cases people left convinced that nothing could be done. Others found a new life of service, and some began to understand the complex forces creating the ghetto. One group of volunteers was assigned to the Cook County Hospital children's ward, where there were many unwanted babies. Their task was to hold the babies and give them the love and affection of a mother. After a short while the women realized these babies should be placed in homes and sensed that no one was taking this responsibility seriously. They smuggled a woman reporter into the hospital as a volunteer. The subsequent articles aroused the community, and a procedure for getting the babies placed was rapidly promoted.

Other volunteers began to question the caliber of public education after they had been assigned to teach a sixth-grade boy to read. Another group of trainees assisted in a freedom school that had emerged when inner-city parents became infuriated over the prejudice and incompetence of an elementary school principal and boycotted the classes. Volunteers gained insights into the school system and their firsthand knowledge made the difference in understanding.

One of the weaknesses in the program emerged after the first year. Volunteers received good orientation and were successfully placed, but there was a need for Bible study and theological reflection on their engagement in the city. In February 1966 we convinced the Illinois Conference of the United Church of Christ that such a staff person might be helpful. Bill Dudley, a United Church of Christ minister, was hired to involve the volunteers in a reflective community that would add this dimension to their work. We hoped those who were related to existing churches would return to their churches with a deep sense of commitment to the city.

While the program lasted, hundreds of suburban people were brought to see and feel the difficulties and frustrations of the slum dwellers. Many people's interest in the city came through this program and they went on to do constructive things. But such bridges to the ghetto were becoming increasingly difficult to build. It was too late.

A meeting in spring of 1965 in a south side storefront basement reflected the dismal outlook for continued bridge-building and made a major impact on me. Seventy-five people attended, among them only three whites: a newspaper reporter, a young Catholic priest, and myself. Black power was in the air. One excited speaker called for a cadre to move into communities and for street corner rallies. "No more meetings for the press!" he said. Another speaker condemned the built-in schools in the newer housing projects. Did luxury housing have such schools? If not, why? A third suggested that black women forget about birth control. On and on came the complaints and angry responses about police brutality, job discrimination, and inadequate training programs. "What other people besides blacks were stopped in their own neighborhoods and the trunks of their cars searched?" From now on there should be no submitting to police who came to search, harass, or arrest. For the future there was going to be black-controlled business and industry. "If the whites want a double society, let's give it to them!" This attitude was spreading.

Seemingly isolated events were signaling an eruption. It was becoming common for police to break up groups and meetings, often with slight pretext. Clubbings, beatings, and unwarranted arrests took place and insulting, undignified, and brutal treatment of those in custody. These practices were not only inhuman, but shortsighted, for they fanned the smoldering resentment into rage.

One Saturday night in April 1965 a dance for young people at the WSO's office on Roosevelt Road was at its height when Bill Darden, the organization's associate director, saw several police officers at the door and went to investigate. He knew there could be no legitimate reason for a police visit unless someone had complained about noise. But if this were the case, why so many? One or two officers could have handled it. He did not want these officers in the room. The sudden appearance of a group of police officers would lead to distrust, alarm, and hostility. In answer to Bill's question the police simply said they wanted admission. He asked if they had a warrant, and when one of the officers replied that they did not, Darden said, "Well, to come in here you need a warrant." Instead of answering, they pushed open the door and went in.

At the sight of the police filing into the room, some of the youths began to scatter. An atmosphere approaching panic spread, and Bill saw that the officers now had their sticks in their hands. "Don't run!" he shouted. One boy was trying to get away and Bill turned to him. "Take it easy, there's nothing to . . ." But now the boy was staring over Bill's shoulder with terror, and a second later Bill was stunned by a blow on the back of his head. An officer had hit him from behind. The boy broke away, and Bill saw an officer catch him by the shoulder. Another officer grabbed a second youth and was hitting him with his stick and the youth was screaming. Bill, still dazed by the blow, saw that Chester Robinson, the WSO director, and Bill Clark, one of its staff members, had come over and were arguing with the police. Bill was taken out and into a police van with the two boys, and a few minutes later Clark and Robinson were thrown in. All five were taken to the station.

The whole thing was senseless. Whenever police appeared at any such gathering it seemed that anyone who spoke or moved was likely to be taken into custody, and anyone who argued was likely to be roughed up or beaten. Any motion was interpreted as resistance.

The real trouble began in the station. The five were lined up in a room and surrounded by officers. Clark was a big, powerful man, and when he moved, several police grabbed him. Bill shouted, "You can't do this to him!" Again Bill was hit from behind on the head. When he came to, he saw the officers beating Clark, hitting him repeatedly on the head, until he crashed to the floor. Then one officer kicked him and told him to get up. But Clark continued to lie there, although his eyes were open. One policeman spit in his face and yelled, "Get up, you dog!" Clark tried to get up but couldn't make it. At this, an irate officer hit him as hard as he could in the stomach with his club. The officers then turned their attention to Darden and Robinson, who were beaten, although not as badly as Clark. Darden was finally thrown into a cell where Clark was lying. Much later that night Clark was taken to a hospital.

This was only one incident. There were many. Certainly the police department must have known that the reports of these outrages would spread like wildfire among the black people, who were now closing their ranks. The bare facts were so raw and brutal they could hardly be blown up. What was blown up was the anger.

29

The West Side Organization for Full Employment (WSO) marked the continuing evolution that had begun with our storefront ministries in East Harlem, Cleveland, and Chicago. I had come to see that white middle-class ministries moving into ghetto communities as leaders would soon have to give way to self-determination, which alone could satisfy the growing racial solidarity. Community organization could no longer be carried on under the name and direct sponsorship of the churches. Within the congregations there were legitimate differences of opinion about political means and ends. I thought the churches now ought to support organizations developing self-determination.

Whenever we met in the early 1960s, Archie Hargraves and I used to have long talks about organizing the unemployed. Archie thought that groups of jobless people should act in community for their own interests. After all, others had organized to promote common concerns and interests. Such organization was a basic American tradition. Unorganized groups had little bargaining power in a highly organized society.

Before my leave of absence for the Urban Emphasis program, I urged Archie to join the staff of the Urban Training Center. By 1964 racial injustice and poverty were worse than they had been twenty years before. The "new" poor were the result of automation and technical change. For years, industries had been moving away leaving behind people who suddenly had become unemployed. Many blacks who had worked to build Chicago were on relief, and over the years a solid core of unemployed city blacks had been increasing. They were capable of work but they could not find it.

We were particularly affected by the plight of this new jobless group. They had a tradition of work, a history of working trades behind them, and society was letting them go. They needed to know that there were other people in the working world who would stand with them. I felt they had to be reached and encouraged to organize.

When Archie came to the Urban Training Center as Director of Missions, he taught a course in mission development. He also started the West Side Organization, in 1964, with two aides, the Rev. Bob Strom, a CCMS staff member, and Don Keating, a graduate of the center. Bob and Don are white and were to work under Archie.

In telling the story of the beginnings of the WSO I am drawing on my own recollections, what I learned from Archie Hargraves and others, and also on a log kept by Don Keating. Much of what follows took place from October 1964 through September 1965, when I was in New York City working on the Urban Emphasis program. Throughout this period I returned frequently and was regularly in touch with the Society staff.

Chester Robinson and Bill Darden, two of the men who turned out to be WSO leaders, were discovered by Chris Gamwell, a West Side Christian Parish minister. Archie, Bob, and Don, by hanging out in local bars and barbershops, found three more men—Bill Clark, John Crawford, and Gene Harris— whom they picked for qualities of leadership. All five were men in their thirties, black, streetwise, ghetto-born and bred, and all were ex-convicts. The Society agreed to finance a storefront office, and the young men were hired at small salaries as a cadre to begin organizing the jobless in the community.

The men had their own idea of how to organize, which was to walk around the neighborhood, go into the hangouts, pick certain people and say, "Man, we're going to have an organization." Archie wanted them to find the unemployed by working with other organizations, aldermen, and through local churches that were concerned, as well as by hanging out, but he was willing to follow the lead of these men. They looked for the hard-core jobless not found at unemployment offices.

In their early discussions with Archie it was decided they would go and tell the local established churches what they were doing. The Church Federation was not to be brought in, nor did they want to join organizations that already had a political or ideological framework. The West Side Christian Parish provided office space until quarters of their own were found at 1527 West Roosevelt Road, an ideal location. Temporary officers were duly elected, weekly executive meetings took place, and a community public meeting was scheduled every Wednesday evening.

The office had someone standing by day and night to talk to people who came in. Some teams went into the neighborhood canvassing for people looking for work, and other teams contacted employers. There was great difficulty with many large employers, because their standards were rigid. A high school education and no police record was specified. Someone once said that a person had to be either a genius or a moron to grow up in that neighborhood and not have some kind of record. But men who could not get jobs at all, whose records were an insurmountable barrier, were emerging as the mainstay of the staff at WSO, many of them working twelve and fourteen hours a day on organizing the community.

30

In the early meetings with the first group of unemployed, Chester Robinson had said that they needed to let the neighborhood see that the organization was doing something. He mentioned tackling a small business, "like the Centennial Laundry across the street." Chester mentioned the laundry as an example of many businesses in the area, but eventually Centennial Laundry became the principal issue. It came up naturally out of stories that had been told in the neighborhood for years. Although many blacks worked there, no black routemen had ever been employed. The starting salary of laundry workers was $1.04, and after four years some were making only $1.19, strictly illegal and maintained, they thought, by payoffs to the union.

WSO waited until it was learned that the laundry was looking for driver-salesmen. A cadre member recruited at the first meeting, Blutcher Bryant, and Bob Strom were delegated to investigate jobs on behalf of qualified applicants registered at WSO. Arranging an appointment was difficult, but they finally made one for August 12 at 10 A.M., with Irving Frank. The laundry was owned by the Brown family, and Frank, married to Brown's daughter, was in charge of the business.

Chester's idea was to have demands prepared and a realistic program. Otherwise, he said, we would be organizing people to be militant just for the sake of being militant. At the laundry, Bryant and Strom were kept waiting forty minutes and then given a tour of the entire plant. Frank obviously knew the purposes of WSO from literature circulated in the area. In each department, selected people had been alerted to answer questions. These employees would step forward and Frank would ask, "What's your name? How long have you worked here? What do you do? Do I treat you right? Are you in charge of this area? How much do you get paid? Do you like your job?" His manner to blacks was different: "This is Willie. This boy has been with us for 25 years." "This is Millie. Her husband is a bum and she needs the job. Right, Millie?"

The dependency relationships were not hard to see. Strom and Bryant were told of employees who went on weekend drunks but were kept on so long as they behaved themselves during the other four days, and also of members of families employed as favors to those working there. It seemed that small loans and favors prevented the challenging of a number of illegal and questionable practices. Lie detector tests were given to suspected employees when garments were missing. Two time cards had to be used by persons working overtime, with straight time rates paid no matter how many hours were worked. Neighborhood kids were used as helpers on laundry trucks at less than a dollar a day. There was no grievance procedure except through the paternalistic relations with Frank and members of the Brown family.

The two WSO men asked about black routemen. None was qualified, said Frank. When pressed to admit that one job was then open, he replied that Negroes were bums and thieves. Moreover, husbands didn't want their wives to deal with black drivers. The laundry was not going to be a pioneer and take chances.

After that, WSO decided to demand eight black routemen and did nothing else except to put out a call for discussion at the next meeting. But the following morning Abe Brown, the owner, and the general foreman called on Strom and threatened to sue him for unfairly charging racial discrimination. There was a heated argument after Strom told them they would have to deal with the organization, not with any individual. Later that day the Rev. C.S. Hampton, pastor of the Lawndale Interracial Baptist Church, made an appointment with Strom. Blutcher and John Crawford went along with Strom. Hampton told them that Brown had asked him to serve as mediator and that he knew the organization was ready to march on Wednesday. He was promptly corrected by Bryant. No action had been planned. A meeting was called only to discuss tactics and strategy. Hampton then offered one driver's job and an invitation to negotiate with Brown in his office. After he was told that such matters could only be discussed with the organization and that they could give him no answer, Hampton tried intimidation, hinting that the mayor and the political machine were on the side of Centennial. With an election coming up, the mayor would not allow any disturbance in the neighborhood, and members of WSO who had police records would be immediately investigated. He said that the request to have Brown talk with the entire WSO organization was out of line; a few always run the organization. The three WSO men felt they were being asked to sell out, and they told Hampton they would get in touch with him after the Wednesday night meeting to let him know what the organization had decided. It was obvious to them that there was a great deal worth investigating if a leaflet circulated in the neighborhood to call a meeting could cause such alarm.

On the day of the meeting, representatives of the Commission on Human Relations called WSO on the phone, saying Centennial had reported that they were stirring up a strike at the laundry. A city electrical inspector called and warned WSO about inadequate wiring on their premises. A sergeant and a detective from the 12th District visited WSO, taking down names and addresses and trying to intimidate those who were there. When they left they drove over to Centennial and went in.

At the meeting that evening three demands were agreed on: eight black routemen be hired by the laundry, "Uncle Tom" Hampton be rejected as mediator, and Brown be invited to the next WSO meeting. Brown rejected the demands and got in touch with Chicago City Missionary Society board chairman Tom Ayers. His complaints about Bob Strom led to a meeting between CCMS and WSO executives. Ayers and Frank Cassell of the board supported WSO and gave helpful advice, including a suggestion that they form an employers' council to get jobs in west side industries. At the next open WSO meeting the people decided to continue negotiations, organize the neighborhood for possible direct action, and plan a selective buying campaign.

On the first of September, WSO met with Brown and his attorney and an agreement was reached. Centennial was to hire two black drivers at $80 a week while training and the union rate later. Centennial agreed to hire qualified people recommended by WSO as other jobs became open. Applicants would not be fired without first consulting with WSO and would be replaced by another WSO member. An experienced presser was needed, and they would hire a WSO member immediately. Brown would be glad to join an employers' council and help get in touch with other businessmen.

But this was not the end of the matter.

Centennial Laundry did not keep to the agreement but used the strategy of evasion and the argument that applicants were not qualified or could not pass tests. The foreman, Demuchio, kept promising to come to WSO meetings to inform the members about the laundry's hiring practices but did not come. He promised two routemen jobs. WSO sent three qualified men but none was employed. He said he would hire drivers but they would have to work in the plant for six weeks first. An applicant was turned down because he was not married. WSO staff members, while sitting in Centennial's office, saw two white men get jobs without having to take tests.

WSO people suspected that Brown was sending spies to their weekly meetings. They were convinced that the reason Brown would never hire black drivers was because blacks were not trusted to handle money. Therefore, the people became more adamant in this demand. Brown, aware of the sentiment and the increasing activity, complained to Tom Ayers that WSO had not sent any qualified men, saying he had already hired one black routeman—the nephew of a laundry employee—and was training others. WSO renewed its demand for eight drivers and started to pass out leaflets in front of the laundry. Brown then threatened to sue the Society but would meet with WSO and give them a chance to avoid it. Many WSO members thought the threat meant that Brown was scared. It's up to him, they said, to find qualified blacks whether we can produce them from our applications or not. There ought to be special consideration for black people, not just equality, to make up for past injustice.

Chester was sure Brown would do nothing so long as customers came, and if business slowed he would run specials. "He doesn't care what we think of him or his laundry," said Chester.

All through this period there was debate among WSO staff and trainees about whether to keep concentrating on the issue of the routemen or on conditions in the laundry—discrimination, exploitation, wages. Chester insisted, "Now, unless you know these folks you don't know what to do. People never could get jobs driving those laundry trucks. But now they've got it into their heads, and they want that work. 'Cause if you're a driver it means you're reliable. It means you are somebody. Folks don't care about those other jobs. Now, this doesn't mean we don't *work* on all the other issues. We do. But we have to concentrate on the routemen so the people see us doing it. Brown hopes we get into conditions on the inside. He hopes we come up against the union. If we go after the union, the syndicate will take care of us fast."

WSO started picketing on October 13 and continued passing out leaflets listing the demands and inviting people to meetings. Jerry Judd and Willis Elliot, of the United Church Board for Homeland Ministries, went out to WSO, talked with Blutcher and Chester, and then joined the picket line. Helen Archibald, too, went out and walked in the line. I was in Chicago on the fourteenth and went to the Wednesday night meeting that week. The Community Council and WSO staff sat at a long table at the front of the room. I was impressed by the solidarity and the spirit. A number of people spoke spontaneously; the action had brought the local residents together. One man stood up and said, "I don't know how many other white people here tonight live in the neighborhood, but I do. I'm pastor of First Immanuel Lutheran. What you are doing I believe is solid all the way. It's Christian and it's moral. I haven't taken my laundry to Centennial for many months."

Betty Perkins, an active WSO member, said, "We want to be people, just human beings, because we are. Demuchio owes it to us. We need to put the facts down and stick together and have a selective buying campaign. We should leaflet the whole neighborhood and talk to the people. If he wants to go out of business, that's fine. We have lots more laundries. We aren't thinking just of ourselves, but the girls that work there. A hundred years ago they took the chains off of us, yes, but some of us let our brains go too. We have to do something. I really mean business. I have five kids—two of them boys—and who knows maybe one day one of them is going to drive one of Demuchio's trucks." This brought great applause.

Chester announced that picketing would start at 1 P.M. the next day and go until closing time. Then, looking down at a couple of people whom he took for "spies," he said, "What time do you close?" A young woman replied, "Seven o'clock."

Some discussion went on about drunks in the picket line. Habitual drinking, taken for granted among the unemployed, was a serious problem for some WSO members and organizers and increased the reputation of the organization in some quarters as riffraff. Blutcher had tried personal appeals like, "You can't do your job reeking of alcohol. You give everybody the impression that the whole WSO is drinking."

When the meeting ended I went away thinking about the primacy of the driver's job issue. It was not a case of people wanting what they could not have, but what they should have, and I thought it went even deeper. It said something about black pride. The demand for routeman jobs was far more fundamental than the insistence on better conditions for those who did menial work inside the plant. The people were indignant enough about the latter, but this was not exclusively a black issue; the demands on Centennial Laundry had united them as a people. They were like Betty Perkins—she cared about the workers inside the laundry, but when her son grew up he was going to drive one of those trucks.

It was not overlooked that keeping the Centennial Laundry issue going was the way to build the West Side Organization. According to Chester, it was useless to canvass without some action on a popular issue going on. For the first time, Brown and Centennial Laundry were doing something positive for the west side community.

But the strange circumstance that Centennial, by resisting, was doing the one thing that would help WSO was countered by the also paradoxical attitude of the CCMS board, who wanted the matter settled quickly. Pressure was building within the Society to get WSO to call off the pickets and meet with the Commission on Human Relations. WSO agreed to meet but would not call off the pickets. The meetings did little good. Brown would make such statements as, "Send me one good Negro routeman and I'll hire him tomorrow morning," or "We have no openings, but if you send us a qualified man we will carry him until we do." Finally, a member of the Chicago Commission on Human Relations asked the question and kept returning to it: "We find it difficult to imagine, Mr. Brown, that in the seventy-five years your laundry has been in business not one Negro has come through your doors who was qualified to be a routeman."

At WSO, as the picketing went on, they talked about investigating the laundry and its directors; interviewing people; filing complaints; studying laws regarding wages, hours, and unions; doing research on other laundries; and building files of case histories. They called other civil rights groups to tell them what they were doing and invite them to participate in picketing. ACT, a militant black group headed by Lawrence Landry, was the only one to respond. Landry called Centennial and tried, in effect, to take over the situation. On October 21, the date of the weekly open meeting, ACT members joined the pickets from 6 to 7 P.M., then came to the WSO meeting. Doug Andrews, their spokesman, said they had come to explain their policy and to see if WSO still wanted them to help. "We do not advocate violence," he said, "nor do we preach nonviolence. We do believe in self-defense. If someone hits us we hit back."

Chester said, "Tell us—is it against the law to sit in front of the doors at Centennial Laundry where the trucks come out?"

"It depends. The laws are geared to perpetuate segregation. Therefore some means has to be found to counter these laws and at present these means might be unlawful."

"We are nonviolent," Chester said, "but if somebody gets hit there is going to be hell to pay."

"If an ACT picketer is molested I guarantee the aggressor will be killed!" Andrews said. "Freedom is death, and death is freedom!"

"This is a young organization and we don't know much about picketing," Chester told him. "The middle-class civil rights people who turn the other cheek—we don't understand turning the other cheek. We have never lived by it. But, is it right? We don't want to start anything. People around here, they just don't like Centennial. We don't want to start a riot."

"ACT is rough and young. We don't advocate violence. But until you realize you are up against the white power structure of this city you will get nowhere."

After more talk about violence Chester said, "I've lived here since 1934. Fighting gets no place. There is some way to do everything. Now, the majority of this community if they get hit fight back. We're not here for violence and we're not here to turn the other cheek. Maybe it will come to violence. We hope not. Now I know I speak for our own group when I say we are going to try and teach nonviolence regardless of whether ACT or anyone else likes it. This community is going to run itself. We don't need anybody else to tell us about violence, non or any other kind!"

The staff and the Community Council gathered in the back of the room after the meeting, and a motion was made and passed to call the ACT office and say they did not want them back the next day in the picket line. The discovery that one of the ACT members was carrying a revolver was sobering.

The morning after the WSO meeting, CCMS executives made it clear to Bob Strom and Don Keating there was going to be a problem with the board as long as the picketing continued. In general, the board agreed with the right of the community to determine its own destiny, but many disagreed over tactics. I was having daily conversations by phone from New York with our executives, so I knew what happened that morning and the night before. I knew Landry and what the ACT people had in mind. Landry had run the angry meeting in the south side storefront basement in the spring of 1965, and what disturbed me most at the time was the way the people had responded. Their rage and resentment didn't have to be whipped up; it had been burning for a long time and was ready to explode. Right after that, I had started to meet for breakfast with some of our board members—usually Tom Ayers of Commonwealth Edison, Lem Hunter of Inland Steel, and Paul Lund of Illinois Bell. I had tried to interpret the intense frustrations of the black community, but they didn't understand the severity of the feeling.

In the afternoon I phoned Strom and told him that ACT's coming in had changed the picture, that ACT was making a play for WSO, and that WSO would have to make a decision right away. I told him we could not tell WSO what to do. We had to leave the door open, but I said I thought Chester would come out all right. If the organization had been inclined toward violence, they would have done it long ago. But now they had to choose. It was up to them. If they took the way of violence, they would latch on to Landry; he had the guns and the men. The other way was to rouse the top people in the power structure to an awareness of the situation.

Strom relayed the message with some embellishment, reminding the WSO group of what they had heard the night before—that "death is liberty, and liberty is death." WSO had no question about the way; it was to be by way of the power structure. WSO was demonstrating its growing maturity.

On Friday, October 23, a meeting began at CCMS in the morning and resumed at WSO in midafternoon. Those present were nine members of the WSO staff and Community Council; six people from the Chicago Business Industrial Project staff and board; Carl Zeisler, assistant treasurer of Inland Steel; Dave Harden, president of Market Facts; Vic Gottbaum, head of American Federation of State, Community and Municipal Employees; and Ralph Helstein, president of International Packinghouse Workers.

Vic Gottbaum told WSO they were kidding themselves if they were looking for legal outlets and that action should be continued. Economic sanctions were costing Brown money. Helstein offered lawyers and office staff. During lunch, Gottbaum met with Ed Marciniak, chairman of the Chicago Commission on Human Relations. When he returned he reported that Marciniak would meet with Brown, that Centennial Laundry was responsible, and that black drivers could be found. The key lay with Ray Shaslan of the Teamsters, who was concerned that no one be fired, but Marciniak's line to Brown was going to be, "You've got to do this. You're in trouble."

But now, Gottbaum said, was not the time for WSO to let up. "You should increase your effort."

"What else can we do?" Betty Perkins asked.

"Stop the clientele at the door. Follow the truck routes in Negro and mixed neighborhoods. The problem will be to know which trucks."

"That's easy," she said. "The ones with the big dogs."

Gottbaum told them to travel in twos, to see which bells the driver rang, and take the addresses and the names. "If he tells you to scram, be polite. Say you don't know of any law you are breaking, but if he thinks you are he has a perfect right to phone the police.

"On the next trip go in pairs, husband and wife if possible. Work out your approach and answers to expected questions ahead of time. Rehearse. Get eight or ten cars ready for early morning, and pads and pencils. Tell the people about Centennial, and request that they call the laundry right now and tell them after the next delivery, that's it. My feeling is that by the time you get that far Brown will have had enough. When a man starts to hurt economically it's amazing how quickly he becomes a pro-human being."

He gave them more advice. "In your leaflets say 'help yourselves' not 'help us.' When you are picketing keep six feet apart; don't stop people going and coming. Don't get into arguments. You don't convince people that way. If they read and agree, OK. If they read and disagree and give the leaflet back, take it with thanks. You can picket and leaflet too. Another thing, and you can spit on me for this—I tell you for what it's worth because it's just the way our society is—wear a shirt and tie."

At 10:30 the next morning Ed Marciniak convened a meeting between Brown and Demuchio of Centennial Laundry and seven WSO members and reached an agreement subject to ratification by both sides.

Centennial Laundry backed out of the agreement. A letter was sent to WSO signed by Abe Brown, couched in general terms, setting forth Centennial's guiding principles: belief in God, equal opportunity, civil rights, and employment on merit. Centennial's lawyer came to the Wednesday meeting on October 28 and read the letter, which went on to say that, according to the policy stated, Centennial would continue to recruit, hire, and upgrade employees without regard to race, creed, or color; that it realized the impact of hard core unemployment on the near west side and had always employed many persons from the area adjacent to the plant and would continue the practice.

Afterward, the lawyer, whom Keating described as "treating us as something less than human," charged WSO with wanting to cross all the *t*s and dot the *i*s. Codozie (Doz) Lyles, a WSO member who had worked for the laundry, got to his feet. "You said Centennial Laundry hires 80% Negro inside. They do the menial jobs, not the ones with positions and pay."

The lawyer told him if the laundry closed there would be two hundred fifty unemployed instead of eight more hired. "Then they might just as well stay home and starve to death as work up there and starve," said Doz.

Bill Clark asked a direct question. "What are the qualifications?" "A man must be honest, trustworthy, and want to sell," was the reply.

"You're saying there're no honest Negroes?" asked Bill.

The lawyer evaded this, and the hiring qualifications were never given.

Afterward, Archie told the cadre they would now have to work to carry the community and to educate the people. "When they see you stick together through this you will be better off than if you had won the first time."

Chester at first was in favor of Vic Gottbaum's idea—following the trucks and getting a quick victory. But many others, including Archie, wanted to continue the strategy of prolongation. There hadn't been enough knocking on doors and mass meetings. They could beat Centennial with a few people, but they could not organize the community this way. What they had done was to pick up some good people, but now they had a chance, given to them by Brown because he didn't come through, to get five hundred or perhaps a thousand. They would go door to door, inviting citizens to participate in a boycott, to sign petitions for the removal of the dogs, and to picket. There would be more leaflets and the West Side Christian Parish would be asked to get the churches to participate.

On October 30 my associate, Dick Schwenke, called Bob Strom to tell him the Society's board wanted WSO to go to Human Relations again and meet with Centennial to find out why they had backed out. The WSO membership decided that Chester should call Tom Ayers and tell him they were the spokesmen on the Centennial Laundry issue, not Bob Strom, and that WSO at this point was not asking Centennial that question.

The situation was strained, because the CCMS board felt capable of giving constructive advice. I consistently urged staying out of WSO decisions while continuing our support, and it was clear to me that the WSO people were absolutely right. I thought we ought to be willing to go all the way to the wall for them. It turned out that in the end we went the distance.

When WSO started the boycott and began picketing again, Centennial got an injunction outlawing both and filed suit against WSO for a half million dollars, naming also the Society; myself; the president, Tom Ayers; and every member of the board of directors. The injunction was so broad that it forbade west side residents and others connected with WSO to do almost anything that directly interfered with Centennial's business or operations. A rally was held at which Archie urged the people as law-abiding citizens to obey the injunction, and Abner Mikva was retained as WSO's attorney.

The Centennial case went all the way to the Illinois Supreme Court and was decided in favor of WSO. But long before settlement, Brown decided to hire black drivers, and WSO recommended twenty young men.

The effect on the Society's board was significant; the board changed its thinking several times and eventually became deeply involved. I think board members initially felt insecure in dialogue with the WSO people; they were accustomed to dealing with churches and clergy. But now they were getting firsthand stories of what was going on. They had preferred to stay in the background, giving orders. But when it came to the test they changed. They would not run out, and they began to realize that while giving support they could not control.

Besides stressing economic issues and acting as an employment service, WSO formed tenants' councils to press for adequate maintenance by slum landlords and eventually inaugurated Chicago's first welfare union.

In one case of the mother of a family on welfare with a legitimate complaint, WSO welfare union workers went with her to the public aid office. When the caseworker refused assistance without explanation the group declined to leave the office until they received satisfaction. Police were called, and all, including the mother, were arrested. Without the financial backing of the Society, this case would never have been fought or justice finally rendered. There were improprieties by the local judge for which he was eventually reprimanded by the Illinois Supreme Court, when it ruled in favor of the defendants.

The welfare union turned out to be a potent tool for organizing, and it was set up on the basis of the grievance procedure that had been worked out at WSO. In one case welfare department workers were so surprised to see recipients demanding their rights and so anxious to get WSO members out of the office that they collected the money among themselves and advanced the cash to the claimant.

Soon public aid recipients refused to go into interviews without a representative from WSO. At one time WSO staff members were told they would no longer be allowed at grievance interviews because the confidentiality of the recipients had to be protected. WSO asked whose confidence was actually being protected. Obviously, it was that of the agency, not the individuals. The delegation stood firm, and an hour before closing time were joined at the welfare office by thirty or forty west side neighborhood people who agreed to stay until they had won the right for their union or neighborhood organization representative to be at the interview with them. The police arrived at about 6:30, but eventually the supervisor relented and agreed to let the representative sit in. The following Monday, WSO representatives were summoned to talk with William Wattie, chief of the Bureau of Welfare Administration, who listened for three hours to grievances of recipients and agreed to the points made by WSO in each case. Most involved inefficiency in the department or a punitive attitude of the welfare worker.

This was the beginning of the union. In some 570 grievances it was proved that the department was in violation of the law, and WSO did not lose one case. A base of people was developed who were willing and ready to move at a moment's notice in direct action.

During the winter of 1964-65 morale at WSO was often low. They were running out of funds, and the staff officially became volunteers again, as they had been at the start. But the activity of finding jobs went on, and basic education courses in reading, typing, and math were instituted. Here the self-help and helping-one-another character of the organization was noticeable. People in the neighborhood were found who could do the training. They did not have to be experienced teachers to help. The educational programs grew and also the organization of teenagers who started their own social clubs.

Early in 1965 WSO elected a board of directors and adopted by-laws and rules of procedure. Among other benefits the board was to free the cadre from fund-raising. Archie Hargraves was the first board chairman. The organization was divided into development and administrative sectors, and task forces were appointed for these and for housing, employment, health, welfare, and education. People were designated to work with various groups, such as storefront churches, informal and formal organizations, welfare recipients, and job recipients. Proposals were prepared and adopted for office and staff procedure.

31

The men who organized WSO were natural leaders. They had the contacts, and they were wise, as well as street-wise. They knew the people and the community. But also they were men who had come out of violence, and they lived on the edge of the law.

The terrible-tempered WSO worker Bill Darden, known as Thirsty, was a man whom few people crossed. Archie recalls one time when WSO people complained about the increased crime. Thirsty called in two men he knew who were doing holdups. "You guys are not right," he told them. "You are not to do anything in the hood, so all the people can be at ease. Otherwise I'm coming after you."

"Yes, Thirsty."

"No stickups. You hear me? No stickups in the hood."

"Yea, Thirsty."

Chester's leadership seemed to reflect the fact of the community's determination. He was always sensitive to it. And I was continually amazed at his skill in confronting people. He knew just how far to go. With one or two others from WSO he would march into my office asking for money, and if I hadn't known his tactics, I might have been intimidated. He could be hard, seemingly inflexible, and yet he never went over the edge.

There was always one little area of reconciliation left open. So I could never get angry at him, and I had to admire his performance. When it was over he would be all sweetness and would say, "Well, I guess we'll just have to go back out there to WSO and go on suffering."

A local newspaper columnist, Jack Mabley, called Chester a Communist. It was not true, and I wrote Mabley indignant letters but never got him to retract, although the only evidence he seemed to have was that Chester's cellmate in prison had been the leader of the W.E.B. DuBois clubs and a Communist.

"I think too many Negroes try to be like white people," Chester would say. "I don't blame the Negro for this. I blame the white people. In order to live in your society, I have to talk like you, I have to act like you. I have to have nine pieces of silver when I eat my dinner, when I ain't never had but one. But I say that if the southerns can say 'ain't' and 'is all' and 'you all,' and all the senators, congressmen from the South can, why can't we do it and be accepted?

"I think Negroes are training people how to be themselves, how to really love, how to really be nonviolent, how to be a passive resistant person, because a Negro, whether people know it or not, is the most nonviolent race in our century. Negroes are the most advanced race in our system. I don't say this out of pride. I say this out of deeds. They are the best in all fields that they participate in, not because they think they are better. It's because they give their best, and I think once we start to really getting Negroes to give their best, I think the whole world is going to benefit by it, because they are going to get something altogether new."

Chester had a natural eloquence and a way of expressing himself freely and directly. Yet he was not always open. Sometimes he would not take part in meetings or get up and leave if he did not like what was going on. When he came back the next day he would not talk. If anyone went too far in opposing him, he was apt to say, "Well, I guess I'll have to get my clippers out," meaning he would go back to barbering, which was his trade.

Except for John Crawford, often called Deacon or Preach Crawford, the original cadre were not openly "religious." At one time, when WSO was considering holding a worship service in front of Centennial Laundry, some of them were asked about prayer. Chester did not like "personal questions," but he said, "I don't pray and never will. I shouldn't say that. My dad did, but he prayed when he was dying."

Bill Clark said, "Prayer. I never did too much praying for myself. I prayed a lot of times for other folks. I've got too much respect for God to pray for myself. I have, and I hate it. I said, 'You get me out of this mess and I will do all kinds of things,' but I was a liar. I'm not ready for church or for God. I don't believe in but I believe of him and I just believe God respects me as I am, as not ready. You should be careful about what you say because you don't know what people are really doing. This is not a religious organization. I thought it was for equality and justice for all. If this was a religious organization I would never have come in that door."

At another time Chester told me, "I have over twenty ministers in my family. I know God is not dead. I fear God more than I do Mayor Daley or anybody else, and when I do wrong I don't think about the police or anybody else. I think about God and what he thinks, and how he is going to take it."

When Chester headed the Chicago delegation in Washington, D.C., during the Citizens Crusade Against Poverty in April 1966, his police record was published in *Chicago American*. Jack Mabley was one of the writers. The story said that Chester had been arrested nine times by Chicago police and had served three years in Stateville for selling narcotics and a year in county jail for possession of narcotics. The latest arrest had been on April 18, 1965, when "two policemen were attacked" entering a dance for teenagers at the WSO. When asked about his record Chester answered reporters, "What about it? I did what I did. I paid for it. I don't think it's anybody's business. I done evil. I seen evil, and now I'm fighting evil. I don't make any excuses."

He also told reporters the latest arrest had been a frame-up. "The police forced their way in. They pushed one teen down and hit another on the head. I told everybody to sit down. They threw me in the paddy wagon and cut both my knees. The officers testified I told the boys to go home and get their guns and kill every white policeman, and the judge said, 'I believe you said that.'"

Sometime later Chester said, "This is the hardest problem I have: to get people to understand me and believe that I want to do something right. And we are here now. We know what is right and wrong. We know because we have been doing wrong all our lives and now we are trying to do right, and we are trying to build people to take our place as leaders and to get more leaders and to build more WSOs and really come up with the answer to the whole social problem on the west side of Chicago."

In addition to its article about Chester Robinson's record, on April 27, 1966, the *Chicago American* ran an editorial that concluded:

> If Robinson were a private citizen, his record as a dope pusher might concern only a prospective employer. But since he is a self-proclaimed spokesman for the poor, his record concerns everybody with an interest in seeing the anti-poverty program succeed.
>
> The program can get results only if people are convinced of its good faith and its effectiveness. When a man with a record like this appears as a local leader, it deals a crippling blow to the credibility of the whole program. Robinson fought poverty in his own way by getting other people hooked on a hideous and destructive habit; how much faith can be put in an organization he speaks for?
>
> We have called attention before to the folly of turning over control of the war on poverty to the poor themselves; that is equivalent to turning over a hospital to the patients. Robinson's record will, we hope, jolt more people into recognizing that being poor is not the only justification for leadership.

The newspaper editorial spoke, I trust, not of sin but of crime, and I think Chester understood this when he said, "I have paid for it." Crime is a social infraction and society punishes it. Of sin we cannot speak. There are moments when we know that all we can do is to "stand beside the sinner in solidarity before God," as Markus Barth of the East Harlem parish put it. "Man," he said, "does not speak against fellow man: he must not do so, even if it should be the 'holiest Joe' dealing with the most insulting backslider."

I think our greatest danger is self-righteousness. I used to tell my congregations, "We are really a fellowship of 'sinners anonymous' standing in need of repentance."

WSO is remarkable as a community organization. Generally, the methods of sociologist Saul Alinsky, executive director of the Industrial Areas Foundation, were thought to be far superior in technique. The Alinsky style was to start with the organizations in an area, hoping to include the poor. WSO, however, started with the poor, hoping to include some individuals who were members of organizations. When the West Side Federation, in January of 1965, began talking to the Alinsky group about organizing the west side, the WSO people did not feel seriously threatened, knowing they would be going after a different segment of the population.

Alinsky had succeeded in several lower-class white ethnic areas and to some degree in the predominantly black Woodlawn community. But in Woodlawn, middle-class people had received the greater advantages and comparatively little had been done to involve the poorer residents. The growth of gangs in Woodlawn was marked during this period. For teenagers, life was a raw jungle and the gang was a means of giving them identity and a kind of "family" support. Their activities were seen in the community as destructive.

Alinsky's premises were these: (1) Local people are more concerned about themselves than any outsider can be. (2) Within communities, there are people of intellect and initiative. Development, therefore, can be in their hands. (3) Controversy and conflict around issues are essential in organizing. (4) The purpose of organizing is to acquire power.

Their organizers attempt to find the self-interest of each group and strike up deals that would make it advantageous to cooperate, even though some differences might be irreconcilable. A constant turnover of leaders guarded against institutionalism. Alinsky people were the architects until the organization became independent, which meant self-financed. They advised against connections with political parties, because this meant losing bargaining power, but suggested cooperating as long as the organization was getting what it wanted from politicians. Their way was to isolate local grievances, create highly publicized protests, and move gradually from protest to acquisition of community power.

My first introduction to The Woodlawn Organization (TWO) came soon after I arrived in Chicago. At first I was slow in grasping the nature of community organizing as it was emerging there. I had been invited by a friend, Msgr. Jack Egan, to a south side rectory, presumably to talk with the Protestant and Roman Catholic clergy about an interchange among the churches in dealing with the problems of Woodlawn. I don't believe Egan planned it, but when I arrived the place was loaded with TWO organizers and I backed off, feeling I was being manipulated into supporting an operation before I knew much about it. It seemed to me the churches and clergy had identified themselves with the organization too easily. They weren't critical enough. I remember going to a church with Nicholas Von Hoffman, who was one of the organizers. He talked to young black kids, trying to get them angry enough to organize. It was the approach known as "rubbing raw the sores of discontent." The organizers talked about how terrible the neighborhood was and told the kids nobody cared about them. Their value system was all self-interest. The people's self-interest was one thing, but what was behind theirs? This was not the gospel, which ought to lift us above self-interest. To me, this method was the opposite of what we were trying to do in the church.

Nevertheless, I was surprised and impressed, perhaps out of temper at the time, because they had gone farther than I had; they had reached farther out, and were succeeding. Because they were doing some of the things we had done or wanted to do in East Harlem, I was attracted but also repelled. They carried things too far and there was a sense that "anything goes" in organizing a community.

Also I was floored by the experience because I felt "out of it," as if I had joined those who used to oppose the sorts of things I wanted to do. I was hardly comfortable in such a role. To suddenly become conscious of the stiff Protestant piety rising up in me was an unsettling experience. In this case I agreed with the ends but not the means. The means were creating hostility and anger—not a real solution—and the problems were being overstated.

Community organizations that had already emerged in the Alinsky pattern were composed of active, above average people—closer to middle class. They claimed to be as representative as possible, that they were as closely identified with low-income groups as anyone—because such groups did not organize.

But WSO was trying to prove that low-income groups could organize. WSO was starting at the bottom and moving up. They began with the predominant group, the unemployed, then included tenants and welfare recipients. Gradually, they spread out to storefront churches and small clubs, asking them to send representatives to WSO meetings so that when given issues came to a head, a number of people could be called to take what action was needed. But the cadre was reluctant to approach established organizations, churches, or settlement houses who would give money, because they were suspicious of too many strings attached.

Perhaps with all the shortcomings of some of its members from the standpoint of traditional middle-class virtues, WSO at that time was close to the ideal stage of the neighborhood organization. It was curiously unpolitical and uncommercial; uppermost was the desire to help one another. The central character was unselfishness. Chester Robinson, although he would have been surprised to hear it, was carrying out the Christian gospel. In this aspect WSO was then the opposite of The Woodlawn Organization.

Chester came to embody the spirit of the group ministry, and he carried this ministry on. He had a strong feeling for the group and the urge to help those in trouble. He was the one most often out in the streets; his contacts were personal. "If someone comes to me for help and I don't do anything, I'm worse than a dog," he used to say. When the cadre met to deal with the problem of low funds, he would say, "We'll cut our salaries." His attitude was one of service and as a leader he was not dictatorial. It was the Community Council, he said, that would "tell us what to do." Chester's influence was undoubtedly the strongest force behind the general concern for the group, and he always stuck to the phrase "helping one another" when he described WSO. Yet he was not religious in the formal sense.

WSO was the culmination of what our group ministry had wanted to accomplish in East Harlem, and Archie Hargraves brought it to fruition. If WSO is a different organization today, it is up to the people. It has moved from protest to development and service, and now operates a health services corporation, a mental health day treatment program, and a drug abuse and rehabilitation project on the west side. It organized two major housing projects with nearly 500 units, and WSO now is developing a commercial strip to cover four city blocks. A number of businesses have pledged to cooperate, and one of the potential coparticipants is Centennial Laundry. Centennial and WSO are now great friends.

32

The development of the freedom movement in Chicago presented a great opportunity to the CCMS board. This attempt of the black community to rise to a position of power had been a long time coming. For years Chicago blacks had worked peacefully and constructively through the Urban League and NAACP, and they would continue to do so. But despite all efforts, reliable surveys showed there was more segregation in schools and housing in the 1960s than in the 1940s. The rising expectations of the black population had driven them toward direct action and, we hoped, direct negotiation.

In Chicago the freedom movement coalesced around the Coordinating Council of Community Organizations (CCCO), which had begun to emerge in 1963. In the summer of 1965 I asked our board to make a decision. I pointed out that CCCO comprised the center of the civil rights movement. Neither the Urban League nor the NAACP were members, because neither could commit themselves to direct action, and the more militant groups were waiting in the wings in the belief that the Daley machine would crush the movement or weaken its capacity to achieve concrete gains.

I was reasonably sure some of the groups who were formal

members of CCCO would escalate civil disobedience if griev-ances were not dealt with. The Society had some relation to individuals in CCCO's policy-making group, which included Archie Hargraves, a member of the CCMS board of directors and director of mission development at the Urban Training Center; Alvin Pitcher, professor at the University of Chicago's Divinity School; Ed Reddick who was on the staff of the Church Federation; and John McDermott, executive director of the Catholic Interracial Council.

I knew it would be unwise for the Society to become a formal member of the Council. We might be a continuing target for damage suits and might be restricting the freedom of action of the movement and ourselves. But in the interests of justice we could hardly refrain from some kind of involvement, so I proposed that the Society contribute funds for three projects: for organizational structure, to support a strong voice for the black community in the city; for a supplementary education program that would bring inner-city parents into the decision process; and for interpreting to suburban people the aims and methods of the growing freedom movement in Chicago. We also proposed to help raise additional funds from those foundations that were interested in education and civil rights.

The board approved this as an inter-religious effort and a continuance of the Society's traditional role as an interpreter of inner-city life.

The Cragin area of Chicago's northwest side was a typical "gray area," the population mostly of Polish, Italian, and German descent. One black family had lived there for years. Within its one square mile were two large Roman Catholic parishes and eight Protestant congregations. The community had about a hundred industries, and most families owned their homes.

In the fall of 1963, when the Cragin Congregational Church closed, the Society made a commitment to continue some form of ministry and asked Don Keating to explore the possibilities. It did not seem wise to continue in a traditional church. The nature of the Cragin community was such that it was neither suburbia nor inner city. Problems were not acute enough for people to be disturbed about them, but at the same time it was a community that showed signs of deterioration. We were interested in it because it represented a typical urban area to which denominations had given little attention.

Don Keating moved with his family into the neighborhood and began looking for activities in which he could participate. Compared with the west side, he found the community relatively dead. Few people showed interest. Most thought he was connected with some church and wanted them to join the congregation. He told them it was the world of Cragin that he cared about, not the church. If he brought up the political situation, they would tell him how bad it was, but if he asked what could be done, residents would usually say something like, "Well, you can't really do anything. Anyway, I get all I want from my precinct captain." But there was one question that always brought great consternation: "How long do you think it will be before the blacks move in?"

In the fall of 1965 Keating began to gather responsible people, and the response from clergy was good. Roman Catholics, Lutherans, and others joined and had developed a modest organization known as Cragin Plus. In the summer of 1966 Cragin was selected as one of the targets for the open housing marches sponsored by the Southern Christian Leadership Conference and the Chicago Freedom Movement. On a Sunday night before the marches occurred the storefront windows of Cragin Plus were broken and the following night the building was damaged by a fire bomb. Some Cragin residents evidently believed that Cragin Plus was related to ghetto organizations through the Society, or else they had learned that Keating had once worked for WSO.

Yet the group was not discouraged. In September twelve clergymen from ten churches met with Cragin Plus members and a neighborhood organization was started, changing the name to the Organization of Northwest Communities (ONC). At the second public meeting seventy people from thirty-five organizations attended. One group began to work on housing code enforcement. Another, the Health and Welfare Committee, held discussions with grade school principals and the Board of Health in an effort to establish the need for a family center. The Youth Committee brought together youth leaders and local businessmen who had had their windows smashed.

The ONC still exists today.

33

By the end of 1965 I had concluded that the Society ought to move from supporting community protest to aiding community development. Community development of inner-city neighborhoods was demanded by the widening gap between them and the growing affluence of some sections of the city. At the ages when the employment ratio should be the highest, we had great numbers of people untrained, uneducated, and unemployed. Another reason for community development was the obvious limitations of the government's War on Poverty. It was difficult for city government to mobilize these particular citizens to work on problems when those problems were the result of city bureaucracy. The Urban Progress Centers set up by Mayor Daley, with their appointed directors and boards, could hardly develop motivated community groups to generate their own programs.

In spring 1968 I suggested that the Society turn to development of community corporations in low-income areas. Such a program would enable the poor—especially the black poor—to assume responsibility and gain management skills while moving toward the full participation in society they were demanding. I argued that if people in the ghetto were going to stand firm in dialogue and negotiations, they had to develop their own institutions serving their own interests.

The idea of a corporation seemed basic to American society, and a statement of principles was accordingly drawn up for a core staff that would work out the program to support only community corporations committed to democratic nonviolent means of change, having open and free discussion with voice and vote open to all residents of the community, with control in the hands of the residents, and that were not controlled by any political ideology or were exclusively political in activity.

A series of events interfered with the realization of this plan. Even as the board debated the wisdom of community corporations, we found ourselves involved in another incident of police brutality toward Society-related staff.

It happened at about 6:30 on a March evening, when the Rev. Bob Strom and Douglas Bryant, a black WSO associate, were walking along Madison Street toward Strom's car. A man called to them saying that Bryant's wife was embroiled in an argument inside a tavern. "You'd better come over here and take care of her," he said. "The guy has called the police."

The two men crossed the street and went into the tavern together. Dorothy Bryant and the owner of the bar were exchanging remarks, but obviously the commotion had cooled. (It was later learned that Mrs. Bryant had thrown some dishes at the wall.) The attitude of other patrons in the place seemed to be curiosity and amusement. Bryant walked over to his wife and began to talk to her, with Strom close behind.

Four officers from the 13th Precinct on Wood Street walked in, and at once the atmosphere became charged. Everyone watched as one of the policemen spoke to the upset tavernkeeper, who pointed out Mrs. Bryant. The police turned toward the Bryants, but Strom stepped between them and the couple, saying that he was a minister and a staff member of the West Side Organization. He explained that he and Bryant had just come in, there had been a quarrel between the manager and Mrs. Bryant, but she was now leaving. An officer grabbed Bryant, shook and shoved him roughly, while another officer grabbed Mrs. Bryant and slammed her against the wall. Bryant and Strom called out in protest. The policeman holding Bryant became irate and shoved him hard against the wall. "You black cocksucker!" he said, "I'm going to fix you!" He pulled out his nightstick and beat Bryant over the head and shoulders, then jerked him around and handcuffed his hands behind him. Another officer had been shoving, kicking, and beating Mrs. Bryant and finally handcuffed her. By this time several people in the bar were protesting. Sirens were heard and other police began to arrive. When she was handcuffed an officer dragged Mrs. Bryant from the wall and shoved her into a booth, holding her there with his knee.

Exclamations of protest burst out around the room, and people who knew Mrs. Bryant came over and tried to tell the police that she was pregnant. The result of this was a rude remark about Mrs. Bryant which Bryant heard. He called out,

"You shut up. I can take care of this. I'm her husband." This drew several officers who jumped on Bryant and began to club him. One infuriated policeman brought his knee up into Bryant's groin and went on hitting him, transferring his club to his left hand, pulling his gun with his right, and uttering a continuous stream of profanity. Bob Strom later said that the gun was resting on Bryant's forehead and that the policeman's "hand was shaking, his face was shaking, and he said, 'You nigger bastard, you black bastard. I'll fix you, cocksucker!'" Strom stood there aghast, hearing a distinct click as the hammer was pulled back, the officer continuing to yell, "I'll kill you, you black motherfucker!" Just then Bryant fell limp to the floor. He said later that he thought he was going to be shot. The same officer began kicking and clubbing him again. The Bryants' hands were locked behind them so that the fingers extended upward, which is the most painful position in which to be handcuffed, and their arms were pulled in dragging them out of the bar, causing great pain. When they reached the door one officer kicked Mrs. Bryant through it.

Altogether there were about twenty policemen around and in the bar by this time and four or five squad cars in the street. On the sidewalk the Bryants were slammed against the car. Bryant kept asking what he had done. Didn't he have the right to speak? Each time he spoke he was slammed again.

Two women were passing by accompanied by the daughter of one, who was of high school age. I had a long talk with them afterward. One of the women, when she saw the treatment of Douglas Bryant, yelled at Mrs. Bryant, "Get his badge number! Report him!" She was immediately seized by a policeman. "Since you're so smart, you can go too," he said, and put her into the car. The other woman asked her niece to hold her handbag so she could get out a dime to make a phone call, but she was caught and, with the niece, was also taken to the station. She said that Bryant had been bodily thrown into the wagon. "We didn't know what was going on. We heard him screaming from outside."

At the station while the three women were standing with Mrs. Bryant at the desk being questioned a man came to the door with a muzzled dog. He said the dog had bitten his mother and that he did not want to keep the animal any longer. One of the policemen, gesturing toward the women, said, "Bring the dog in here. We'll turn him loose." At this the women began to scream. One climbed up on a table and the others ran to hide behind officers. The policemen, however, had been sufficiently amused and the dog was not unmuzzled.

Strom had been thrown into the wagon after Bryant, and at the station the two were taken to the interrogation room and told to stand against the wall. Eight officers faced them and it looked as if further violence was intended. One of the officers and two detectives began demanding name, age, occupation, and also asked questions such as, "What kind of organization is this West Side Organization?" Throughout they kept up the stream of profanity. They wanted to know the nature and activities of the WSO and the welfare union, and also "What communist organization was Rev. Strom a member of?" Strom refused to answer until the handcuffs were removed, but Bryant said, "The West Side Organization is an organization of some people who have united together. We are trying to see that everybody can set their own table every day. Maybe today I can set my own table, but I feel that the next man and woman should be able to set theirs too."

Despite the interrogation the customary booking procedure had not been carried out. Obviously, the questioning was strictly harassment. After the handcuffs were taken off Strom said, "I will now tell you what kind of organization we have. I am not a Communist, and I believe in the possibilities of America and democracy. Our organization has found over six hundred jobs for people. We work on violations within the Cook County Department of Public Aid, on welfare laws, and the like. We have programs for teenagers, educational programs, and so on."

One of the detectives said, "How are you going to teach people who can't learn? How do you deal with people who are lazy and won't work?"

After this Bryant and Strom were booked and locked up in different cells. Later Strom was brought to the front room, where several policemen were gathered and another interrogation began. During this time one of the officers said, "We have the Ku Klux Klan. Maybe we should let them take care of your kind." Another standing by said, "We don't have the KKK—we have the PNA" (Polish National Alliance). Bryant was also brought out and questioned again. He kept repeating that he was working for unity and harmony and for putting bread on the table.

"If you're so interested in unity and harmony and organizing people," said one policeman, "why in hell did you tell me to shut up?"

"I told you to shut up because I could handle my wife," Bryant said, "because we had already settled the argument, and because we were already leaving the tavern."

"You mean you told him to shut up?" yelled another policeman. "Listen, nigger, if you had told me to shut up it would be a different story. You'd better get down on your knees and thank the Lord you didn't tell it to me because if you did you wouldn't be alive to talk about it."

A third officer said to Bryant, "You aren't any organizer. You're nothing but a black prick, and a prick always ends up in a box and that's what we've got ready for you. We got a coffin ready for you."

Bryant replied, "Well, we are all going to die and there are worse things than death."

Strom and Bryant were then put into the same cell, and by that time Bryant was feeling the effects of the severe beatings. His head was swollen and extremely sore, and he could barely move his left hand. He had pains in the groin and his body was covered with bruises. Strom told a turnkey that Bryant needed a doctor and shortly afterward he was taken to Bridewell Hospital, where he was given a pill and a glass of water and told he was "all right." By the time he was returned to the station Strom had been able to call his attorney. One of the charges against Bryant was that of carrying a concealed weapon. He had a straight razor, but it had not been in evidence either at the scene of the arrest or at any other time.

Immediately after the arrest some of the people at the tavern had called Chester Robinson at WSO. Chester, Archie Hargraves, and I all went to work, and by midnight we were able to get the prisoners released. Strom and the Bryants got into my car and I drove them to the home of Dr. Quentin Young. Mrs. Bryant, bleeding around the head, with lacerations in the leg, and pregnant, had been left for four hours with no attention. She remained under Dr. Young's care for several weeks.

Early the next day I called the superintendent of police, Orlando Wilson, and left word that it was extremely important that we see him as soon as possible. Within a week a group of us talked with Wilson and three of his deputies. We described the racist, sadist tactics used by some of the men on his force and informed him that there were about twenty-five witnesses willing to testify to the truth of our allegations. We were told the department was carrying on an internal investigation of the incident and that we would be informed of the results. No report ever came; we heard nothing further from the department.

With the increasing complexity of urban problems, the interpretive task was becoming crucial. We had discovered during the summer of 1965 how difficult it was to keep abreast of developments in the civil rights movement. The mass media interpreted areas of immediate conflict but seldom reported in depth or analyzed the underlying factors that could affect public policy. We wanted a more direct relation to the overall civil rights movement. Through the Coordinating Council of Community Organizations we had been supporting the Chicago Freedom Movement in working toward an open city. But we also saw the issue of civil rights involved in almost all the major urban problems, and we felt that we needed a person who could stand in the civil rights movement and interpret these urban issues directly to the churches. We were fortunate in securing the services of the Rev. Kenneth Smith, who had developed a new church on Chicago's south side. The interpretation program became a joint project of the Northeast Association of the United Church of Christ and the Chicago City Missionary Society, with the two organizations sharing in the support.

Smith's primary assignment as our Minister of Urban Affairs was to represent the Society and the Association in citywide meetings concerning the freedom movement and other public issues, report to both boards, and develop position papers and public statements that the boards might want to adopt. The secondary assignment was to interpret the aspirations of the freedom movement to the churches. This meant a great deal of speaking to church congregations as well as arranging for people in the movement to form contacts with groups of suburban churches in an effort to halt the polarization of opinion and encourage more involvement in metropolitan issues.

The Puerto Rican riot in 1966 came as a surprise to many, although our workers in Casa Central had been reporting the problems to us: inadequate, crowded, expensive housing; lack of remedial and bilingual reading facilities in the schools; a market of low-paying jobs, with few opportunities to learn real skills; and for over a year more and more incidents of police harassment. When a youth was killed during a Puerto Rican Day celebration there were several nights of open rioting in the barrio along Division Street on the city's near northwest side.

It was this rioting and looting that brought Mayor Daley's famous shoot-to-kill order. Anyone found looting would be shot, and the police would shoot to kill.

The atmosphere of the black and Latino neighborhoods was heavy and charged when Martin Luther King Jr. came to Chicago in the spring of 1966. Andrew Young, a United Church of Christ minister, had telephoned from Atlanta to ask my opinion about the advisability of King's coming. I thought that he should come. He was committed to nonviolence, would not only preach in the name of justice, but he would work for change, and I thought by addressing major issues he would help relieve the growing anger. Those who were still calm and reasonable would be watching him, and this was what I felt was needed. Dr. King had a great personal power, a gift for convincing and motivating those who heard him. But the will of the people had hardened.

When he arrived Dr. King formed a policy-making agenda committee on which I sat. He preached in a number of churches, soon gained a large following, and we felt it was time for him to have a conversation with Mayor Daley on the issues to see if concessions could be gained without further pressure. The city officials would hear what King had to say, but that they would really listen was doubtful. Nevertheless, the meeting would be historic, it would have its value, and I hoped would be widely reported in the press. We met on July 11 in the mayor's office.

When we came in everyone was tense and expectant. The mayor met us with his principal staff and the heads of city departments, including the superintendent of police, Orlando Wilson, and School Superintendent Benjamin Willis. Dr. King and Al Raby sat at the mayor's right. Raby was a former Chicago schoolteacher, who had quit the school system and was working with the Coordinating Council of Community Organizations (CCCO). At this time there was a movement against the school system and against Willis. The rest of us were seated in a semicircle around Mayor Daley's desk, and the city department heads and mayoral staff people stood behind us, along the walls. Newspaper photographers came in, took a few pictures, and left; they were not permitted to stay. I took notes on what was said.

Dr. King opened formally, thanking the mayor for agreeing to see us, saying he had not singled out Chicago but thought of the city as typical of every large northern city with dual standards in housing, income, employment, and education, all adding up to de facto segregation. He explained that the aim of the freedom movement was to achieve one city for all people, and said that we must declare Chicago an open city. He spoke of the ghetto as invisible—most people in Chicago did not understand its despair—and reiterated his hope that a non-violent movement would mobilize the discontented. He addressed the mayor as a man of great power but noted that some of the real demands might well be beyond even his power. "Mayor, you know you can use your power creatively," he said. "None of us created this problem. It was left to us by a prior generation. Yet we must deal with it in a massive way."

King began going down the list of grievances. Housing was the main issue, he said. "Also we feel we need a police-civilian review board. We have a fine superintendent, but we know of serious reports of police brutality. Such a civilian review board would give a psychological lift to the nonwhite community." He pointed out that Philadelphia and New York City had such boards and warned that riots had started over police incidents.

Here the mayor called on Superintendent Wilson to reply. Wilson said a civilian review board was not needed. The problems were being handled within the department. He explained that he had asked Herb Smith, senior member of the bar association, to act as consultant, that Smith had followed these cases and reported that the department had dealt adequately with them. A civilian review board, Wilson said, would damage department discipline rather than improve it. He had found that when police were accused of brutality the police association closed ranks around these men. "We may fail in some cases," he said, "but we feel we are penetrating the blue curtain."

"From my experience with the police last summer," Al Raby said, "I feel you have not penetrated the curtain. I know of at least fifteen men who contribute to the bad image of the department."

"I am sure there are many more than fifteen," Wilson replied smoothly, "and I am trying to rid the department of these men."

Mayor Daley began a little speech, remarking that he was glad to hear Dr. King say that the problems were not only to be found in Chicago. "We are working on these things, and we are moving," he said, "and we need help from everyone. We need the cooperation of all the people in the community. We have demands for more public housing and at the same time demands to tear down slums. We are not proud of slum buildings, and we didn't create them, but we are dedicated to the task of correcting them."

Then, to my dismay, Mayor Daley brought up the usual old complaint about tenants in city slums. He talked about problems with tenants and said that Dr. Hilliard and Mr. Brooks of the Public Aid Department had tried to find ways of making people better housekeepers. The city had visited some 225,000 people in its rodent-and-insect-control program.

It is true that housekeeping programs and rat control are necessary, but the conditions are effects of poverty and racism.

Throughout my years of work in the ghettos I had grown tired of hearing this argument perpetually cited unfairly by city bureaucrats as one of the causes, if not the principal cause, of all the difficulties. Many were convinced that this segment of society lived together because it was disorderly, lazy, and neglectful, and that whatever was done for such people would fail. Structures built for them would be ruined. I was disappointed at the trend that this gave to the interview and at the appalling lack of understanding in bringing up the matter of tenant problems here with Dr. King, who had come to discuss fundamental issues and questions relating to the life of the whole city. The problem was not tenants, but discrimination in housing, education, jobs, and treatment by the police.

"We are committed to a decent home for everyone," the mayor continued. "We have the finest program for demolition of any city. We tore down nine hundred dilapidated buildings in 1965 and this year we will tear down twelve hundred."

As the discussion proceeded I noticed that the mayor was employing his usual techniques. I had watched him do this many times. He was hard to confront. He would turn to his department heads for replies to criticism, and when he spoke it would be to tell all the great and good things that were happening in Chicago. All through the conversations, when Dr. King tried to engage the mayor in broad issues, he never got a direct answer as to what would be done specifically by the city. Mayor Daley kept asking King what they were doing about these things down in Alabama. "How are you doing down in Montgomery?" the mayor would say, or "What is happening in Atlanta?" The implication was clear that Dr. King ought to set things right in his own area before coming up to Chicago. I could see that King was not going to get the mayor to look at any issue as a whole.

Daley used another technique. Many times in the past I had noticed that he always tried to get at the specific case. If none could be given, that settled the matter. If there was a case, he would isolate it and refer it to someone. Whenever a complaint was made publicly he would simply say, "Give me the date, the time, the place, the person involved," and then to his assistant, "Take this down. Write this address down. Let's look at this building." This was an effective routine, always making a good impression on the crowd or before the news cameras. It gave people the feeling that the whole issue and all the problems were going to be solved, or it gave people the idea that this particular problem was exceptional, that normally everything was running well.

I remember one time a year or two later when Daley called me on the phone. "I'm having some of our religious leaders in," he said, "and I'd like to have you come to the meeting." When I got there he began to accuse the clergy of fomenting riots. "The ministers are out there in the neighborhoods just trying to get the people to riot," he complained. This was something I could not take, so I said, "Mr. Mayor, if you will just give us the names of these ministers, the dates, the times, and the places, we will certainly try to do something about it." Daley was speechless. He blinked, opened his eyes wide, and glared at me, his jaw set and his face slowly beginning to turn pink. For a moment he kept up the silent, cold stare. When he finally spoke his voice was harsh. "Benedict," he said, and his hand came down flat on the desk, "you know who these people are better than anybody else in this room!"

Now the mayor went on to assure King that moderate-income housing had been planned by Chicago. The City was attempting to open up receiverships. "We are seeking answers to housing problems too," he said. "We have the desire and we are trying, and we need your help." In answer to Dr. King's request for a racial head count in city hall, he said, "We will do it when all government agencies do it."

King tried to stress structural changes. "The mood of the Negro won't wait," he said. "Almost ninety-eight percent of the Negro population lives in the ghetto. Whenever a minority is separated it will be discriminated against and that is a structural problem. We have to persuade business to see our plight. The common market countries are bringing new workers from other countries with complete language barriers and giving them skills in two weeks."

"We have called business leaders in," the mayor replied, "but we can only urge them. We cannot make demands."

"It has to be done and on a massive scale," Dr. King

continued. "We must boycott businesses that do not integrate, and we ask that the city cancel contracts with firms that refuse to hire Negroes."

Mayor Daley's response was that the city was doing all that could be done. When the discussion turned to police brutality, Al Raby tried to get the mayor to answer by asking him if he agreed with Mr. Wilson. "I'm opposed to brutality," the mayor said. "The decision is Mr. Wilson's decision."

Raby persisted, saying, "We were told several months ago (in the Strom-Bryant case) that we would hear the outcome of the investigation, but we have heard nothing. We have not been told of any disciplinary measures taken."

Arthur Griffin, pastor of Mozart Baptist Church and a member of the West Side Federation, spoke up, saying that thousands of people were not satisfied that the police could restrain themselves.

The mayor again glanced at Superintendent Wilson, and Wilson replied, "Thousands may think I am wrong, but hundreds of thousands think I'm right. You can appeal cases through the FBI, the state's attorney's office, or the courts."

This official attitude gave me a queasy feeling about the future, even though no defiant words had come directly from the mayor. Evidently, he wanted Wilson to say it.

When King asked the mayor for his concrete responses to the demands Mayor Daley said he agreed with the program, but that the city would need to move through orderly processes, which would take time. It could not be done overnight. "But I am in agreement," he said.

In Dr. King's closing statement he declared he was against Black Power, but spoke of black people losing faith in democratic processes and in nonviolent means of change. He hoped that someone in power would make a bold approach. "We cannot wait," he said. "Young people are not going to wait. This is a moment of challenge. We need a peaceful revolution, but concessions must come. We need victories. We must be able to say to the youth that we are making progress."

After that, in an attempt to bring together the various civil rights groups in Chicago and solidify the Chicago freedom movement, Dr. King held a mass rally at Soldiers Field. With other members of the agenda committee I sat behind Dr. King on the platform, and I remember that as he rose to speak the Blackstone Rangers started to walk around the seats at the top of the stadium. While he spoke they continued their slow measured march around the top. There were about five hundred of them. What their purpose was no one knew, unless it was intended as a show of strength, and if so, it was dramatically effective. Blacks were overcoming the feelings of powerlessness.

Nevertheless, a force was moving that would eventually have to be recognized by the city administration, and Martin Luther King's advent was one of the signs of this strength. His way had been to confront the mayor with the demands in a friendly and rational manner. But the only chance for an orderly approach to change would be for the city administration to respond quickly and positively. This would give King the promise of victory he needed. I did not think the administration would do this. I thought it was hopeless.

The day after the stadium rally the west side erupted in the first of a series of urban riots.

<h2 style="text-align:center">34</h2>

There had been a week of sweltering heat. On the near west side children waited to get into the city swimming pools. Hours for swimming were regulated according to age, but the fire hydrants were opened. It was an old summer tradition in the slums. Police had always been lenient, permitting it during hot muggy spells for a reasonable period. Usually, a spray was contrived by propping a board up against the gushing water so that more children could play around it. Their pleasure would be short-lived, because when the street was flooded, an officer would come along and turn off the hydrant. But recently the police had become intolerant. One Tuesday afternoon (July 12, 1966) squad cars cruised through the neighborhood, seemingly bent on turning off every hydrant, and as soon as they drove away the residents would open them again.

Late that afternoon Chester Robinson was sitting outside the WSO doorway when two police cars pulled up and a sergeant asked if he had any influence with the youths in the area. He explained that some boys were creating a disturbance a couple of blocks away. The report was that someone had been robbed and that teenagers were stopping cars, pulling people out of them, and throwing them into the water. Chester said he would go along with them and talk to the youths.

When they reached the corner of Roosevelt Road and Throop Street the trouble was over. It had concerned an ice cream truck that had gotten stuck in a hole. While the driver was telephoning for a tow truck a group of youngsters gathered around the hydrant, broke into the truck, and helped themselves to ice cream bars. But now the youths were again splashing one another in the water. The street was flooded and the hydrant was off. One of the police cars left, and Chester remained in the other car with two officers.

Then, paying no attention to the police, the youths opened the hydrant again. Two more squad cars drove up, and a dispute got started about leaving the hydrant on. The kids were arguing that the hydrants were allowed to run on Taylor Street, the main east-west artery in a small Italian community. Chester asked the officers to delay shutting off the water. The youngsters were excited, and more and more people were stopping and gathering because of the number of squad cars. Some might say that this was the moment when the riot could have been prevented, but I think it was bound to happen. Nothing could have prevented it, for the police themselves had gradually incited the people. They were ready, tempers were high, and now for seven days there had been no relief from the oppressive, stifling heat. The explosion was overdue.

Chester's warning went unheeded, and the water was again shut off. But the disturbance had attracted a crowd, who clustered around the hydrant as cover for someone turning on the water. Chester, still sitting in the car talking to the policemen, saw the water suddenly gush out, and the three watched it for a few minutes. Then one officer handed a wrench to his partner and told him to close the hydrant. While doing this the officer was dowsed by one of the teenage boys. A burst of laughter followed, and the policeman seemed to take it as a joke. He joined in the laughing, but his partner got out of the car, grabbed the boy, and pulled him over to the police car.

Instantly there was a rush of people, pulling the boy free, pushing and shoving the police, preventing them from chasing the youth. Faces had turned angry, and bricks and bottles were being thrown. The officers radioed for help while Chester got out of the car. About thirty squad cars arrived. The crowd was growing larger and angrier, and the police were plunging in, swinging their clubs. They hit five or six teenagers on the head, and blood flowed as some were subdued and arrested. Most of the rioters were boys in their early teens, but older persons who had come into the street to see what was going on also found themselves being roughly pushed and beaten. Chester saw that the people were not giving way. Officers were prodding at the crowd, shouting at them to move. One cop yelled out, "Why don't you go home?" and a voice from the mob called back, "Baby, we are home!"

The disorder increased. Chester decided to go back to the WSO office on foot. He phoned the district police station, asking that someone be sent to stop the police action. If the police could be held, he would try to control the people, he said. He also called Human Relations, but no one from this division appeared at WSO until the riot had been going on for five or six hours.

John Crawford and Gene Harris went to the area to try to help cool the situation. They found the people standing their ground, lined up facing the police, shouting and throwing missiles. The police were trying without success to disperse the crowd, but a taunting chant had begun, low at first, then swelling into the theme of the "Volga Boatman." It was a wordless chanting, and Gene, seeing a way to get the crowd to move, put words to it. They had been chanting, "Dah-dah-daaaaah-dah-ugh!" and he began singing, "Come on to WSO—ugh!" John Crawford, the song leader at WSO, joined in the chant, and finally more than a hundred people began to move, marching up the middle of Roosevelt Road.

The police went along. Soon masses of people had gathered in front of the WSO storefront, with police lining the streets on either side. At first Chester thought the anger and trouble might be stopped, but when he heard that teenagers were looting at the Blue Island shopping center he concluded that a serious riot was on the way. After he called me I tried to reach Superintendent Wilson, without success. I located Archie Hargraves, who went to WSO, but I had no luck in reaching either Ed Marciniak, at the Mayor's Commission on Human Relations, or Sam Nolan, of the Police Department of Human Relations.

WSO leaders—along with James Bevel and James Orange, of the Southern Christian Leadership Conference (SCLC)—talked to the task force captain, trying to get the police to withdraw to a point a block away so they could attempt to deal with the people, and also they tried to get the teenagers released from custody. But the police refused to pull back or to release anyone.

WSO became the center of activity. While crowds milled in the street, newspaper and television reporters, precinct officers, ministers, policemen, and community residents pushed through, going in and out. WSO was neutral ground for belligerents from street gangs as well as police officials to consult the WSO staff in a desperate attempt to stop the riot. Around 10 P.M. a meeting was to be held at Shiloh Baptist Church two blocks away, and WSO and SCLC staff people worked to round up teenagers to attend the meeting. Word was given that Dr. King and other notable people were to make speeches, and a great effort was made to move the crowd, especially the young men, to the church. Chester went with Dr. King, Andrew Young, and the others, while John Crawford, Jim Orange, Bill Darden, Archie Hargraves, and several other WSO workers remained outside, circulating among the hundreds who refused to enter the church.

But King was unsuccessful. Many would not listen to him, crying out that they did not want to be taught about non-violence when they were faced with the brutality of the police. Earlier King had obtained the release of six teenagers who were among the first to be arrested, and Chester wanted to organize a march to the police station where he thought the others were being held, but none of the civil rights leaders at the meeting would agree. Speakers were not holding the audience, and eventually the meeting ended in confusion.

In the meantime at least a thousand people had converged

outside the church, and a roadblock was built up with garbage cans and barrels on Ashland Avenue between Hastings and 13th Street. When a car with three men inside came up to the roadblock and was trapped by the crowd, someone yelled, "Let's get them!" A mob of youths began a fierce attack on the car, throwing garbage cans and breaking the windows. They pulled out the passengers, three Latino-Americans. If it had not been for Bill Clark's courage the three would have been badly beaten, perhaps killed. Bill jumped instantly between the victims and the crowd, yelling at the top of his voice, "If you want to get them, you'll have to kill me first!" It was either his huge powerful figure or the fact that many of the young men knew Clark and respected him that stopped the mob for a moment. But the moment was long enough for Archie Hargraves and two others to break through and stand at Bill's side, forming a human shield for the three Latinos. According to Archie, only Bill Clark could have done what he did and survived. But when the police came they began to club everyone in sight. Archie yelled that they were trying to save the Latinos, and he did manage to stop one officer from clubbing a WSO member.

The rioting that night grew more serious, with police shooting into the air and people rampaging in the streets. Dr. King returned to WSO with Chester. They felt nothing more could be done out in the neighborhood. King and his staff used the WSO office as headquarters, as did Commander Hackett and a police Human Relations detachment. Coming and going also were youths who had been sent by Chester to communicate with gang leaders. WSO was the command center for the rest of the night.

The next morning Dr. King and his staff tried to organize a neighborhood meeting of businessmen, community agency representatives, ministers, civil rights leaders, and some of the gang leaders who had come in the night before. It was to be held during the noon hour at the Community Presbyterian church. This church, in a storefront across the street from WSO, was the last remaining church of what had been the West Side Christian Parish. Dr. King, Andrew Young, and Chester Robinson were to chair the meeting, the purpose of which was to prevent a recurrence of the rioting, and a press conference was to follow. The press and television people did not wait and began to question gang leaders, businessmen, and Dr. King as they came in at noon, creating confusion, which worked against any possibility of an effective, orderly announcement being made in due course after a collaborative discussion.

When the press conference ended at 2 P.M. both the WSO and the SCLC staff fanned out into the neighborhood to talk to the people. The hot weather continued and hydrants were again turned on in the back streets. The people jeered as police cars drove by, but it was not until evening that officers began to turn off the hydrants. With this, the bricks began flying again, and finally the water maintenance department was ordered to shut off the hydrants so that they could not be turned on again.

This was Wednesday, and many neighborhood people crowded into WSO headquarters for the regular Wednesday night meeting. Youths presented their complaints to Task Force Commander Hackett. One after the other they told their side of the story and described incidents of excessive force and cruelty, callousness, and unjust treatment. But Hackett and his associates stuck stiffly to defending the police and calling for obedience, law, and order. The gang leaders walked out after that.

That night Chester Robinson and entertainer Dick Gregory patrolled the neighborhood, as Chester put it, to "talk sense into people's heads." Also two teams of fifteen men each, with Crawford and Hargraves as leaders, went out to get the people off the streets. It was agreed that these teams would use the police patrols. They worked from 11 P.M. until 1:30 or 2:00 A.M., by which time the fighting, window-smashing, and fire-bombing had ended. Except for sporadic looting, the rioting on the near west side was over for the rest of the summer. WSO people believed their effort succeeded because the people knew the volunteers or recognized them as neighbors.

On Thursday morning the Society and the Church Federation of Greater Chicago set up a hotline so that WSO people could speak directly with ministers and other persons around the city. Staff people and volunteers were sent into the neighborhoods to interview those who had seen the fighting and would be willing to testify. Each account revealed a pattern of excessive force used against any black person who was less than cooperative or who was just at the scene or in the way. A few residents admitted that some of the teenagers were at fault and should be punished. Comments often heard were that the police "enjoyed" it, and that they had been "waiting for this chance for a long time."

Dr. King called another meeting on Thursday afternoon at Shiloh Baptist Church for clergy from all over the city. Many of the WSO people opposed this move, feeling the presence of ministers would be inflammatory. The people were only going to be irritated, they said, at any hint of blame for the rioting. When the meeting began Chester talked about keeping the situation under control, warning that the people were armed as well as the police, and that innocent people were suffering. He, too, was concerned about witnesses. "What the police have done is they have brought in some Negro killer cops, people who will bust open heads and stomp you in the face. I know some of these people," he said. "I am an ex-convict and I have known some of them for twenty years. We must go through the neighborhoods and tell them to keep the children at home. And, most important, we must watch the police."

Martin Luther King brought up the charges of the mayor and the *Chicago Sun-Times* that he and his movement had incited the rioting. He went on to describe his meeting with the mayor on Monday, when he had asked for an end to police abuse and requested a civilian review board, and told of the mayor's insensitivity to the needs of the people. "Now," he said, "we are being blamed because the people's resentment spilled over." He cited Chester Robinson, Bill Darden, and other WSO people for their leadership during the troubled nights, and credited their action for averting a much worse situation, and he repeated that he was afraid of losing his leadership because he had not produced a victory for the people through nonviolent means. He quoted President Kennedy: "Those who make a peaceful revolution impossible make a violent revolution inevitable," and then said, "I'm trying desperately to lead a nonviolent movement. I must say, I need some help in getting this faith across." If a strong emotional response and long resounding applause could cheer him, it was certainly there that day. But I'm not sure he was cheered.

The near west side was one of the quiet places on that Thursday night. A number of teenagers, organized by WSO, had gone from door to door telling the people to stay indoors. But several miles westward rioting broke out in the Lawndale-Garfield Park area, and eventually the National Guard had to be called in to restore order.

Black Power was decisively in the air. One day after a meeting of the agenda committee, when King had just returned from the South, where Stokeley Carmichael had confronted him, he was really dejected. As we left the meeting I followed him through the door into the hall and made some sympathetic remark about how difficult it must have been for him to face the Black Power challenge in the South. He nodded and shook his head without saying a word. Dejection was written on his face.

The rioting was taken seriously by the business community. In general, the religious community had not given Dr. King open support but embraced the position and attitude of the mayor: There were problems, admittedly, but they were being worked on. The Conference on Religion and Race was always used by the mayor as a counterbalancing force against the movement. It was a strategy on his part to blunt the religious imperative in what King was saying. Because poverty funds, controlled by the city, were so important to the existence of many inner-city churches, it was impossible for the established religious groups and some of the major black churches to embrace King and the movement wholeheartedly.

I had some reservations about the long-term effect of the movement. Although King was superb in rallying people, giving them confidence, and stimulating their imagination, I thought there was not sufficient staying power in the form of organization behind it. But I felt because of his prophetic stature, King was to be supported regardless of whether or not a continuing organizational structure emerged.

Several years later this same critique of organizational style led me into a confrontation with Jesse Jackson. A Baptist minister, Jackson was the founder of Operation Breadbasket, a joint project of the SCLC and the CCCO. I had known him since he was in seminary, and following the death of Dr. King, when he was promoting Operation Breadbasket, he had asked for an opportunity to talk about getting the support of the Society. I arranged for most of the senior staff to meet with Jesse, and after he had made his proposal I quite thoughtlessly, in white bureaucratic fashion, proceeded to tell him how to run his operation. In retrospect, I know that while I may have been right in pressing him to set up a board and certain orderly procedures, it was certainly not the time or place to make such observations. I had put him down in front of both black and white staff. As soon as the meeting was over, he left immediately, and I realized that I had exhibited the white racism that so often lurks below the surface in all of us.

One of the most successful programs to come out of Dr. King's movement in Chicago was Operation Breadbasket. Even with a total blackout by the mass media, it developed a selective buying campaign in the black churches that opened up several major companies for black employment, and obtained millions of dollars of new income for the ghetto. The procedure was to investigate the number of black employees in a particular company. If only token integration had occurred, a negotiating team of clergy went to talk with the management, and in most instances additional jobs were opened. On some occasions picket lines were called out at the retail outlets to demand that a product be removed from the shelves. At the same time congregations were urged not to buy a particular brand because of the employment policy of the manufacturer or processor.

On one occasion long afterward, when Mayor Daley spotted me leaving a meeting, he called out, "Hello, Don! How are you?" in his friendliest manner. Then he came across a crowded room to shake my hand. I had to assume the greeting was genuine, and I returned it in a like spirit. As we talked I found myself drawn toward him. I realized how easy it would have been to become a close friend of this man. But I knew that in the long run such a friendship would have required unquestioning loyalty. During that moment I felt the attraction and my own regret. In my pastoral character I could see Richard Daley as a human being rather than as the mayor. I was not always right, and he was not always wrong. But I had drawn the lines, and anyone who does this has to appear to be right, although knowing the opposition has its point. As I walked back to my office I had a sense of alienation, of not being free. I stood with the unemployed and the underprivileged and against the majority by my own choice, but I felt a sudden wave of loneliness.

After the summer of 1966 blacks had closed their ranks and were on the move, and to a lesser degree, Latinos. In Chicago the realization was dawning that concessions would have to be made. These riots had been different only on the surface from the riots in Detroit in 1943, when black and white citizens had clashed directly. The rioters in 1966 had attacked the police, but the target was fundamentally all whites. The police stood as the white racist line of defense. They had been trained, encouraged, and drilled so that the white community could feel secure. Blacks instinctively felt this. The police were the fortified symbol of entrenched white racism, and police brutality was the bludgeon of white racist cruelty. The whole police system was a white fortification. It was not there to protect the blacks. White citizens did not see what went on in the segregated ghettos every day, nor did they inquire. Lack of understanding on both sides was creating a systemic force that had lost its restraint and its judgment.

This rioting had not reached the white areas. Blacks had spread destruction in their own neighborhoods, and small shopkeepers had suffered the losses when black people decided to take the merchandise dangled before their eyes daily on television screens over the years. Here again the police stood between them and the good things of American life.

It was becoming increasingly clear, especially to business and to the churches, that ghetto residents would be taking control of future development of their communities. The experience of the riots left me with a renewed conviction that independent neighborhood organizations were the only possible solution. WSO had been invaluable in reducing the rioting and interpreting the issues that led to it. WSO proved that local neighborhood people, given the opportunity, could build community.

Casa Central, directed by Rafael Martinez of our staff, had been organized in 1958 as a ministry to the growing Latino population. The original mandate included concern for immigrants, and after the Bay of Pigs fiasco, numbers of Cubans had come to Chicago. When Rafael left to teach at Northwestern University we recruited Dan Alvarez, who had been a social worker in Cuba, as director. Alvarez was instrumental in getting the Spanish Ministerial Association to organize a complaint center on Division Street. Over the years Casa Central has aided Latino efforts to build a stable community on the northwest side of the city, and it has spawned at least three churches. Now it is one of the most respected Latin-American social agencies in the country. Recently, it has concentrated on housing problems and has organized a senior citizen program, a nursing home, two or three day-care centers, and a shelter for runaway girls as well as battered women and children.

In mid-June of 1966, when the massive publicity given to Mayor Daley's shoot-to-kill order had confirmed the mood of police belligerence, Dan Alvarez and Art Vasquez of our Social Welfare Task Force helped to calm the disturbance in the Puerto Rican West Town area. Art Vasquez knew the area intimately, and he worked as an on-the-spot communicator, finding out what was really happening in the streets and relaying it to public officials and news media. His perceptions and timely organization work helped avert a serious clash between civil rights organizers and teenage gangs. At Casa Central, although outside the troubled area, Dan Alvarez served as one of the community spokesmen. He and Vasquez collaborated in getting a serious community organization, involving Catholic and Protestant clergy, launched in West Town, the scene of the riots.

When violence breaks out community organizations are often blamed by citizens who do not know the facts. Those who take the long, hard route of helping the poor and use their anger constructively in attacking the causes of poverty are in the middle, blamed for their allegiance to nonviolence by the violent-minded and blamed also for "sowing the wind" by those outside the community. I continually pointed out to our board that organizations like WSO and Casa Central are criticized in part because they are there. But because they are there, someone is around who can help restrain violence and restore order.

In some respects it might seem that I was out of my element by this time, always situated at least once removed from the direct action. My temper, character, and experience would draw me to the city streets and neighborhoods. I ought to have been out there at WSO during the thick of their troubles, working side by side with the staff, talking to the people, arguing with the police, trying to think ahead and make plans. But now, they did not need me there and that was good. They had leaders now— their own.

I was convinced that neighborhood development based on self-help and self-determination was the key to authentic citizenship for ghetto people. The role of the Society now was to seek and transmit funds and technical know-how to the best indigenous leadership that could be found. This meant taking large risks, but there was no workable alternative. The riots encouraged us to renew our mission.

35

In 1967 the Chicago City Missionary Society changed its name to Community Renewal Society. The understanding of the word missionary had changed. Originally, the missionary was one sent to live the life and continue the work of the apostles in the world and for the sake of the world. But the old meaning was not generally understood and our name was often misinterpreted. The new name—Community Renewal Society—was determined by our program direction. Our mission was an action-reflection commitment to the world's human problems. The structure of the church would emerge around those problems.

Peggy Way, the Society's first program director, understood these principles well and applied them in programming. She said, "If our task is to work with God in the areas of human decision-making, then the problems in the world are our focus, not the religious understanding of the sponsoring organization. When part of the problem is a change in social structure, those affected become a necessary part of the programming decisions."

The mood during the late 1960s and the continued incidents increased the caution of our board members. A committee headed by Paul Lund proposed a new set of guidelines that emphasized the Society's commitment to nonviolent social change, which had always been implicit, and stipulated that we would concentrate on areas where we could make significant contributions. This was, among other things, an attempt to keep me from getting into everything that was possible. I took it as being helpful.

I was ready with a program to aid community development that would put the people of the slums into the principal roles. In a report to the Society's board in fall of 1966, I noted that through attitudes of distrust, the Chicago antipoverty program had avoided reliance on residents of the inner city. They were still an untapped energy. Dollars had been substituted for initiative, with professional "poverty fighters" doing the work of serving the poor instead of providing the means and offering them the responsibility of serving themselves. Still worse, the fight against poverty had become separated in some aspects from the fight against the slums. Federal programs had tried to prepare the poor for a remote middle-class world they would not inhabit for a long time. Slum dwellers had been encouraged to prepare for jobs elsewhere, ignoring the struggle to renew their own neighborhoods and press for local jobs, better schools, and better services where they were living.

The high cost of this kind of bureaucratic approach could be seen in the Job Corps, a national program that removed youths from their communities and immersed them in an alien world at a cost of $10,000 to $14,000 per year per trainee. Locally, a "Jobs Now" project planned to find employment for three thousand inner-city youths over sixteen months at a cost of $754,000. Yet in the same length of time WSO had found jobs for six hundred people at one thirtieth the cost.

What we needed to do, I explained, was to encourage inner-city residents to regain control of their communities by giving them the opportunity to act. We had to trust them. Although much had changed since 1940, the slums remained, with one important difference: The urban slum, and particularly the black ghetto, had now become recognized as America's major domestic problem. We were wasting millions of lives and billions of man-hours in nonproduction, nonconsumption, and nonparticipation in our society. Perhaps we would never be able to eliminate poverty altogether, but we ought to attack systemic poverty, which was a malfunction of our social, political, and economic system.

It would take money. But America was spending billions on a welfare system that nourished slums and poverty. However, money alone would not do it. If we continued the nation's strategy, we would not eliminate the problem, because this strategy was doing things for people instead of with them.

I proposed that we train and educate people to become useful in their own neighborhoods. Of course we wanted to encourage integration into white communities, but we were recognizing that this would be a slow process.

I was not thinking of attitudes of trust, but of a practical program of entrusting the people with responsibility and funds for managing their own affairs, and about business investments based on calculations of risk and return. Attitudes of trust would come later, based on performance. It was true that good employment programs had come along which offered equal opportunities. But they all required a certain readiness, motivation, and initiative on the part of the slum community and its individuals.

A survey of selected slum blocks in mid-1966 found 47.7% of adult potential workers unemployed. Among the unemployed, 70.3% were not seeking work, and of these less than half expressed interest in job training. Job opportunities were not going to dissolve the culture of dependency.

The urban programs demanded even more readiness. They seemed to imply that whole communities would be organized and ready to play an active part in slum renewal. But would they? There were only a few community organizations in such neighborhoods and they were struggling to exist. The people in the slums had to be encouraged to join and to organize. But they would not do it until they saw some point, until they had leaders whom they knew and trusted. They would then need the freedom to act on what they were concerned about.

One big question was whether the slum neighborhood would accept help from the community at large. Anger naturally follows apathy and despair when the slum dweller first discovers he or she can do something. But I felt we ought not to be too alarmed about such anger. It could be the fuel of progress if we let it alone. The WSO certainly had begun in anger against "the system," and yet it had been one of the few effective forces for peace in the previous summer's riots. Its members had a vision of community renewal through local self-help that riots could only destroy.

Liaison could be developed between the business and professional world and the church agencies. The church was not trusted in the slums any more than it deserved to be. After all, it had started welfarism. But the churches were growing away from paternalism and beginning to help people fight their own battles. Church agencies could be the bridge across which money and know-how could move into the inner city, the brokers to bring the resources together. The most serious technical risk would be poor leadership, but this risk I worried about least. I had seen WSO's leaders become self-made lawyers, self-made employment agents, self-made community organizers.

What emerged from this was the most ambitious program the Society had ever undertaken, finally limited to one neighborhood. The program, meant to be a prototype, was called Toward Responsible Freedom (TRF). We planned to ask for open support for free enterprise in the ghetto.

A long-range organizing drive was to be inaugurated in a selected slum area, and we decided to ask the city's cooperation. With John Gallagher, a management consultant who was then president of the Society's board, I met with Mayor Daley to describe our intentions. The mayor listened attentively and pledged his full cooperation, but we were to receive more harassment than help from the city. We spoke also to Deton Brooks, Chicago director of the Anti-Poverty Program, in the hope that he might find ways to be of financial and technical assistance. In the fall of 1967 Garry Oniki and Reuben Sheares came to Community Renewal Society as staff members: Garry to do research and planning, especially for the new program, and Reuben to direct it. Tom Keehn was engaged to assist in fund-raising and program development.

The Society resolved not to intervene or do anything that hinted of paternalism. We would provide funds for an organizing campaign and seed money for enterprises, agencies, and technical assistance. We were going to raise funds to be placed in the hands of neighborhood people. A project area with at least fifty thousand residents was to be chosen where there was urban blight, unemployment, limited business opportunity, inadequate housing, high delinquency, and broken homes. A black consortium composed of the staff of local community organizations recommended the Kenwood-Oakland area, and Reuben Sheares suggested to the existing Kenwood-Oakland organization that they apply to the Society for designation as the nucleus of the TRF project. The organization, founded by Jesse Jackson when he was a student at Chicago Theological Seminary, was at this point virtually defunct. In due course the Kenwood-Oakland Community Organization (KOCO) was designated, and for the duration of the project we appointed a community development committee of the board with an overwhelming black majority, staffed by Reuben, to act for the Society in all decisions pertaining to TRF. We made certain all decisions about spending money were firmly in the hands of black people.

The Kenwood-Oakland area is a severely depressed part of Chicago, bounded by Lake Michigan on the east, Cottage Grove Avenue on the west, 35th Street on the north, and 47th Street on the south. Like most inner-city slums, it was not truly a neighborhood. People moved in and out rapidly, and there was little interest in building a cohesive social network. The few churches had little or no connection with one another. Thirty percent of the adult male labor force was unemployed, over a third of the families received welfare assistance, and almost two thirds of the adults had not completed high school. There were only six doctors in the area. No playing fields, parks, or recreation spaces existed despite the fact that over half the population was under twenty-five. The Black P. Stone Nation, a south side gang commonly known as the Blackstone Rangers, had started a push north from their base in Woodlawn and had made more progress in organizing the area than KOCO.

Reuben had great difficulty in bringing KOCO to the point of negotiating a basic covenant with the Society because of animosity among the groups of local residents. Churches would not meet with secular agencies, the young would not gather with the old, and businessmen did not care to talk with gangs.

A press conference was scheduled for November 21, 1968, to announce TRF, but the Chicago Police Department scooped the story a week earlier. At a ceremony elevating him to the rank of captain, Lt. Edward Buckney revealed that a new privately funded program called Toward Responsible Freedom had started in Kenwood-Oakland. Buckney's announcement centered on the hiring of Jeff Fort, leader of the Blackstone Rangers. "They are hiring known gangsters as organizers at substantial salaries for doing nothing," was his charge. This was before the program had started, and Buckney's remarks were the first hint of police surveillance and infiltration of Society programs.

The Blackstone Rangers were but one of nearly thirty organizations and groups in Kenwood-Oakland participating in TRF negotiations out of which a new KOCO was to emerge. The Rangers were an organization of youths of various ages. They were feared and respected, and all kinds of stories were told about their activities. Nobody knew the extent of the membership, and the Rangers' girl friends had been formed into an auxiliary. TRF had hired a staff of twelve from among different organizations. Jeff Fort was one of these, and his particular assignment was as a youth coordinator.

Earlier in our negotiations with community groups I had gone along with Reuben and Garry for a meeting with Fort. The place was a parish house next to a church that the Stones had taken over, and while we sat there waiting we watched them coming and going. They were young black men of all types, wearing red berets and tight bands around their foreheads. The bands carried different insignia that seemed to indicate their rank. We waited a long time, and when the word was finally passed around that Jeff was on the way, the place seemed to become busier. When he came in with three or four bodyguards they sat in chairs across from us. There were no introductions. We were supposed to know him. He was small in stature, rather quiet, but he was articulate.

He got down to business at once, saying he wanted to sign the covenant with the Society. Reuben replied that the covenant had to be signed with the KOCO. Fort said that the Stones already had the entire area organized. "We are ready to sign now," he said flatly. Reuben repeated that the covenant had to be made with the entire KOCO organization, not just one group or committee. I explained to Fort that the key to the whole program was widely shared interests. The point was to put the people in the community through the development process—not to install a certain designated, ready-made chain of command but to find and encourage many leaders. We were going to turn over the money and bring in the expertise because we wanted to see the whole community organize itself, take over the responsibilities and work in its own interests. It would mean development of tenants groups and parents groups to bargain for quality education, and possibly community-owned local business enterprises. A broad base was necessary.

Discussion went back and forth, but neither of us moved. Fort didn't argue or try to persuade but maintained his dignity and the attitude that he was offering us a great advantage. Finally, Reuben said, diplomatically, something about giving further thought to the matter. At this, Fort and his bodyguards got up and walked out, leaving us sitting there. It was clear that we were not going to sign a covenant with the Blackstone Rangers or give them money or designate them as the youth division, but we were not excluding them from participation as a neighborhood organization.

Buckney's remarks printed in the *Chicago Daily News* gave the false and damaging impression that KOCO was to be of, by, and for the Blackstone Rangers. My phone began ringing. One after the other, board members and corporate contributors called. Two weeks later Jeff Fort resigned from KOCO because he felt his presence on the staff would create continuing embarrassment.

The covenant was signed between KOCO and the Society.

KOCO agreed to organize the community with the understanding that the Society would provide funds and technical assistance.

This would be a real test. Hitherto most urban community organizing had been done in the style of Saul Alinsky, focusing on the more cohesive lower middle class. But KOCO's aim was not to win concessions, but to create a self-sufficient organization of the poor. The organizing plan was for twelve men and women to fan out among the residents to develop units that would then coalesce in a communitywide council of organizations. Locally controlled business enterprises would be started, and we thought the initial organizing effort would take a year or so. Resource boards were envisioned to bring in expertise from outside. There were skills in black and white communities that were indispensable here, but in the tense racial atmosphere at the time the problem of how to impart such help in a spirit of equality remained formidable.

The full-time, salaried chairman was a local black Mennonite pastor, a former addict and prison inmate, the Rev. Curtis Burrell. He had chaired KOCO in its infancy and stood out as the only active clergyman willing to take on the difficult tasks.

The press did not miss the appointment. On November 13, 1968 the *Chicago Tribune* headlined "Kenwood Leader Is Ex-Convict" and announced that the president of a community group (KOCO) receiving $100,000 a year was an ex-convict with a long record of arrests on charges of burglary, possession of narcotics, and larceny. The writer, William Jones, reviewed Burrell's history, including various arrests, prison terms, and enrollment at the Goshen College Biblical Seminary from which he was graduated before becoming assistant pastor at the Woodlawn Mennonite Church on 46th Street. Burrell was quoted as saying he became a Christian in prison.

The *Tribune* stated that in addition to the $100,000 for the first year, the Community Renewal Society would eventually raise $3.5 million to finance KOCO projects for the next five years, and that initial funds had been solicited from businesses, foundations, and individuals, including the Inland Steel-Ryerson Foundation, the Illinois Bell Telephone Company, and the Sears-Roebuck Foundation. The Rev. Donald L. Benedict, the story continued, served two terms in a federal penitentiary during World War II for refusing to register for the draft.

Not long after Curtis Burrell's election it was decided that another person was needed to oversee the work of the block-by-block canvassers. With the approval of Reuben Sheares, Leonard Sengali, a local resident and a meatcutter in one of the slaughterhouses, was elected by KOCO. According to our covenant, Sheares as project director could approve only the two top positions, all staff jobs being under direct control of KOCO. But Sheares was frequently consulted.

Funds were slow in coming, and only a fraction of our budget of $2.8 million was on hand when we started. The number of organizers had to be cut from twelve to six. The problem of KOCO's public identification with the Stones had intensified, because Leonard Sengali, although maintaining he was not a member, was a public spokesman for them. Also, Sengali at this time became interested and involved in Jesse Jackson's effort to get welfare increases through the Illinois legislature. He proved his mettle as an organizer in the area for this drive, but energy was diverted from the TRF organizing effort. The irony of marching for welfare increases while deploring the welfare system as debilitating was common, because the welfare funds were necessary for survival in the slums.

KOCO participated with other organizations in a unified action on the issue of jobs for black construction workers, which took place downtown, and at one point the protests shut down Loop construction. The result of the demonstrations was the Chicago Plan, forged by Mayor Daley and the construction unions, which apportioned a certain number of jobs to black workers, including some from Kenwood-Oakland. Soon after this, the police arrested Leonard Sengali for the murder of one Phillip Chroman. Sengali's arrest came on the same day that two Black Panther leaders, Fred Hampton and Mark Clark, were killed in a raid, which the local papers alleged to have been engineered by States Attorney Edward Hanrahan. These events were viewed as more than coincidence. Sengali claimed that when he saw him in prison, Hanrahan attempted to strike a bargain on the murder charge in exchange for information on black coalition leaders who had helped to initiate the Chicago Plan.

Now KOCO was widely attacked in the news media again, and black leadership across the city rallied behind Sengali. Edwin (Bill) Berry, executive director of the Chicago Urban League, Jesse Jackson, and I supported Sengali and testified to his character. Eugene Pincham was our attorney. From the beginning, the state's case was confused and weak, bearing all the earmarks of harassment. The state asked for numerous continuances before the bail hearing to keep Sengali in jail as long as possible. The complaint had not even been signed by a witness.

When the time came for the state to call its first witness during the bond hearing the district attorney asked that the court be cleared because witnesses feared they might be intimidated. Pincham objected strenuously to no avail and then pointed out that Sengali had never been placed in a lineup or confronted by an accuser. If the court was cleared of all but Sengali, the witness would identify him because he would be the only person seated at the defense table. The judge offered to let Sengali's wife and two other black men drawn from the bullpen sit in the courtroom. After more argument the judge ordered two men from the bullpen to sit at the defense table and said that Sengali could sit with his wife in the spectator seats.

The witness testified that he had seen Sengali get out of the murder car and run past him. Asked to pick out Sengali, he said that he did not see Sengali in the room. The second witness testified that he saw a man get out of the murder car after he heard a shot. He then identified Sengali in the courtroom as the man.

As Pincham pointed out later, both witnesses said they saw the shooting but told no one about it until they "just happened" to talk to a policeman and an assistant district attorney eleven weeks after the incident.

Other witnesses testified that they saw a male Negro, but their descriptions did not fit Sengali. During cross examination of two police officers by the defense attorney it became clear to everyone that the state had no case. The judge released Sengali on his own recognizance and reprimanded the district attorney.

Sengali's arrest and hearing dealt a severe blow to KOCO and to the Society's fund-raising drive for TRF. Yet the business community was responding. Contributors knew, with smoke rising on the west side, that a fresh approach was necessary, however risky it might seem. Some corporations made three-year pledges. Most adopted a wait-and-see attitude. Many of our corporate donors had been impressed by Sengali when he spoke at luncheons. He was a persuasive speaker, a gifted organizer, and had brought management skills to the organizing process. His charisma and his direct trusting relationship with the Stones meant that he could communicate with the neighborhood as well.

In spring 1969 people in Kenwood-Oakland were complaining about gang oppression. The fear and concern over violence, extortion, and intimidation had increased. In early June, Burrell was confronted in his office by one of the Blackstone Rangers, a KOCO organizer, demanding a raise. Burrell, who interpreted his manner as threatening, took a gun from his briefcase, fired several shots into the floor as a warning, and left.

On the 15th of June the KOCO office was bombed and gunshots were fired into Burrell's home. Burrell began leading "walks against fear." There were four walks. On the first, Curtis Burrell and Reuben Sheares walked along one side of the street and about a hundred Blackstone Rangers marched on the other side, with police cars driving along slowly. On the second day the two were joined by a dozen or so residents, and again they were paced by the Rangers. On the third day Burrell had about a hundred followers, and on the fourth, a much larger turnout. The demonstrations were widely publicized as a response to fear of violence in the neighborhood, but they were also intended to establish a new image for KOCO as independent of the Blackstone Rangers. Many residents who had been reluctant to affiliate with KOCO came forward. Support also was given by hitherto silent citywide and community groups. KOCO was demonstrating leadership capacity and a true instinct for community control, but such basic issues as the civil rights of the Stones remained unresolved.

In about three weeks an almost totally new staff reopened the office, and the split with the Stones was complete. The Rev.

John Barber, head of Black Men Moving, was hired as Burrell's administrative assistant. Leonard Sengali, who had run into problems as go-between, resigned before the walks, pleading his loyalty to the Blackstone Rangers. His letter explained, "I believe in redemption instead of detention for our young people. The youths are our future. They need us. We need them for survival. . . . We must not annihilate them." His resignation was a major blow to KOCO's organizing effort.

KOCO had become more unified as an anti-Stone organization, but Burrell was becoming more and more estranged. In his restaffing he hired only people he personally trusted and accordingly developed a tight inner circle. Later he drifted away from active politics, organized the First Church of Man, and began espousing his personal philosophy. After two months of charges, meetings, and controversy Burrell tried to enlist the Society's support for his position and became vindictive when we remained neutral. We were reluctant to intervene in what we viewed as an internal matter at KOCO. Robert Lucas, coordinator of the Leadership Training Program at KOCO, was named the new chairman in April 1972 by the KOCO board. Funding for 1973 was dependent on the results achieved by the new leadership. In 1974, with assistance from Society personnel, KOCO would have the primary fund-raising responsibility.

During the time of travail for KOCO its development projects had been going on. Self-determination was our principle in transmitting technical assistance. In each activity there was a committee of community residents, a chairperson of the group, a technical assistance staff person, and a KOCO community organizer. The biggest problem was lack of continuity because of constant turnover of professional technical staff owing to the upward mobility of black technicians.

The leadership training program was more successful. We hoped to train local people in our workshops as leaders to identify urban problems, make decisions, and help develop a healthy community. Of the 134 trainees graduated, some took leadership roles at KOCO but many went on to other jobs and moved out of the neighborhood.

In housing, KOCO made some valiant efforts. Prefabricated units would have provided good housing for low-income residents, but the city building codes would not allow cheap housing. In the Oaken Rehabilitation Project some forty-eight units were completed, and KOCO participated as a limited partner in a 164-unit project at Lake Park Manor. KOCO worked through the local block club to successfully oppose massive demolition of the Drexel-Ingleside-Ellis complex of thirty-seven buildings with over five hundred units. Residents developed an alternative plan, and it was easier to halt the demolition than to execute new housing plans.

Economic strategy was crucial to KOCO's future, and we encouraged profitable enterprises owned by KOCO. A for-profit corporation, True People's Power Development Corporation, was set up for this function. One of its plans was for a shopping center, but we discovered that apparently no enterprise of this sort could be undertaken without involving the local alderman as a partner. Although the project was planned with expertise, KOCO could not get the land for it. The plan was rejected by city hall. Obviously, the contract had been promised to the local alderman.

The major effort of the True People's Power Development Corporation was a plastics plant known as New Horizons Plastics. Here KOCO made two great mistakes. The first was to put money into a high-technology business with a tremendous investment in machines that employed at the most fifteen people. The second mistake was to take on a building and put in machines on this scale when it ought to have started in someone's garage. Although governed by a black board of directors, it had not grown up through the people. Nevertheless, the company probably would have been successful had it not been for the Arab oil boycott. Plastic suppliers, largely the big oil companies, allotted their plastic to customers of long standing. The failure of New Horizons Plastics was a heavy blow for our board. Not only had $200,000 of TRF money gone into it but we had guaranteed another $100,000 line of credit. A number of board members plunged into the struggle to save this company.

The concern for health among the people led to health planning in cooperation with Michael Reese Hospital. The city finally planned a new health center in the Kenwood-Oakland area as a result of KOCO's intensive effort, and KOCO was instrumental in developing a health maintenance organization, which received federal funds to create the center operating on 47th Street. KOCO's program with state funds for mentally retarded children was eventually transferred to the Abraham Lincoln Center, a settlement house on the south side, because of political maneuvering as well as its characteristic fault of overextending itself.

The paramount issue in education at this time was neighborhood control of schools, but KOCO found itself powerless to effect changes in the system, although it won a free lunch program. Other groups had the same experience, and most Chicagoans agree that significant change in the school system will require massive parent organization and possibly a major boycott.

KOCO still lives today as an expression of the Kenwood-Oakland people.

TRF was an attempt to get local people to take charge of their communities instead of leaving them. Perhaps Irwin France was right in insisting that Kenwood-Oakland was too far gone. Yet TRF reinforced my belief in the self-help, self-determination concept. Management must be learned through having something to manage. But learning it within the strictures of complex governmental regulations is not easy. It is remarkable that so many ghetto programs administered by local residents have been reasonably well run. I think funds provided to community organizations can be managed and accounted for with integrity and in an orderly fashion. Prior to TRF few businesses or foundations would make grants directly to neighborhood groups. They saw TRF as a way of giving to local communities with the Society taking the public responsibility and pressure. Today they have little hesitation in giving to most community groups. TRF proved there is a remarkable reservoir of local leadership.

It is significant that community organizations, the major bulwark against victimization of Chicago neighborhoods, were founded and originally supported mainly by churches. During the 1970s the Society continued its support of the West Side Organization, North Lawndale People's Planning and Action

Conference (progenitor of Pyramid West), Westown Concerned Citizens, and the Voice of the People in Uptown. Also grants were made to several Latino groups on the northwest side and in the Pilsen neighborhood. Two organizations with great development capability, The Woodlawn Organization (TWO) and Pyramid West, were originally funded outside the authority of the mayor. TWO received major grants from the Ford Foundation and from Catholic and Protestant church groups. Pyramid West received grants from Community Renewal Society, churches, the Wieboldt Foundation, and other private Chicago foundations as well as one of the last major national impact grants from the Office of Economic Opportunity. The mayor's signature was required, but the administration was centered in the neighborhood group. Thus independence makes significant participation by local people possible. Yet I think neighborhood democracy remains a precarious dream.

Progress against racism, too, is far from steady. Some years ago I attended an evening meeting held in a church gym, called by a coalition of black social workers and west side leaders. One after the other they proclaimed that no longer could white organizations, agencies, or churches expect to operate branches in black communities. The only way would be to operate with black personnel. Black people were no longer going to stand for white people coming in and running special agencies. "You whites have got a problem. It's the black condition, and the white problem!" "The idea is—you write the checks and give them to me!" "We don't want whites studying us anymore. If you want to study something, study why you are racist. That's going to make a good study!" The tone was vehement, angry, and resolute.

I have never forgotten the empty chairs at that meeting. Telegrams of invitation had been sent to civic leaders and to heads of public agencies and private groups. Three rows of chairs had been placed in an open square and a name placed on each chair. With the people facing one another around the square, it was easy to see who had not come. The chairman pointed to the empty places. There, he said, were the names of the people who did not take blacks seriously enough to come and listen. School representatives and police officials had not come. There were few politicians or people from city agencies. Yet this was shortly after the riots that followed Martin Luther King's assassination.

36

In 1971 Don Rumsfeld, a Chicago congressman, was appointed director of the Office of Economic Opportunity (OEO) by President Richard Nixon. A short time after he assumed office I was asked to consider the position of midwest regional OEO director. The chance to work from within government attracted me. At the very least I could put more money into community-based organizations.

When it seemed likely I would be appointed the Society board agreed to give me a leave of absence. Then a phone call came from Alfred Taylor of Rumsfeld's office, who said that all necessary intelligence data had been cleared for my appointment. I knew the only mark against me was my prison record, but they discovered that President Harry Truman had pardoned me, presumably when I went into the army.

"But," said Taylor, "information from the *Chicago Tribune* will stand against your appointment." I asked for the details, but he said he didn't know what they were—just that the newspaper had derogatory information about my activities. In view of probable adverse publicity, Rumsfeld could not proceed with the appointment.

I had no idea what he was talking about. I should have been outraged. It was not until 1975 that I found out the whole story.

In late 1973, as our TRF program wound down, Reuben Sheares accepted a call to the Office of Church Life and Leadership at the United Church of Christ headquarters in New York. This was a great loss, but we were fortunate in securing Rodney Wead to succeed him. He turned out to be a unique community developer. Not long after he joined us he became interested in the Organization for a Better Austin (OBA), which had a new executive director, Mark Salome. They toured the Austin area, and Rodney got acquainted with the organization. He introduced Salome to our community development committee, and after several meetings the committee decided to fund OBA.

Several days later Mark Salome was revealed in the local press to be an undercover agent for the Chicago Police Department. The shock sent OBA into a tailspin. Suspicion was created throughout the group. Our board members, trying to act as good stewards of Society funds, began to wonder if other organizations we were helping harbored undercover police. We knew that the neighborhood groups were seen as enemies by Chicago authorities.

I had some suspicion of police surveillance now and then but still was not aware of the extent of it until the Swim II case. Swim II was a full police investigation of Community Renewal Society, the Urban Training Center, and of me, undertaken by some forty intelligence agents. The Better Government Association and the Alliance to End Repression developed the case in 1975 and asked the Society to join in a lawsuit against the Chicago Police Department, the Federal Bureau of Investigation, the United States Army, Mayor Daley, and others, charging political surveillance of community groups. The CRS board, after its experience with Mark Salome, was glad to consent. When the judge ordered the police department files opened we examined their file on the Society and related groups.

The records consisted of twelve volumes, 989 pages long. The first volume contained an index in which 1,669 individuals and groups were mentioned. The primary objective given was to "identify and outline the complete structure of CRS and its affiliated organizations." The investigations were carried out between October 1969 and February 1970. Most of the information came from program membership lists, financial statements, and newspaper clippings, and a limited amount from actual interviews and observations.

How the intelligence division obtained the internal documents included in the file remains a mystery. Most of it is dull, containing lists of names of anyone who had anything to do with Community Renewal Society, the Urban Training Center, or a community organization. There also were newspaper clippings and records of talks with informants. Swim II included fifty-three surveillance and twelve interview reports.

I was outraged and shocked to see index cards with my name and the name of the Society labeled "subversive" and stamped

"GANG" in large letters. I read that "the Community Renewal Society is primarily associated with the United Church of Christ based in New York City. Union Theological Seminary is the educational arm of this church." There is, of course, no direct connection with either. "The Director and other personnel of Community Renewal Society were trained at Union Theological Seminary." (At that time only Jim Mason, Walt Ziegenhals, and I were Union alumni.) The investigators reported that Union promoted communist, radical, and subversive ideologies; because the leaders of CRS were trained at Union, they promoted these ideologies.

Noting that CRS organized, staffed, and financed various community organizations, they asserted that "following the establishment of CRS youth organizations, each area has become a nucleus for youth gang activity and in some cases a gang problem has arisen where, prior to the arrival of CRS, no well-organized gangs existed." To my knowledge, CRS never contributed one dollar to any gang in the city of Chicago. Did the Chicago police department also believe that development of gangs in ghetto neighborhoods throughout the nation was due to the activities of social agencies and churches? The bias of the investigators was clear when I read that the Society was funneling money into the "Black Belt," and that CRS was among the names in an appointment book belonging to Leonard Sengali.

The Urban Training Center was defined in the file as the educational arm of CRS. While I assisted in developing the center and served on its board, it was completely independent and funded primarily by major Protestant denominations and national foundations. Furthermore, the investigators concluded that the Urban Training Center was the Chicago counterpart of Union Theological Seminary and could well be the center for radical education in this country. One report said that the Urban Training Center was "the recognized meeting place of street gangs and radical organizations." The file included lists of Center officers and committees, memos, form letters, and minutes. Department investigators had been in touch with police departments across the country requesting investigation of similar urban training centers, obviously in order to set up a conspiracy charge.

CRS was also alleged to be connected with the Black Strategy Center. In fact, we had no connection, having felt it would be a high-risk venture for us. The Strategy Center was Archie Hargraves' idea and was brought into being by efforts of top executives of Commonwealth Edison, Inland Steel, and the Continental Bank, but in the police file the leaders were said to be CRS staff who would "probably continue in a joint effort to secure political and racial revolution in the United States."

The investigation of our Model Cities Technical Assistance Program concluded that CRS had substantial or complete control of major community organizations in the four Model Cities target areas. In one memo, investigators noted that a report summarizing the Model Cities program "conceals and distorts the actual relationship between the Community Renewal Society and the community organizations which they assisted." I suspect this meant nothing incriminating had been found. The files revealed no understanding of the feelings of the black community during this period. It seems impossible that the police would believe that a predominantly white, church-related agency could control black organizations at that time. It never occurred to the department that black people might organize or belong to an organization for any purpose other than gang activity.

In volume twelve I read, "It is known and documented in this report that many of the individuals associated directly or indirectly with the Community Renewal Society have views and goals diametrically opposed to those of the administration of this city." Now that one was true!

Later investigations by *Chicago Tribune* reporters revealed that a ten-day personal surveillance of me had been carried out by the Chicago police department. My house had apparently been watched from early morning to the late hours of the night and my movements monitored. Phone calls were made to my home to find out if I was there at various times. The account of my exemplary behavior as recorded makes dull reading except for one passage describing me as leaving my home accompanied by a white female with red hair "believed to be his wife."

The personal file gave details of my "criminal record from 1940 to 1943." March 23, 1966 seems to be the day the police department became interested in investigating me. An entry on this date observed that a year before I had spoken to a police department group identifying myself as an ex-convict, stating that I chose to go to jail during World War II rather than go into the armed services. The memo continued, "We did not know if he was telling the truth" and called for a complete investigation: ". . . recheck FBI, request fingerprint information, check army intelligence, check New York Police Department, try to get photo from army or prison records. . . . Expedite as quickly as possible!"

Why the sudden interest on this date, and why the great urgency? Another March 1966 memo revealed I was at the police station with an attorney for Strom and Bryant, arrested for fighting in a tavern, and that we were charging police brutality.

"The principle of the spy operation is clear—politics," said the *Chicago Tribune* (June 19, 1977), commenting on the story.

Also appearing in the police files was an Internal Revenue Service plan to investigate tax-exempt groups, specifically, the Community Renewal Society and the Urban Training Center. That the IRS was used for political purposes during the Nixon years has been established. The intent was made clear in a memo by a Nixon aide, Thomas Huston, in 1970, saying, "What we cannot do in a courtroom via criminal prosecution to curtail the activity of some of these groups, IRS can do by administrative action. . . . Moreover, valuable intelligence type information can be turned up by the IRS as a result of their field audit."

Before beginning his audit the IRS field agent went to the Chicago police department for information on CRS activities. It was clear to us soon after the agent began his work that he had already made up his mind. He insisted repeatedly that we had given money to street gangs. He wanted to see those vouchers. We had not done this and had no vouchers to show. Finally, he was forced to conclude that we were properly exempt as a religious urban mission agency. Many other organizations in the city were plagued by such audits during the Nixon years.

37

After the death of Martin Luther King it became increasingly clear that a major task for whites was to confront white institutional racism. Although it was a white rather than a black problem—and blacks pointed this out—racism was and still is difficult for whites to acknowledge. After the riots I was to speak to the Illinois Conference of the United Church of Christ. The conference minister urged me not to talk about racism. "It turns them off," he said. In the early 1970s whites were tired of hearing about the minorities, and blacks were tired of being studied and programmed. But those who thought the country had made much progress against discrimination were shocked by the Kerner Commission's report that ours remained a racially and economically divided society.

Our first attempt to consciously address white racism was a program called Toward an Open Society. Harley Cook, a young seminary graduate, was hired to investigate housing discrimination in the suburbs. He began by aiding in the establishment of HOPE, a voluntary organization in DuPage County that bought old houses, rehabilitated them, and sold them to minority families. Not much was known about how suburban zoning ordinances frustrated construction of low- and moderate-priced housing to prevent migration of underclass citizens to middle-class areas. We did quite a lot of work on this, and Harley proved so talented that he was soon hired by a housing developer.

About this time John McDermott, former executive director of the Catholic Interracial Council in Chicago, who had served for a year on our board, was thinking about returning to the city. He wanted to start a publication aimed at institutional leaders to help them work toward racial justice.

As John began his work with us, I agreed to confine ourselves to Chicago rather than to try for a national publication which might reach everyone. John brought in Lillian Calhoun, a black journalist who proved invaluable in training students who, by and large, were the only reporters available to the budding publication. *The Chicago Reporter,* which published its first issue in July 1972, has contributed significantly to change in racial attitudes and practices.

When the *Reporter* revealed that ten of the city's thirty-six ambulances lacked telemetry and other life-saving equipment, that nine of those ten were stationed in black and Latino communities, that the two busiest ambulance companies had no telemetry, and that one of these served the Dan Ryan Expressway, the most traveled section of road in the country, what happened? Racism was officially denied, and nine months later all ambulance companies were properly equipped. Another *Reporter* story exposed for the first time the high rate of neonatal deaths in Chicago hospitals. The Board of Health's response focused on a key problem that the *Reporter* had stressed: Too many high-risk pregnancies were handled by hospitals that did not have the necessary staff and experience.

The February 1978 issue called attention to Chicago's high fire death rate and to the record and problems of the fire department. This led to an overdue fire department shake-up. Fire Commissioner Robert J. Quinn resigned, and the new commissioner, Richard Albrecht, pledged a sweeping review of policies and procedures. A propitious outcome was the new administration's decision to end the city's resistance to federal court orders on minority hiring.

It is not for shock and sensation that these stories are published. The intention of the *Reporter* is to lay the ground-work for constructive systemic change. The circulation is only thirty-five hundred, but it goes where it counts. Aimed at leaders, policy-makers, and managers, it directly affects the centers of responsibility and influence.

The *Reporter* calls attention to good and bad by giving details of successful race relations programs and sharing information among community institutions and leaders. Once a year it prints charts of comparative figures on minority employment by individual organizations and companies and also minority purchasing and transactions by businesses and banks in Chicago. Companies demonstrating progress are cited.

Whatever I do, wherever I go, I am bound to have a "Bill Webber" as a close associate. Such a person, inclined toward prudence and practicality, usually materializes from among the inner circle to play this necessary, often repressive, sometimes dream-shattering role. If no one did, I would go out and actively search for someone, I am sure. Various people have come on cue for this part. The Society's board and executive committee sometimes played the Bill Webber part with good effect. When the board voted down my proposals there was never any confrontation. I expect other people to be as strong in their feelings and convictions as I am. I have come to see the value of dialogue—where feeling and reason can be reconciled. But not always. There have been times when I have been reasonably persuaded against a course of action but went on feeling that it was right. In such a case I am inclined to suspect the reasoning.

During the 1970s Walt and Harriet Ziegenhals came from Cleveland to join the Society. From the moment he joined the staff Walt began to remind me of the need to preserve and encourage the local congregation. I pointed out that the churches were turning inward and most church people were trying to rediscover faith within their own congregational life. Should we reinforce this insularity? But Walt talked about basic values of our civilization communicated generation after generation through the churches. Although I was resisting, his reiterated argument, "It was in the churches that we first heard the gospel," could not be dismissed. The Society had been heavily involved in community development and we were beginning to deal with institutional racism. Perhaps it was time to give attention to inner-city church congregations.

Walt went ahead and made a study of the effects of racial change on urban congregations. He discovered that if the trend continued the United Church of Christ would see thirty-four of its 177 Chicago churches closed by 1985. His plan to help these churches was based on the establishment of a covenant between partners, to do away with paternalism, with the inevitable strings attached. The covenant was not legally enforceable, but a formal acknowledgment of mutual promises made in the sight of God. The partners would be the Society, the Chicago Metropolitan Association of the United Church of

Christ, the Illinois Conference of the United Church of Christ, the United Church Board for Homeland Ministries, and the local churches in racially changing neighborhoods.

Again I was in a dilemma. I saw the need for this action, and I knew our board would like it. But not only was this plan wholly against my general inclination, there was something personal in my resistance. The personal aspect made my opposition stronger but more suspect. The storefront church concept was still my preference. The best way to use the money was to spend more on people and activities and less on buildings and maintenance. The storefront had succeeded where the traditional churches had failed. But now, even if such storefront churches were still practical, white ministers could no longer go there. The storefront church had given way to the community organization. I remembered that the original organizing group at WSO had thought of the West Side Christian Parish as their only sponsoring religious organization and wanted a neutral office that could belong to the unemployed no matter what their religion or politics. It was significant that when self-determination had come through WSO, the West Side Christian Parish was finished. Had its parishioners gone back to the churches?

I was drawn toward those who felt, as Archie once put it, "Churches gathered for worship and organized for 'life together' made little sense. They are not where the action is nor do they comprehend it." Archie also used to say frequently that the world was like a floating crap game, and that the church should be a confirmed gambler and go where the action is. It seemed to me that hunger, suffering, unequal opportunity, and segregation had to be addressed first of all. Perhaps after that, the church congregations, accepting everyone, would be truly Christian. Yet the churches that did not accept everyone had given us support. Could we stand by and see so many of them die? There were still people there, hearing the reading of the gospel. I had to admit that in the history of social justice, progress is not a regular forward march. The pendulum sometimes swings back.

We proceeded with the covenant, and subsequently the concept proved to be a good way of relating churches and funding agencies. Both parties were able to be open about their genuine problems.

Lilly Endowment, Inc., while interested in our proposal because they viewed the loss of churches in the inner city as a national problem, was disturbed about our United Church of Christ denominational approach. But we convinced them it would be a model of future strategy for other denominations, and funds were set aside to make the findings available to others. The Churches-in-Transition program, led by Walt, with Bert Campbell as its program director, gave program assistance, direct aid for salaries, and lay and pastoral training to help seven churches change from all white to predominantly black or Latino constituencies. Also a pretransitional training program was provided for eight other congregations where the change was imminent. One of the projects, "Curriculo Hispaño Bilinque," by Maria Fiallo and the Rev. Sally Scheib, is now being studied nationally. Following our agreement with Lilly Endowment, a Churches-in-Transition national consultation in 1977 gathered nearly one hundred church leaders from denominations all over the country.

The Society is free and not free. Not being completely under denominational control meant that we were free to assist churches like the Fellowship Missionary Baptist, on Chicago's south side. It was after King's activities in the city that the plight of this church came to our attention. The Rev. Clay Evans, its pastor, had been active in the freedom movement, and membership in his church had grown to the point where its old building, inherited from a white congregation, proved inadequate. He thought if he managed to get some construction started he would be able to obtain a bank loan, so with funds from his congregation the steel girders were put up. But he found he could not get a loan and in desperation turned to the Society.

He felt that local banks had refused him because he had been involved with King. I thought it very probable, and it was this likelihood of political intervention that made me interested in helping. Clay needed a loan guarantee of $300,000, and the loan was finally secured by the Society, assuming half the guarantee, the United Methodists and Presbyterians, taking one quarter each. The church has continued to grow and has never missed a payment.

But that was an exception. Since coming to Chicago my support has come primarily from one denomination. The Society is in covenant with the Chicago Metropolitan Association of the United Church of Christ, and therefore its church strategy is denominational. When I arrived in 1960 the Society had broken its relationship with the denomination as a result of its opposition to the formation of the United Church of Christ. Consequently, under a "division of labor," the Association worked with local churches and the Society with neighborhood agencies and other missions.

Shortly after I came to Chicago I talked with Jim Smucker, association minister of the Chicago Metropolitan Association, and Clarence McCall, conference minister of the Illinois Conference. We thought there could be a more amiable relationship among us. But problems existed. The Society had financed the founding of more than 90 church congregations prior to 1954 and held a $120,000 revolving fund for new church development. I recommended it be turned over to the Illinois Conference with the stipulation that priority be given to the metropolitan area. The board was shocked at my proposal to give the money away but approved it; this meant the Conference could develop a new church without Society approval.

Another point of conflict was the grant mortgages the Society held as liens on church property. These were mortgages placed on churches when program grants were made. Although they became payable only if churches ceased to function or joined other denominations, I thought it was wrong to do this when giving money for a mission. I had no interest in making churches repay the Society for past support. So I proposed that we forgive these program-related mortgages. The board approved and instructed me to explain the action to the churches. In doing so I found that there had been great resentment against the Society for its old policy of giving with strings attached.

In 1963 we agreed that at least fifty-one percent of our board be chosen from the United Church of Christ and that the

Illinois Conference be consulted on the choice of subsequent Society executive directors. Half our nominating committee was to be elected by the Chicago Metropolitan Association. So over the years an open break has been averted, trust has developed, and now an area of creative tension exists between the Society and the denomination. I am sure that more ecumenical and mission-centered movements will be needed in the future, although we cannot predict the way in which they will emerge.

While she was in Cleveland, Harriet Ziegenhals organized and directed a chorus of inner-city and suburban singers. She wanted to try it in Chicago. I hesitated, but because I did not like to refuse Harriet, attempted to find good reasons for such a project. It seemed more suitable for a solid, conservative, traditional organization. But then I realized that this was the very thing to counteract our "bad image" in the eyes of many local congregations. It would help to offset some biased and narrow opinions about our connections with community organizations by carrying our name into various religious and secular communities while demonstrating that we cared about music and worship. Now Harriet has about 150 people of all ages in the Community Renewal Chorus and its youthful counterpart, All God's Children. She has begun a tradition I hope will go on for a long time. The singers come from all sections of the city and suburbs, and each year the chorus performs five or six concerts in churches and every spring a major benefit performance in Orchestra Hall. Its quality is professional, and on tours to Rumania, Poland, and Russia the group's interracial and interethnic character has presented an ideal image of America.

Pleasant Valley Farm is one of the last pieces of natural prairie, with the tall prairie grass that once covered large areas of Illinois. Except for the farm, it has been left wild and natural. Two ponds are stocked with fish.

Getting city children off the streets in summer was no longer an adequate reason for maintaining Pleasant Valley, but Jim Mason brought in an ecology program, and also emphasized intercultural, interracial, and interethnic activities. Now we try to encourage children to watch things grow, teach them about ecosystems and educate them in the use of our natural resources, instilling reverence for the land and some understanding of the doctrine of creation—that the earth belongs to God and we are stewards.

Some summers there is a survival camping trip, taking canoes up the Wisconsin River, living in tents, and learning to cook. A night camp is held where the children sleep during the day and stay awake at night, learning what happens in the small hours, hearing the night sounds, discovering which animals are out, listening to the forest. Also, they visit night workers and shops that are open at night.

The Pleasant Valley property was purchased in 1953 and more land acquired in 1961, for a total of 460 acres. The purpose is that of Community Renewal Society itself: to be an agency of renewal by providing ways and means for the church and its people to become consciously involved in the world.

Many of Jim Mason's programs were unique in involving all ages simultaneously and also integrating the deaf, mentally ill, handicapped, and retarded with so-called plain, ordinary folks whose only handicap, as Jim used to say, "might be moral." Experimental efforts included a weekend country school (anthropology for seventh and eighth graders), teen work-study, and ecumenical weekends. School dropouts were employed as part of the staff.

Jim tried a new educational form in which learning was tied up with leisure, not work or the work week, and included weekly forums, a weekend college, man and nature studies, and teen programs in natural and social sciences. His ideas included developing a community ministry, bringing in more summer-type programs during fall and winter, and becoming more closely associated with specialized groups, mental hospitals, special and ghetto schools, and always making the farm a renewal center for individuals and families.

The partly underground solar building we constructed at Pleasant Valley brings many visitors who want to see how it works and take away ideas. Vegetables grown in the garden are used at the farm table, and we encourage groups to take an acre of land and explore productive enterprises like cooperative canning and preserving.

In America we have made a break between city and country. For many people, going back to the country is restoration or an adventure. There is often a connection between mental health and outdoor experience. For city people there is less noise, less distraction, and different kinds of diversion. We did not want to use camping exclusively for sports, or the development of crafts and gimmickry, or for a vacation, to turn a person around or change one's outlook. Our idea, rather, was that of considering environment in terms of thought—of human beings in nature and the nature of humanity—as well as work and recreation. We emphasized the community aspect of camping with its own kind of political organization.

Someone once said that one of the positive influences on those who come to the farm or the camp is that they feel welcome, but I think it is more than that. They feel they are part owners, even trustees. Our staff, rather than having a possessive attitude, makes everyone who comes feel part of it.

38

The Great Depression and the history of the bloody conflicts accompanying the rise of organized labor were at the base of my keen interest in management-labor relations and in the influence of work on societal values. It seemed difficult to find ways to relate the gospel to the ethical problems emerging in the workplace.

In East Harlem we had fairly close contacts with some of the trade unions, and in Cleveland I had worked with members of the machinists' union and the Rev. Bob Raines to organize several labor-management retreats that were helpful in opening up communications. My first attempt in Chicago was in the exploratory program with John Noble, when the executive committee acted before much of a defense could be made.

One evening I spoke at the Winnetka Presbyterian Church where Bill Cohea was associate minister. He had been meeting in the Loop with some of his parishioners on the problems of ethics in business and was convinced that working with businessmen was an important ministry.

Bill developed the Chicago Business and Industrial Project

and ran it for seven years, supported by the Society and the funds he raised directly. It met to discuss problems in the industrial setting and formed a coalition of concerned business executives, business schools, and universities. They used case studies—presenting the problem of a particular company or individual for the group to solve. The aim was to discover how a worker in the world of business and industry could live to the fullest human potential.

The Chicago Business and Industrial Project did not attempt to instill values but encouraged business and industry to determine what values were implicit in their policies and attitudes. While the project was not called "religious," its staff workers assumed that people who are shaping the lives of others through the values they are creating or upholding need to engage in dialogue with those others.

As a result of this work some corporations modified their images in the community, and education policies for workers were improved. Some business executives and union officials redefined their roles. Unions began to think about the social meaning of the fact that union members are far outnumbered by unorganized workers. Union and business leaders began to recognize their feelings of alienation from the job and to provide opportunities for reflective thinking. Many corporations had often stated publicly that they wanted their people to have wide views and see themselves in the context of the total society but seldom practiced it. The project provided a ready mechanism for this kind of search.

Richard H. Luecke conducts the Society's current program of inquiry into the problem of unemployment and the future of work. He is a Lutheran minister who came to the Urban Training Center in 1964 as director of studies.

Throughout the 1960s it was assumed that social problems would be resolved from Washington, and there was little disposition on the part of our board members to get into an unemployment program. They saw unemployment as a high-level priority for economists, business, and government on a national scale. I was dubious about programs whose good effects were expected to trickle down to the poverty areas and decided our board members needed time and a more relaxed setting to pursue this. Ann and I invited them in groups for chili suppers and evenings of conversation on the question of unemployment. Our discussions made it clear that the old ways of solving the problem were inadequate. Programs that stimulated business left the underclasses unemployed or with low-paid work of which more was being done by machines. I felt the key issue was jobs and proper pay, which meant enough money so that people could buy the housing, education, and health services that were now coming through very costly bureaucratic government programs. When we did not pay people enough the market went down, local business declined. We got unemployment and underemployment, and more government programs. We found we had to talk not only about more jobs but about tying those jobs to families and communities. Essentially, that would be carrying on the Community Renewal Society's tradition of concern for the inner city. But how was it to be done, with industries fleeing and automating?

After several months, in the fall of 1976, we formed the Committee on Unemployment and the Future of Work. Dick Luecke would serve as staff director. He conducted many neighborhood seminars of five or six weeks each on the question of work and the role of the church in the work of communities. Two major metropolitan meetings for religious leaders were held at the First Baptist Congregational Church on the west side in cooperation with the Church Federation of Greater Chicago, of which I was then president.

What we feared has come to pass. Unemployment has not been halted through expansion of industry, and expansion of services, including public services, obviously is not going to end it. According to Dick, the committee's study confirms our belief that creative thinking and planning at the neighborhood and community levels to encourage reinvestment and even retooling in those places will be required. The seminars have moved into discussions on conservation and on new kinds of work dealing with energy and weatherization.

The committee has had discussions with the Economic Development Commission, keeping an eye out for smaller businesses where most of the new jobs are found. It works with others to get legislation passed that brings funds to communities and also with the city at developing links between publicly funded training, public jobs, and public contracts. The city budget for capital expenditures and capital investments is reviewed in connection with jobs for people who live near those installations, and the effect of public service monies is studied. Poor neighborhoods have a great deal of money going through them, but it doesn't stay. A good community is one where it is spent a few times in the community before it leaves.

The study has laid hold of major new realities confronting the city in terms of finances, the flight of industry, and the closing down or diminishing of services. It seems that we will need to work first, not at some "solution" to the problem of unemployment, but at finding what goes into making self-sustaining work as opposed to public programs that supply work for a little while and then stop. It will require understanding and activity at the community level.

This program confirms my feeling that if we do not look at the economy from the viewpoint of those who suffer from its systems, sooner or later we all suffer. We do not need more high technologies with a socially irresponsible approach to efficiency and mechanization, but manageable operations with work that gives people status. This is a program not measured in immediate results, but it is essential.

I believe the right to employment is a constitutional one that grows out of a natural right. Land and resources are God-given. People must have access to land, tools, and resources to make a living. Life, liberty, and the pursuit of happiness are constitutional guarantees, but under our economic system pursuit of happiness is in jeopardy without income. To deny employment is to deny that access, and therefore unconstitutional.

39

Jesus wept over the city saying, "Would that even today you knew the things that make for peace! But now they are hid from your eyes."

I refer to this association of knowing and feeling when I call myself a "born-again radical." For me, "born again" means both being born into a world of poverty and suffering and also feeling what it means to be despised and rejected; and "radical" pertains to the root. The radical person gets at the roots, searches out the source, cause, or principle.

I do not see how one could be "born again" in this sense without being radical. This would mean seeing and feeling with those who suffer injustice without the disposition and the determination to uproot the causes of evil. To be born again is to manifest more than a passion of sympathy. It is to be more than a tender-hearted spectator who weeps at the personification of tragedy, tosses money to the beggar in the street, and then goes to dinner. Jesus wept, but he was also radical. The radical is deeply committed to liberating the victims and confronting oppressors in the name of justice.

For me, rebirth happens daily. Because progress is slow and the evil remains, one must be born again, not once and for all, but continually to an unfinished task. Paul wrote, "I die daily in Christ." To die daily in Christ is to be reborn again each day to deeper engagement.

Wherever there is individual human suffering, especially in poverty, I find the strongest appeal to both the priestly and prophetic aspects of Christian ministry. The two functions become correlative, one acting in compassion, the other impelled to speak out for justice. Compassion expressed only as pity or paternalism is like love without justice, a pale imitation of the real thing. In true compassion there is partnership, solidarity, and identification.

Some say we can come to faith only through worship. I came through my concern for the unemployed and the alienated, through understanding the deadening weight of ghetto existence on young people, comprehending the effects of dilapidated housing on family life, witnessing privation, discrimination, and violence. I have found worship more significant in times of struggle, more a celebration of the power of God. A great moment was the time of prayer with all the tenants in the freezing building before we went to the housing authority. Another was the time when I was in solitary, utterly alone with my inner conflict. And I remember one night in

Newark when several homeless men and women were with us for dinner. They were moved because we had taken them in, and soon there was a general spirit among us, a feeling of jubilation and a kind of paean that seemed ready to burst into a Te Deum of friendship. It was almost as if we were drunk, yet we had nothing intoxicating to drink. Suddenly, everyone seemed to come alive; we began to talk and to share some of the most meaningful experiences of our lives. I remember saying afterward that it had been a kind of upper-room pentecostal experience.

For all who think and act in the light of the world as it is, there is a connection between the gospel and politics, and between the gospel and democracy. Certainly today no one would say that economic well-being should not be an important goal. The problem is not economic feasibility as a rule in itself but the absence of democracy in determining it and the narrow extent in applying it. What is economically feasible for one segment may not be economically feasible for others or for the whole society. In fact, it is almost certain not to be. Democracy, when it takes precedence, can be the correcting principle. Christianity looks at decisions from the standpoint of those who will be victimized. And democracy, in guaranteeing for the victims a right to speak and participate politically, educates the whole society in self-discipline and justice, and looks to informed human reason for decision. These victims must be heard. They must be brought into the process. I see no solution being formulated within either capitalist or communist ideologies. I think more solutions will be found in moves toward decentralization and alternate technology geared to the human scale. That is why it is so important to search for local neighborhood initiatives using such technologies, and also for worker-owned structures like cooperatives, and to match such economic control with moves toward neighborhood governance and political communities where individual voices speak with effect. As an ideal, we seem to subscribe to a faith in political democracy but not in economic democracy.

Therefore I believe the Christian should be informed and involved in politics, although this is not to imply that Christians possess better remedies for the problems of poverty and racism than are offered by those outside the church. In political work, as Christians, they do not properly come into a group and say, "We have arrived with the answers." In a community organization they do not always identify themselves, but in working with other people, who may or may not be Christians, they bring a great sense of judgment that comes from their opposition to idolatry and their faith and hope in a perfect kingdom of God which always stands in judgment over human institutions. As Christians, they are continually confronted with the radical dimensions of their faith.

While the individual Christian often takes a partisan stand, I believe that the church itself, as a whole, should do so only in some great extremity. Its position transcends any particular side of a controversy. The church should reach through to the moral imperative, continually pointing to a higher justice and calling for still better solutions. The great danger is insulation. Captivity of the church by the middle and upper classes is potentially fatal; it means nothing less than the absence of the living Christ and the emptiness of the claim to be a center for caring and redemption.

As a community of the faithful, the church can move away from internal institutional aggrandizement toward a role of servanthood in a world seen as the arena of God's activity. Perhaps more functional congregations will arise, organized around questions of justice, devoting themselves to service through action and reflection. But structure is not the primary consideration. New living structures will emerge only insofar as they are expressions of a new response to Christ's call; and a new understanding of the word and the sacraments will emerge only out of the encounter with the world.

I know that some individuals reject any thought of participating in politics, and others take positions on certain issues that they defend as absolutes. Although the goal of the born-again radical Christian—achieving liberty and equality for the poor, oppressed, and rejected—is in a sense absolute, all who pursue the goal should be prepared for argument, discussion, and compromise with regard to the means of achieving it. One model only of perfection exists in the history of the world, incarnate in Jesus Christ.